On Transits and Transitions

On Transits and Transitions

On Transits and Transitions

Trans Migrants and U.S. Immigration Law

TRISTAN JOSEPHSON

RUTGERS UNIVERSITY PRESS

NEW BRUNSWICK, CAMDEN, AND NEWARK, NEW JERSEY, AND LONDON

Library of Congress Cataloging-in-Publication Data

Names: Josephson, Tristan, author.
Title: On transits and transitions : trans migrants and U.S. immigration law / Tristan Josephson.
Description: New Brunswick : Rutgers University Press, 2022. | Includes bibliographical references and index.
Identifiers: LCCN 2022007388 | ISBN 9781978813564 (paperback) | ISBN 9781978813571 (hardcover) | ISBN 9781978813588 (epub) | ISBN 9781978813601 (pdf)
Subjects: LCSH: Asylum, Right of—United States. | Emigration and immigration law—United States. | Transgender people—Legal status, laws, etc.—United States. | Sexual minorities—Legal status, laws, etc.—United States.
Classification: LCC KF4819 .J67 2022 | DDC 342.7308/2—dc23/eng/20220624
LC record available at https://lccn.loc.gov/2022007388

A British Cataloging-in-Publication record for this book is available from the British Library.

♾ The paper used in this publication meets the requirements of the American National Standard for Information Sciences—Permanence of Paper for Printed Library Materials, ANSI Z39.48-1992.

www.rutgersuniversitypress.org

Manufactured in the United States of America

To my mom, Sally-Anne Jackson,
for her support and persistence

CONTENTS

On Transits and Transitions

On Transits and Transitions

Introduction

In 2000, the U.S. Court of Appeals for the Ninth Circuit decided *Geovanni Hernandez-Montiel v. Immigration and Naturalization Service*,[1] which became the first successful published case that dealt with a trans asylum seeker. Geovanni Hernandez-Montiel was awarded asylum in the United States as a "gay man with a female sexual identity." Hernandez-Montiel had migrated to the United States at age fifteen from Mexico, fleeing physical and sexual violence from family members and police officers. The Ninth Circuit's precedential decision reversed a decision two years earlier by the Board of Immigration Appeals (BIA), which had dismissed Hernandez-Montiel's appeal for asylum. But in this moment of legal success, the plaintiff at the center of the case was missing and unaccounted for. After winning the case at the Ninth Circuit, Hernandez-Montiel's attorney had to hire a private investigator to track down his client and share the good news. The disappearance of Hernandez-Montiel at what is arguably the climax of the case, at the very moment that a federal court recognizes and validates her asylum claim, serves as a fitting illustration of the relations of mobility and immobility that structure the legal category of transgender. Trans migrants are marked by changing legal and social status, often in relation to changes in sexed/gendered embodiment and to geographical movement, yet immigration law insists on fixed categories for the granting of rights and recognition.

Hernandez-Montiel v. INS sets the precedent for future asylum cases involving trans migrants and therefore marks the beginning of the process through which the category of transgender becomes incorporated into U.S. asylum law. In the decades since *Hernandez-Montiel v. INS* was decided, transgender has become a category institutionalized in other areas of immigration law and policy as well as in social services, public health, and other legislative contexts. Yet celebrations of the "transgender tipping point"[2] have occurred at the same time of heightened debates and anxieties about immigration. *On*

Transits and Transitions explores what the increased visibility of trans people in the public sphere means for trans migrants and provides a counternarrative to the dominant discourse that the inclusion of transgender in law and policy represents the progression of legal equality for trans communities. Focusing on the three key areas of asylum law, marriage and immigration law, and immigration detention policies in the early twenty-first century, I track the movement of trans bodies across the physical and metaphorical borders of the nation-state, alongside trans migrants' changes in embodiment and shifts in legal status.

Attending to the intersection of immigration and trans rights, this book traces how the trans migrant becomes a legible legal subject across these areas of U.S. immigration law and policy. Moving from Geovanni Hernandez-Montiel's grant of asylum as a "gay man with a female sexual identity," to the recognition of "transsexual marriage" in immigration cases, to the inclusion of "transgender" in federal immigration detention standards, I show how the incorporation and consolidation of the category of transgender in U.S. immigration law and policy functions as a process of state regulation and violence. These three areas of law and policy interface with each other to determine the grounds for recognition and for forms of differential inclusion for trans migrants. Immigration law and policy regulate different types of movement and displacement that center on the construction and acquisition of citizenship, both as a formal legal status and as a cultural status and mode of belonging. The title of this book, *On Transits and Transitions*, highlights how questions of mobility are central to the production of trans migrant legal subjectivity. *Transits* gestures to the movements of trans bodies across the physical and metaphorical borders of the nation-state, such as the U.S.–Mexico border and cages in immigration detention facilities. *Transitions* invokes changes in sexed and gendered embodiment and the shifting legal and social status of trans migrants as they make themselves legible to state institutions to obtain rights and recognitions. Together, *transits* and *transitions* capture the insecurity and precarity produced by U.S. immigration control and related processes of racialization. Asylum grants recognition and freedom of mobility to exceptional trans migrants as a symbolic gesture of inclusion. This gesture offers protection to a relative few of the most vulnerable trans migrants while legitimating the mass detention and removal of others through immigration detention policies. Marriage offers access to citizenship for more privileged trans migrants who are able to meet the normative gender and class-based requirements. Considered together, the transits and transitions of trans migrants across these three legal regimes illuminate how relations of mobility and immobility constitute citizenship and national belonging in the United States.

The book begins with the institution of asylum because asylum is a key immigration strategy for trans and queer subjects who have few options to access documented status in the United States. As individuals who are often rejected by their families, trans migrants are marginalized by the heteronormative family reunification biases of the 1965 Immigration and Nationality Act.[3] Trans migrants also face obstacles with other modes of legal entry that require high amounts of cultural, class, and economic capital such as labor migration, which prioritizes visas for highly educated professionals and wealthy investors. Asylum law offers protection to individuals who are fleeing persecution or who have a "well-founded fear" of persecution by their government or by groups or individuals that their government is not able or not willing to control. Hernandez-Montiel's story exemplifies the forms of violence and persecution many trans migrants, particularly trans women, experience from family and from state actors. As a young child, Hernandez-Montiel suffered reprimands and disciplining from family members in Mexico and was eventually kicked out of the house after she was expelled from school for not conforming to gender and sexual norms. From age twelve onward, Hernandez-Montiel was frequently harassed and arrested by Mexican police officers for walking down the street or for hanging out with other gender nonconforming youth. At age fourteen, she was abducted and raped on two different occasions by police officers. Shortly after these sexual assaults, she was attacked by a group of young men on the street and spent a week in the hospital recovering. Hernandez-Montiel attempted to flee this violence by migrating to the United States; she crossed the border in 1993 but was arrested and deported back to Mexico within a few days. She made a number of other attempts to migrate to the United States, and successfully entered without inspection in October 1994. Hernandez-Montiel submitted an application for asylum in February 1995, and after her application was denied by an immigration judge and then by the BIA, the Circuit Court of Appeals decided in her favor in 2000.

To apply for asylum, migrants have to cross the U.S. border and apply from within the United States. As a result, asylum is often depicted as a back door to the regular U.S. immigration system, which prospectively screens immigrants through a visa application process. Yet the asylum process itself requires applicants to adhere to prescribed gender, sexual, and racial narratives of identity and persecution in order to be legible to asylum adjudicators, as Hernandez-Montiel's characterization as a "gay man with a female sexual identity" demonstrates. Beginning this book with an analysis of asylum law and asylum cases allows me to approach the question of mobility by examining how immigration control regulates not just trans bodies but also the processes of transition from one place to another and from one legal status to another, for trans subjects who must argue that they deserve protection due to their transness.

Marriage law also serves as a key site for the articulation of and production of national belonging. Throughout the history of the United States, ideas about marriage have been inextricable from ideas about the formation of the nation. Marriage law is central both to the reproduction of gendered, sexualized, and racialized forms of being and to the reproduction, along with immigration law, of the state itself.[4] At times, marriage is equated with citizenship, demonstrating how marriage and the immigration and citizenship regimes are intertwined. Examining the intersection of marriage and immigration law reveals the relationships amongst rights, citizenship, and mobility for trans migrants in the United States.

As a third area of law, the immigration detention regime interfaces with asylum and marriage law in the production of citizenship and national belonging to mark those populations of migrants who are deemed excludable. If asylum can be posited as type of entry into the United States for trans migrants, immigration detention must be understood as the corresponding form of displacement and incapacitation for trans asylum seekers and other trans migrants. More importantly, the purportedly protective asylum system serves to legitimate the rapidly expanding immigration detention and deportation regime.

Bringing together these three areas of the law allows me to map the unevenness of recognition for trans migrants across social, cultural, and legal determinations, and to show how relative freedom for some trans subjects is founded on the unfreedom of other trans subjects. This book seeks to draw out how the state-sanctioned violence, repression, and discipline experienced by trans asylum seekers and detained trans migrants serve as the necessary backdrop and conditions for the rights and state recognition gained by trans subjects who may be able to able to access national and gender normativity through marriage.[5] However, I also show how these same state logics and violence structure, in differing degrees, the quotidian lives of more privileged trans subjects. My own history as a white trans immigrant reflects the hierarchies of socioeconomic class and racialization that condition access to mobility and documented status in the United States. A work visa granted through my father's employer made it possible for my family to move from England to the United States in the early 1980s, and sponsorship from a family member enabled us to qualify for lawful permanent residency within a decade. My position as a white, trans masculine permanent resident facilitated my gender transition, and access to subsidized federal student loans in the early 2000s helped me afford the legal filing and application fees for changing my name and sex/gender marker on my immigration documents. I still had to navigate the quotidian violence built into legal processes of recognition, which required me to present myself to medical and legal authorities through prescribed normative narratives of gender and sexuality that did not necessary reflect my identity, and forced me to negotiate with multiple therapists, doctors, and diagnoses in order to justify my access to transitioning technologies. Yet my relative privilege contrasts sharply with the experiences of many undocumented trans migrants and trans migrants of color who struggled in this same time period to access safety and legal status in the United States. The immobility of some trans migrants forms the basis of this project, a project that both allows for and is a consequence of my own mobility. As such I can become an alibi for the liberal state, evidence of trans subjects who can migrate to find economic opportunities and successful careers.

On Transits and Transitions argues that the recognition of trans migrants in immigration law is specific but not exceptional to trans subjects. Mobilizing trans studies as a mode of analysis, I use trans as a critical lens to show how binary sex/gender and normative gender undergird racialized categories of citizenship.[6] The biopolitical management of trans migrants needs to be understood as emblematic of how U.S. immigration and asylum institutions manage gendered, sexualized, and racialized populations, illustrating how recognition and incorporation are premised on narrow and restrictive categories that affect all migrant subjects, not just those who are trans. At the same time, focused attention on trans subjects and trans legal cases in these three areas of immigration law does reveal the specific ways that transgender circulates to discipline trans migrants and how immigration law participates in the consolidation of transgender as a legal category. Transgender becomes articulated as a traumatized subjectivity in asylum law, as a form of normative citizenship in marriage law, and as a category of vulnerability deserving of state "protection" through incarceration in immigration detention policy.

Trans Migrations and Mobilities

This book approaches the question of im/mobility by interrogating the ways that state and legal institutions regulate not just the movements of trans bodies and identities but also processes of transition and shifting legal statuses. The tensions between mobility and immobility that structure the relationships of trans migrants to citizenship and national belonging in the United States occur both at the level of the subject and at the level of state institutions and actors that regulate transition and movement for trans migrants. Trans becomes a conceptual framework with which to think about the change and movement that constitute trans migrants in the areas of asylum law, immigration and marriage law, and immigration detention policy. Trans is also a way to highlight the violence of naming and classification through the designation of certain bodies and identities as "transgender" or "transsexual" by state institutions, social services, and community and nonprofit organizations.[7] I am attentive to how "transgender" and "transsexual" often circulate as particularly Western categories of racialized, gendered, and classed identity that cannot account for the diversity of gender and sexual identities and ways of being. In this book, I use trans to refer to the range of gender-variant expressions, identities, and practices of gender nonconforming subjects, and to theorize processes of change and movement as well as the collisions that occur when trans subjects interact with legal institutions.

Mobility is a familiar trope in the field of trans studies. Changes in gender identity and changes in sexed/gendered embodiment are often theorized as a form of movement for trans subjects. Even if one's trans identity is conceptualized as immutable and innate, modern trans subjects are usually marked by changing social and legal status. Many trans narratives render this movement as a form of both metaphorical and literal travel and border crossing. The linkage of social and medical transition to travel is a particularly common theme in Western mid-to-late twentieth-century transsexual autobiographies. Within these narratives, travel is associated with sexual and gender freedom in ways that reproduce colonial tropes of travel and discovery.[8] In his analysis of trans and gender nonconforming mobility in relation to gender reassignment surgeries, Aren Z. Aizura argues that "Imaginaries of transness as movement carry the freighted meanings of transnational mobility with them, colonial and imperialist imaginaries as well as stories about how geographical mobility maps onto social mobility, self-transformation, and possibilities for reinvention."[9] When theorizing trans mobility, therefore, we need to recognize how political economy and different processes of racialization shape trans movements and the production of transgender subjectivities.[10] Like Aizura, I focus on how the conditions of possibility for trans mobility are shaped by neoliberal capitalism, neocolonialism, and the interactions between immigration law and trans subjects. *On Transits and Transitions* attends to the displacements, migrations, and movements of trans subjects that may or may not be voluntary in the context of forced migration, detention, and deportation.

I am indebted to the rich body of scholarship on queer and trans migrations that has emerged over the past two decades, theorizing processes of migration in relation to questions of sexuality and gender, formations of race and nationality, and theories of citizenship. This field has brought together research on immigration law with queer and trans studies to investigate both how sexuality and gender inform processes of migration for queer and trans migrants as well as how border crossings and immigration policies regulate and produce sexual and gender identities.[11] Eithne Luibhéid's scholarship on histories of sexuality and gender at U.S. borders, and her work on the shifting lines between legality and illegality for queer migrants, has been particularly formative for this project.[12] Trystan T. Cotten provides a capacious description of transgender migrations as "movements of desire, agency, and generativity without unitary subjects or foundations. They are heterotopic, multidimensional mobilities whose viral flows and circuits resist teleology, linearity, and tidy, discrete borders."[13] *On Transits and Transitions* contributes to the existing research on trans migrations through a sustained, multilevel analysis of U.S. immigration law and policy. In addition to thinking about how trans migrants cross borders, I track how legal cases, legal categories, and immigration policies also move in relation to trans migrants. I attend to the classification of trans migrants in legal and policy texts to show how the incorporation of the category of transgender reveals the specific relations of im/mobility and displacement that are central to trans subjectivities.

To develop my multiscalar analysis of mobility and immobility in U.S. immigration law and policy, I draw on the insights of mobility studies. Caren Kaplan calls for scholarly work on displacement, mobility, and immobility to historicize discourses of movement in their specific contexts in order to understand the transnational structures of exclusion that frame movement in the modern era.[14] In her description of the "new mobilities paradigm," Mimi Sheller writes that mobilities research "focuses not simply on movement per se, but on the power of discourses, practices, and infrastructures of mobility in creating the effects of both movement and stasis, demobilization and remobilization, voluntary and involuntary movement."[15] Mobility studies recognizes that the mobilities of certain bodies is dependent on the immobilization of others, challenging the equation of mobility with freedom.[16] Mobility is a central organizing theme for this book, which theorizes im/mobility on the scales of the body, the law, and the nation-state. My use of mobility as a critical lens allows me to make connections across changes in sex/gender embodiment, the movement of bodies across borders, shifts in legal status, and the circulation of the category of transgender in immigration law and policy.

Trans migrants are often figured as hypermobile subjects who travel across borders of gender as a spatialized category, traverse national borders, and cross the prescribed boundaries of the liberal subject. The movements of trans migrants across borders and within the United States, as well as changes in embodied sex/gender, constitute two types of movement that help us think about the relationships of gender and migration. I also attend to what can be understood as the micromobilities of gesture and of desire. For example, my analysis of trans migrants' personal narratives in their asylum declarations explores their strategic deployments of desire, in which desire is constructed both as excess, something that drives movement and becoming, and as attachment, something that anchors and makes possible a sense of belonging.

In addition to thinking about the movements of trans migrants themselves, I examine how legal cases circulate and condition other cases, shaping the construction of the category of transgender in immigration law and the recognition of trans migrants as legal subjects. I borrow Bruno Latour's concept of "immutable mobiles" to theorize circuit court decisions and other immigration cases as traveling inscriptions that produce trans migrants as legal subjects.[17] I track how immigration law and policy is also shaped by the circulation of other state logics. The inclusion of transgender in the *Performance-Based National Detention Standards 2011*,[18] for instance, exemplifies the mobility of carceral logics of criminalization. Across the different chapters, I juxtapose the mobility of legal documents and court decisions to the immobility of actual trans migrants. In Geovanni Hernandez-Montiel's asylum case, legal documents stand in for her when her attorney decides to file an appeal at the Ninth Circuit Court of Appeals, despite not knowing where his client is. In the legal realm of immigration detention, trans-inclusive detention standards circulate as a proxy for the actual inhumane conditions of immigration detention facilities.

Law, Governance, and the Limits of Recognition

On Transits and Transitions analyzes U.S. immigration law and policy as a site of subject production. Law defines national borders and marks the internal spaces of the nation-state, but it also constructs the subject positions of citizen, asylee, detainee, alien. The law mediates the relationships of individuals to state institutions, disciplining subjects and granting rights and recognition.[19] I model my orientation to the law on Juana María Rodríguez's analysis of law as a discourse that produces particular racial and sexual subjects and identities as it regulates and determines the material conditions and fates of those subjects.[20] My argument about the emergence of "transgender" as a legal category is indebted to David Valentine's incisive analysis of the creation and institutionalization of the category of transgender in the United States in the early 1990s. Valentine traces the adoption of "transgender" in public health, social service, and scholarly contexts, showing how this category is premised on the assumption of ontological separateness of gender and sexuality as they are divorced from race, class, and nation.[21] He situates the production of the category of transgender in the larger development of selfhood under neoliberalism in the late twentieth century United States, in which the emergence of transgender exemplifies how the neoliberal state deploys identity and recognition politics to push for a politics of liberal equality rather than a politics of justice.[22] I extend Valentine's framing of "transgender as a *category of knowing*" to U.S. immigration law and policy to show how the legibility of trans migrants is premised on normative binary understandings of sex/gender and fails to protect those gender-variant subjects who are often most vulnerable.

My analysis also builds on feminist, queer, and trans scholarship on biopolitics and governmentality to understand the law as a tactic of racialized and gendered governance. Michel Foucault characterizes biopolitics as a technology of power that works through state apparatuses and civic society to regulate large populations by intervening at the level of general phenomena rather than at the level of the individual through disciplinary mechanisms.[23] As "the power to 'make' live and 'let' die," biopolitics provides a useful framework to mark the connections across these different areas of the law and how they work together to produce trans migrants both as worthy of protection and inclusion and as excludable and disposable. Achille Mbembe's necropolitics develops Foucaultian biopolitics to consider the centrality of death in social life and how some populations are marked for death while others are given resources for life.[24] I draw on queer and trans of color scholarship that has taken up Mbembe's arguments to theorize a queer necropolitics that examines "regimes of attribution of liveliness and deadliness of subjects, bodies, communities, and populations and their instantiation through performatives of gender, sexuality, and kinship, as well as through processes of confinement, removal and exhaustion."[25] C. Riley Snorton and Jin Haritaworn theorize biopolitics and necropolitics as "technologies of value extraction" to make sense of how "visibility, legibility, and intelligibility structure a grid of imposed value on the lives and deaths of black and brown trans women."[26] Snorton and Haritaworn's analysis of the ways that the deaths of trans women of color circulate "as raw material for the generation of respectable trans subjects"[27] helps me think across the three different areas of immigration law I examine, particularly the relationships between the circulation of narratives of suffering and violence in asylum cases, the disposability of trans migrants in detention, and the consolidation of trans legibility and citizenship for marriage-based immigration.

By attending to the biopolitics of U.S. immigration law, this project contributes to critiques of rights discourses and liberalism by feminist, queer, and trans studies scholars. Wendy Brown and Judith Butler, among others, have shown how identities within liberalism are formed on the basis of injury, which then allows subjects to seek sanctuary and recognition from the state within a framework of rights.[28] Elizabeth Povinelli provides a helpful interrogation of liberal governance and how liberal discourses like individual freedom and social constraint serve as the "motivating logic" for recognition by settler colonial societies.[29] I utilize her framing of the autological subject, the self-made subject of liberalism in tension with the genealogical society that constrains their freedom, to think about how trans asylum applicants in particular have to position themselves against a transphobic, violent country of origin that will not grant them the freedom to exist. Similarly, Chandan Reddy's formulation of "freedom with violence" as a central contradiction in the modern nation-state also offers a useful framework for my analysis of immigration law. Reddy highlights the failed project of inclusion in the liberal state and how the process of inclusion shores up and expands the forms of state violence that produced inequalities in the first instance. The modern nation-state claims to provide freedom from violence but that freedom for some depends on the deployment of state violence toward racialized others. "Freedom with violence" draws attention to the legitimization of state violence and the attachment of emancipation and citizenship to forms of institutionalized violence.[30] I also build on Dean Spade's critique of liberal trans politics that are more invested in obtaining rights and recognitions rather than in transformative justice.[31] Spade argues that seeking inclusion in state institutions and in legal frameworks is a limited political goal that will not transform the material conditions that produce the poverty, criminalization, violence, and incarceration experienced by many trans people in the United States. *On Transits and Transitions* draws on scholarship critiquing rights discourses to think specifically about what the incorporation of transgender in immigration law makes possible for trans migrants as well as the limitations of these forms of legal recognition.

This project is also in conversation with scholarship within transnational feminist studies and postcolonial studies investigating the role of heteropatriarchal structures in citizenship and nationalism.[32] Trans subjects often have a vexed and contradictory relationship to the heteronormativity that undergirds dominant formations of citizen and nation in the United States. My focus on legal documents explores how trans migrants articulate themselves in relation to the U.S. nation-state as a site of (strategic) identification and how trans migrants feel citizenship in a bodily sense, as a form of "passionate attachment."[33] *On Transits and Transitions* contributes to this scholarship on citizenship as a legal status and as a cultural status related to national belonging. In the realm of political participation and state recognition, citizenship operates as a legal category that mediates the relationship of subjects to state institutions. Feminist and queer studies scholars have shown how the figure of the liberal citizen-subject is premised on regulatory structures of race, gender, and sexuality.[34] My project develops this analysis by highlighting the centrality of a stable binary gender and notions of bodily integrity to the construction of the citizen-subject in Western liberal thought. Trans migrants illustrate the fiction of a stable and consistent sex/gender and trouble the norms of bodily integrity that undergird citizenship as a legal and political category. Throughout my chapters I mark how discourses of criminalization and racialization mediate forms of differential inclusion and exclusion to condition citizenship as a legal status. Devon Carbado's "racial naturalization" provides a framework for understanding how racism produces forms of simultaneous inclusion and exclusion in the United States.[35] Nicholas De Genova's work on the production of "deportability" and Eithne Luibhéid's research on the shifting lines between legality and illegality for queer and trans migrants demonstrate how the temporality of immigration statuses means that immigration laws produce differentiated and stratified categories of legal status.[36] Gender and sexuality are central to understanding how state institutions configure the lines between citizen and noncitizen.[37] For example, gender and sexuality shape how immigration officials evaluate the legitimacy of migrants' claims for legal status by distinguishing a "marriage for love" from a "bogus marriage" and an "asylum seeker" from an "economic migrant."

Archive and Methodology

The book's archive consists of a range of legal documents, including published court decisions and supporting briefs, immigration court hearings, asylum declarations, expert witness statements, federal detention standards, immigration legislation and statutes, and U.S. Citizenship and Immigration Service (UCSIS) policy memos. I also analyze congressional hearings, USCIS training and guidance manuals, immigration attorney handbooks, and human rights reports. I put these legal and policy documents into conversation with news media on trans migrants and with statements by LGBTQ legal advocacy organizations and trans migrant grassroots activist organizations.

I gathered my archive from a variety of published and unpublished sources. My analysis of trans asylum cases in the first half of the book relies on legal documents related to mostly unpublished asylum cases. In 2009 and 2010, I reached out to several national and local San Francisco Bay Area immigration organizations that work on LGBT asylum cases, as well as to individual immigration attorneys who had represented trans asylum applicants, primarily located in California. From those organizations and individuals who were willing to share case files with me, I obtained a range of legal documents related to about twenty-five trans asylum cases. The number of files I received per case varied. For some cases, I only received the asylum declaration, which is the personal narrative written by an asylum seeker that details the applicant's experiences of persecution and the reasons they fear returning to their countries of origin. For other cases, attorneys also shared legal briefs, expert witness statements, amicus briefs, and psychological and medical evaluations. Robert Gerber, the attorney who represented Geovanni Hernandez-Montiel in her precedential asylum case, sent me the transcript of the initial hearing with an immigration judge, the immigration judge's decision, the BIA decision, and other case files related to Hernandez-Montiel's case. My discussion of trans marriage immigration cases and immigration detention policy in the second half of the book is based on published legal cases and policy documents that are publicly available on the websites of the U.S. Circuit Courts of Appeals, the BIA, and the various departments of the U.S. government.

The U.S. Circuit Courts of Appeals and the BIA only publish a narrow range of cases as precedential, although nonprecedential cases are available on the courts' websites and in immigration law databases. The relatively small number of asylum cases that are published as binding precedent demonstrates how the usable legal archive is structured by the court system's decisions about its own visibility, which in turns shapes how transgender as a legal immigration category circulates to make visible some trans migrants and not others. The trans asylum cases in the first two chapters of the book deal mostly with trans women from Central and South America, and my discussion of immigration detention policy in chapter 4 invokes several stories of trans Latinas who have died in detention facilities. In my chapters, I attend to the specific histories of Central and South American migration to the United States, and how immigration law, criminalization, and policing have functioned as key sites for the racialization of Latinx immigrants. The pairing of increasingly restrictive immigration laws with increasing economic integration across national borders under neoliberal globalization has meant that Mexican and other Central American migrants have fewer options for legal immigration to the United States in the late twentieth and twenty-first centuries. Poor migrants who do not qualify for skill-based immigrant visas are routed into undocumented status and criminalized as national security threats. The criminalization of Latinx migrants in U.S. immigration law and political discourses reflects and produces social and cultural constructions of Latinx people as threats to the U.S. nation, often as "invading force[s] from south of the border."[38] As many immigration studies scholars have shown, immigration law functions as a site for racialization and the reproduction of racial hierarchies, constructing Latinx migrants as nonwhite, as inferior, as perpetual foreigners.[39] The U.S. asylum system also contributes to the racialization of Latinx migrants, as I discuss in the first two chapters. The more recent racist anti-immigrant politics of the Trump administration capitalize on these historical constructions of Latinx migrants as violent criminals and threats in order to push for the dismantling of the asylum system through practices like the "Remain in Mexico" policy and for the continued expansion of the immigration deportation regime.

The overrepresentation of trans Latinas in published asylum cases[40] and in the asylum declarations I examine contributes to the invisibility of other trans migrants in immigration law but also in news media, public discourses, and activist work around trans migrants, especially in the larger context of public and legal discourses on immigration that tend to center on the U.S.–Mexico border and on Central and South American migrants. The predominance of trans women in my archive may also contribute to the increasing visibility of trans women in political discourses as exemplary vulnerable trans populations. My focus on trans Latina asylum seekers in the first two chapters thus risks holding up trans Latinas as emblematic of trans asylum applicants, and my archive potentially limits the book's analysis of how nation, culture, and racialization shape the experiences of trans migrants from other regions. For example, Black trans migrants, including Black Latinx migrants, are often not foregrounded in political and activist discussions around immigration and criminalization in the United States.[41] Programs like the Black LGBTQIA + Migrant Project (BLMP) at the Transgender Law Center and grassroots organizations like El/La Para Trans-Latinas and Southerners on New Ground (SONG) are working to shift these conversations and to create stronger collaborations amongst trans, immigrant, and Black racial justice activists.

Similarly, the gender disparity in my archive also shapes my analysis in this book. It is difficult to determine whether the overrepresentation of asylum cases by trans women reflects gendered migration patterns. Given that individuals' ability to migrate is conditioned by gender, social class, race, and nationality, the predominance of trans migrants who were assigned male at birth in the legal cases I examine may reflect familial and cultural restrictions on the mobility of trans and gender nonconforming individuals who are assigned female at birth. Sharalyn R. Jordan notes that gender disparities in LGBTQ asylum cases may be caused by the fact that in many countries, people who are assigned female at birth often have a limited ability to leave their homes and/or travel independently.[42] In a research study with LGBTQ refugees in Canada, Jordan found that some trans women chose to migrate with a more masculine gender presentation consistent with their legal documents. None of the declarations by trans women in my archive mentioned this migration strategy, but the declaration by Alejandro, a trans masculine asylum seeker from Peru, narrates many difficulties he experienced trying to leave Peru. He was turned away at the airport on at least two different occasions because the sex marker and name on his identity documents did not reflect his gender identity.[43]

In their cross-national study of published trans asylum cases, Laurie Berg and Jenni Milbank found a thirteen to one ratio of applicants who were assigned male at birth to applicants who were assigned female at birth. Like Jordan, the authors suggest this ratio may be a result of the greater access that individuals who are assigned male at birth have to both mobility and resources.[44] However, this study is based on a small sample size of thirty-seven published asylum cases, which are not representative of all asylum applicants since the BIA in the United States and similar judicial bodies in other countries engage in selective publication of court decisions for precedent. And as I note in chapter I, many asylum cases are adjudicated by asylum officers and do not reach immigration courts. There is a lack of data on the gender of asylum applicants. The Department of Homeland Security's immigration statistics on asylum seekers only provide demographic data on binary sex (female, male, unknown) as well as age, marital status, and country of origin.[45]

The content of my archive means that my analysis tends to focus on particular forms of interpersonal and state violence that target femininized bodies. Regardless of how representative the cases in my archive are, this gender disparity may restrict my ability to theorize how other trans migrants, specifically those assigned female at birth, narrate their gender identities and experiences of gender and sexual violence to U.S. asylum adjudicators. Throughout the chapters, I am attentive to how the content of my archive constrains the book's ability to theorize how gender, culture, nation, and racialization inform the experiences and legal legibility of trans migrants from other regions. Yet the shape of my archive also allows me to interrogate in more depth the particular forms of transmisogyny and state-sanctioned violence directed at trans feminine migrants.

One of the theoretical problems I grapple with in relation to this archive is how to think critically about the forms of state power and judicial violence that trans migrants experience in U.S. immigration regimes without reproducing the structures and narratives of violence that constitute those same institutions. Saidiya Hartman poses this question in her essay "Venus in Two Acts": "How does one revisit the scene of subjection without replicating the grammar of violence?"[46] Hartman asks if it is possible to write about archives of slavery in ways that do something more than just expose violence, given that the archive itself cannot be separated from the relations of power that produce that violence.[47] She wrestles with her desire to "exhume the lives buried under this prose," to be able to provide a form of redress by recovering a fuller account of the humanity of enslaved subjects.[48] I also have a political desire to do justice to the trans migrants in my analysis, to be able to present their stories and lives beyond the narrow confines of their legal legibility as trans subjects, which is often premised on narratives of trauma and violence. Yet the actual materials of my archive limit my ability to do this. Legal documents like court decisions and policy statements represent trans migrants through the logics and priorities of state institutions, and documents like asylum declarations, the personal narratives of trans asylum applicants, must conform to prescribed parameters and modes of representation. Given this, I work to read the legal archive against the grain in order to interrogate the relations of power that structure the production of legal subjectivity for trans migrants.[49]

This approach enables me to examine the law as an instrument of state power and violence on several registers. Using mobility as a lens, I show how asylum law and immigration detention policies cause physical forms of violence through the displacement, incarceration, and deportation of trans migrants. At the same time, I highlight the material effects of legal interpretation and examine how the production of legal subjectivity is itself a process of violence. The judicial process and the writing of court decisions and immigration policy do violence to the complexities of the identities, embodiments, and histories of their subjects. Critical legal scholars have built on Kimberlé Crenshaw's theory of intersectionality to analyze how the law disaggregates vectors of identity and social power to recognize legal subordination and discrimination on a single ground, such as gender or race.[50] Legal studies scholar Robert M. Cover maintains that "legal interpretation takes place in a field of pain and death" and cannot be separated from the violence it causes.[51] Academic analysis forms another layer of interpretation that brings the corresponding violence of re-presentation. The stripped-down subject of law and policy—and of rights discourse more generally—is at odds with feminist and queer theorizations of subjectivity. Wendy Brown marks this when she notes the difficulty and near impossibility of theorizing "a socially stigmatized legal subject that is not single and monolithic."[52]

The field of cultural studies offers a way to open up these questions of legal subjectivity. Unlike conventional legal scholarship, cultural studies stands outside legal reasoning and looks at legal texts and legal questions in different ways. Lawrence Grossberg argues that a practice of "radical contextuality" defines the field of cultural studies.[53] Through its focus on context and its refusal to separate the discursive from the material, cultural studies offers a productive approach to understanding and making visible the violence of legal subjection, which often compounds the other forms of physical, sexual, and psychological violence that trans migrants have already experienced. This book's methodological approach consists of a Foucaultian discourse analysis of both legal and cultural texts. Although most of my chapters begin with the legal and the juridical, the project challenges the privileging of the law as a definitive arbiter of trans migrant subjectivity.

On Transits and Transitions contextualizes asylum law, marriage law, and immigration detention by illustrating how these legal regimes interface with neoliberal economic practices, cultural discourses of sex and gender, and the racialization and criminalization of immigrants in the United States. Analyzing legal texts in conjunction with cultural texts and discourses allows me to consider the law and legal paradigms as cultural productions themselves. This approach challenges the expertise of the law and marks the legal archive as partial and limited. Hartman argues that attempting "to jeopardize the status of the event, to displace the received or authorized account" can be a method of intervening in the violence of the archive.[54] I prioritize legal and juridical texts to understand how state institutions and actors produce the category of transgender as a legal category, but I also situate the legal realm in relation to news media and the work of activist organizations to flesh out the production and circulation of legal, civic, and cultural citizenship and national belonging for trans migrants. My approach is grounded in a cultural studies of the law approach, which aims to make the law accountable to the cultural categories and assumptions on which it rests.[55] This project also seeks to move beyond a critical denouncement of the law as a repressive force and tries to highlight how trans migrants use the law strategically to present themselves to immigration institutions for recognition. I take seriously the work of legal practitioners who advocate for trans migrants, but I also bring the insights of queer theory and critical race theory to bear on the efforts of legal practitioners and legal advocacy organizations to mark the spaces that exist for intervention and transformation.

Chapter Outline

On Transits and Transitions begins with the figure of the trans asylum seeker and the incorporation of the category of transgender into asylum case law. Chapter I takes up *Hernandez-Montiel v. INS*, the first precedential court decision involving a trans migrant, in more detail. My analysis focuses on the role of immutability and visibility in the case, which submerges (trans)gender identity into gay sexual identity. I argue that dialectics of absence and presence, and mobility and immobility, structure the production of the trans asylum seeker as a legal subject. This chapter also considers how trans migrants fall out of the bureaucratic and judicial deliberations about their own cases, through tensions between the substantive and procedural elements of a case, in which procedural issues often sideline or distort the central substantive issues. These procedural questions, however, are just as integral to the constitution of the legal subject as the actual substantive issue of whether the trans migrant will be granted asylum. *Hernandez-Montiel v. INS* reveals how discourses of immutability shape the mutual articulation of racial, cultural, and national identities with sexuality and gender within asylum cases, and illustrate the contradictions of asylum law in relation to trans embodiment and mobility.

I expand my analysis of trans asylum in chapter 2 through an examination of asylum declarations, the personal narratives that detail asylum seekers' experiences of persecution in their country of origin, and the reasons they fear returning. As sworn legal documents, declarations have a prescribed form and content, and as such produce a particular traumatized subject. My argument shows how the law confines the conception of self to a liberal rights-bearing subject, one who is free of all ambiguity and marked instead by stasis and a teleological self-sameness. This subject brings together the discourse of the asylum seeker as a victim of persecution and suffering with the discourse of a transgender person as a self-actualizing subject who becomes who she has always been. Yet by highlighting trans migrants' strategic deployments of desire and complicity, I demonstrate how trans asylum seekers displace and potentially disrupt normative discourses of nationalist desire for the United States and thus offer alternative ways to understand the relationship between migrants and the U.S. state.

Chapter 3 turns to the area of marriage law as it intersects with immigration law, focusing on a precedential case in which U.S. marriage law is reconfigured in relation to bodily difference. *In re Lovo* (2005) is a BIA case that confirmed immigration benefits for marriages involving transgender spouses. This case marks the incorporation of marginalized subjects and the expansion of citizenship rights through the vehicle of marriage. I use *In re Lovo* to address key questions about trans citizenship as it is shaped through marriage, immigration, and neoliberalism. Through a close reading of the BIA decision and its implementation and incorporation into USCIS policy, I show how the process of normalizing and disciplining trans subjects is dispersed across different institutions and sites. This approach emphasizes the mobility of the law and of legal regulation compared to the immobility of trans migrants.

The last chapter examines immigration detention as a space that regulates the im/mobility of trans migrants who are criminalized as deportable. Although all detained migrants face extreme violence, trans migrants are especially vulnerable to specific forms of abuse, including rape and sexual assault, humiliation, solitary confinement, and denial of HIV treatment and hormone therapy. In 2012, Immigration and Customs Enforcement (ICE) released its *Performance-Based National Detention Standards 2011*, which for the first time mention transgender migrants and contains trans-specific provisions, largely due to the work of LGBT immigration advocacy organizations like the National Center for Transgender Equality and Immigration Equality. Chapter 4 conducts a close reading of these standards to explore how state institutions like ICE respond to critiques of their own violence by incorporating discourses of the vulnerable trans subject. I show how the inclusion of transgender in the national detention standards functions as a reformist reform that legitimates the continued incarceration and deportation of trans migrants. I also gesture to the ways that these detention standards can be mobilized as an abolitionist tool to highlight the failure of reformist reforms and inclusionary politics, and to push for the dismantling of immigration detention for all migrants.

In the final pages of the book, I ask how this history of the incorporation of transgender into U.S. immigration law and policy over the past two decades can help orient contemporary trans and immigration movements in relation to the law. Rather than embracing the law as a means to equality or rejecting the law as a repressive force, I consider how grassroots trans immigrant activists are engaging with immigration law strategically to advance liberation movements that do not fall back on legal recognition as the solution to the racism, sexism, and transphobia experienced by trans migrants.

1

Visibility and Immutability in Asylum Law and Procedure

This chapter returns to the precedential Ninth Circuit Court decision in *Hernandez-Montiel v. INS* (2000)[1] to frame my discussion of how U.S. asylum law and procedure constructs trans migrants as legible legal subjects. Geovanni Hernandez-Montiel was granted asylum as a "gay male with a female sexual identity," a formulation that submerges (trans)gender identity into gay sexual identity. While this court decision set the precedent for future trans asylum cases,[2] it restricted recognition to those migrants whose feminine gender identities could be read through their sexual identities. Discourses of immutability structure the legal recognition of trans asylum seekers. In *Hernandez-Montiel v. INS*, these discourses shape the mutual articulation of Hernandez-Montiel's racial, cultural, and national identities in relation to her sexuality and gender identity. My close reading of *Hernandez-Montiel v. INS* reveals the contradictions in asylum law for trans migrants. These contradictions include the law's insistence on an abstract, disembodied subject who is granted rights even as historical hierarchies of power and inequality inform the very production of that law. Importantly, these contradictions are not exceptional to trans subjects but are made more obvious in relation to these subjects who do not conform to existing legal categories and normative constructions of sex and gender.

The chapter opens with a brief historization of U.S. asylum law and a discussion of the legal process of applying for asylum. Then, using *Hernandez-Montiel v. INS* as my central text, I examine the circuit court decision as a genre in which legibility operates in two modes: through discourses of immutability and through the tensions between the substantive and the procedural. In the first mode, immutability and visibility are key categories that organize the legal reasoning in trans asylum cases in which trans migrants must claim an essential sexual and gender identity to be recognized as legitimate asylum applicants. The immutability of sexuality and gender is dependent on the rendering of culture and country of origin as oppressive, violent, and static. I use Bruno Latour's concept of "immutable mobiles"[3] to think about how the circuit court decision circulates as precedent, in conjunction with the circulation of the immutability of discourses of gender, sexuality, and culture. The second mode of legibility occurs in the tensions between the substantive and the procedure that structure circuit court decisions, in which procedural issues of jurisdiction often sideline or distort the central substantive issue of whether the asylum applicant should receive protection from the state. I contend that these procedural questions are just as integral to the constitution of the trans asylum seeker as a legal subject. Thinking about these two modes of legibility in relation to mobility reveals the role of embodiment in trans asylum cases. The entire asylum legal system is set up to refuse the presence and messy embodiment of the asylum applicant, yet my analysis of these two modes of legibility makes clear that the body of the asylum seeker is central to asylum proceedings and acts as a disruptive excess to the operation of the law and to the proposed liberal subject itself.

The Refugee Act of 1980

The Refugee Act of 1980[4] forms the basis of asylum law and procedure in the United States. The passage of the Act was preceded by three years of congressional hearings on the development of a systemic legislative refugee policy.[5] These hearings were motivated by several political and economic concerns, including the need to maintain the balance of power within the U.S. government; the need for the U.S. refugee policy to adhere to the U.N. Convention and Protocol Relating to the Status of Refugees, which the United States had signed in 1969; and the desire for the United States to serve as a leader and example for other countries. While refugee and asylum law is grounded in international human rights law, the establishment and implementation of asylum law in the United States reflected the political imperatives and interests of the federal government in the late 1970s and early 1980s, many of which continue to animate the administration of asylum law in the contemporary moment.

The language of human rights pervaded congressional discussions of the proposed legislation that culminated in the Refugee Act. In these discussions, the earliest of which occurred in 1977, the figures of the refugee and asylum seeker were mobilized in relation to the construction of the United States as a democratic country that promises liberty and equality.[6] Many of the state representatives in these hearings emphasized the U.S. national tradition of accepting immigrants and providing new opportunities for them as well as protecting those in need, what Hon. Leonard F. Chapman Jr., Commissioner of the Immigration and Naturalization Service (INS) at the time, called "our national tradition of humanitarian concern."[7] This rhetoric, however, existed in tension with nativist discussions about how to limit refugee flows and how to quantify that national commitment to helping others while prioritizing the needs of U.S. citizens and preserving federal and state resources for U.S. citizens.

Congressional hearings in the late 1970s on refugee policy were concerned with the standardization of the categories of refugee and asylee as legal, political, and social subjects who are accorded certain rights but who are also clearly and discretely classified in relation to U.S. citizenship. This emerged in conversations and testimonies on issues such as whether (and when) refugees should receive lawful permanent residence status, how healthy they should be, whether there should be a category of "special concern" for refugees who are politically valuable or to whom the United States has a historical obligation or responsibility, and who qualifies as a refugee and not as an economic migrant.[8] These hearings reveal contradictory attitudes toward the relationship between foreign policy, refugee policy, and human rights. Even as government representatives like Attorney General Bell argued for human rights as the basis of refugee law, they also emphasized refugee policy as foreign policy. Ultimately, the hearings make apparent the political economic priorities of the Cold War continued to animate the proposed refugee legislation.[9]

The Refugee Act in 1980 adopted the human rights standards outlined in the 1951 Convention Relating to the Status of Refugees and led to the establishment of a separate system for the admission and resettlement of refugees and asylum seekers.[10] The Refugee Act codified the United Nations' definition of a refugee as anyone who is fleeing persecution or has a "well-founded fear" of persecution "on account of" race, religion, nationality, political opinion, or membership in a particular social group.[11] This persecution must be committed by the government or by individuals or groups that the government is "unwilling or unable to control."[12]

Gender and sexuality began to be recognized as grounds for asylum claims in the 1990s, through cases dealing with gay and lesbian applicants as well as with women fleeing domestic violence. These cases were successful in opening the category of "membership in a particular social group" for gender- and sexuality-based asylum claims.[13] Chandan Reddy argues that these cases allow the United States to "draft U.S. citizenship as a formally protective apparatus against patriarchy, homophobia, and supposed 'illiberal' cultures."[14] Asylum plays a key role in the construction of citizenship, as increasing protections for sexualized and gendered asylum seekers allow for the articulation of U.S. citizenship as a guarantee of "individual liberty and sexual freedom."[15] Discourses of asylum support the liberal ideals of freedom and liberty inherent in universal notions of national citizenship while obscuring and perpetuating the racial, sexual, and gendered hierarchies historically embedded in the practice of citizenship.[16] At the same time, asylum also enables U.S. citizenship to be positioned against the so-called patriarchal, homophobic, and sexist cultures outside of the United States.

Like gay and lesbian asylum seekers, trans migrants make their asylum claims on the basis of "membership in a particular social group." Hernandez-Montiel's grant of asylum as a "gay man with a female sexual identity," not as a transgender woman, demonstrates how trans asylum seekers in the 1990s had to draw upon already established legal categories of gender and sexual identity to build their cases. "Transsexual" and "transgender" are explicitly acknowledged in precedential asylum case law in 2007, when the Ninth Circuit Court of Appeals refers to a trans asylum applicant, Nancy Morales, as a "transsexual" and uses female pronouns in the published court decision.[17] And it is only in 2015, in *Edin Carey Avendano-Hernandez v. Loretta E. Lynch*, that a trans migrant is granted relief as a "transgender" person.[18] There are however successful unpublished (and therefore nonprecedential) asylum cases that recognize trans asylum seekers within the categories of "transgender" and "transsexual."[19]

It is important to note that I am not advocating for the imposition of transgender or transsexual as universal categories, or that the legal recognition of transgender as a category signals the existence of some sort of "real" trans identity. In fact, I am interested in how the history of trans asylum cases opens up ways of thinking about trans subjects and identities that push against the reification of the categories of transsexual and transgender in other legal arenas and in cultural forms. As I discuss in this chapter, creative legal strategies— formulations like "gay man with a female sexual identity"—used in early trans asylum cases to make the applicants legible within existing legal paradigms frustrate the law's tendency to posit trans subjects as stable, and reference the interrelatedness of gender and sexuality in ways that is often flattened by the category of transgender. Tracing the incorporation of the category of "transgender" into asylum law in the early 2000s illustrates how the recognition of "transgender" as a legal category has its own regulatory effects. As I noted in the introduction to this book, "transgender" and "transsexual" are U.S.-centric categories that fail to capture or translate the diversity of gender and sexual identities and ways of being. The adoption of transgender as an established legal category in asylum law happened quickly in the early 2000s, aided in part by the increased circulation of the language of "transgender" in national and international human rights discourses and by the advocacy efforts of immigrant rights organizations.[20] For example, USCIS worked with the national LGBTQ immigrant rights organization Immigration Equality for two years to develop a training module for asylum officers to learn how to better adjudicate asylum claims by LGBTI persons.[21] This module, "Guidance for Adjudicating Lesbian, Gay, Bisexual, Transgender, and Intersex (LGBTI) Refugee and Asylum Claims," was released in 2012, and provides definitions of "transgender" as well as recommendations on how asylum officers should consider trans asylum applicants in relation to the formulation of "particular social group."[22]

Applying for Asylum

This section of the chapter details the steps involved in applying for asylum in the United States, in order to theorize how this procedure discursively constructs the figure of the trans migrant as a legible legal subject. Asylum begins with the materiality of a body on the land, since applications for asylum can only be filed by persons who are in the territorial United States, unlike refugee applications which are processed abroad. Individuals can apply for asylum either affirmatively or defensively, depending on whether they file their application on their own initiative or file it before an immigration judge after being placed in removal proceedings.[23] As trans asylum seekers move through the application procedure, they are increasingly codified and abstracted in legal representations as well as increasingly removed from their cases in terms of their physical presence and their voices. While this is the process of legal subjection for all subjects, the experiences of trans subjects can help us understand this process better since the sexed and gendered trans body tends to disappear and then reappear at key moments in the legal process. The moments in which the applicant's sexed, gendered, and racialized body is invoked (and simultaneously produced) in asylum legal procedures illustrate the centrality of the body to the asylum claim and to the production of the trans legal subject, despite liberalism's understanding of personhood as disembodied. The particularities of the trans body and the harms experienced by trans applicants—before, during, and after their asylum cases— center on their sexed and gendered embodiment. I use embodiment to refer to the cultural, social, legal, and political processes through which meanings are attached to the bodies and bodily practices of trans asylum applicants, in order to highlight how these asylum cases do not just produce legal subjects who have trans identities but also produce the trans body.

Affirmative applications for asylum are from persons who are currently in the United States and who decide to apply for asylum prior to the initiation of removal proceedings by the government.[24] After an asylum seeker submits an application, an interview with an asylum officer is scheduled. Although asylum officers receive specialized training in conducting interviews with persons who are fleeing persecution, most asylum officers are not attorneys.

The second type of asylum application procedure is a defensive asylum application. In such cases, the government has issued a Notice to Appear, which requires the noncitizen to demonstrate that she is not removable on the basis of committing removable offenses, entering the United States without proper documents, or living in the United States without legal status. Noncitizens whose affirmative asylum applications are denied and who are not in lawful status are also placed in removal proceedings. Once in removal proceedings, noncitizens can argue for an asylum claim as a defense. Asylum applicants who file for asylum defensively when charged with deportability are placed in detention centers and prisons while their cases are decided, a process that may take months or even years.[25] Defensive asylum cases go directly to immigration court, where the applicant appears before an immigration judge who hears the evidence and issues a decision.[26] Hernandez-Montiel's asylum case began at this stage of the procedure in immigration court. The immigration hearing covers the same material as the asylum interview with an asylum officer in terms of establishing persecution, credibility, and so on, but unlike an interview with an asylum officer, removal proceedings are adversarial, and an attorney from U.S. Immigration and Customs Enforcement (ICE) is present to argue the case against the applicant.

Both the asylum interview and the immigration court hearing work like a Foucaultian scene of confession.[27] The asylum officer or the immigration judge is the authority to whom the applicant has to present a certain narrative of persecution and identity that fits the requirements of the law. There is a prescribed form, and the legal adjudicator is looking for certain aspects of the applicant's experience. This aspect of the asylum process parallels the history of medical professionals' assessments of trans people seeking access to hormone therapy or surgeries, in which trans people are required to attest to a life-long history of gender dysphoria and subscribe to a "wrong body" narrative to qualify as "transgender."[28] Similar to the immutability required for medical recognition of trans status, trans asylum applicants must enter into the particular mode of language mandated by asylum statute, which is grounded in discourses of immutability and necessitates clear distinctions between identities, groups, and experiences. Immutability operates as a central category within asylum cases, especially for those sexuality- and gender-based cases involving claims of "membership in a particular social group."

The main purpose of the asylum interview and immigration hearing is to determine credibility. After the interview or hearing, the asylum officer or immigration judge will review all the documents of the case to prepare the decision. The burden of proof is on the applicant to establish that she is a refugee in accordance with the law. The applicant's testimony alone may be enough to meet the burden of proof, but only if "the applicant's testimony is credible, is persuasive, and refers to specific facts sufficient to demonstrate that the applicant is a refugee."[29] According to the statute, a credibility determination may be based on "the demeanor, candor, or responsiveness of the applicant or witness, the inherent plausibility of the applicant's or witness's account."[30] This section of the Immigration and Nationality Act presents these highly subjective criteria—demeanor, candor, responsiveness—as neutral and empirically determinable qualities, thus belying the ways that they are embodied traits read through culturally and nationally specific ideas about gender, race, sexuality, and class. These criteria also highlight the importance of bodily gesture in the asylum interview and immigration court proceedings. Qualities like "demeanor," "candor," and "responsiveness" are signaled (and evaluated) through bodily gestures like tone and volume of voice, eye contact and movement, body posture and movement, and dress and appearance. These qualities, while included in asylum statute as a way to verify credibility, also provide clues to the applicant's embodied identity for asylum officers and immigration judges, and therefore serve as a measure of the immutability of identity.

Paradoxically, as measurements of immutability, these qualities are themselves about movement and mobility. Gestures and bodily performances like these are fleeting and contextual, yet these are gestures that confirm an identity that is supposed to be fixed and constant. During her 1996 immigration court hearing, Hernandez-Montiel is questioned about being dressed in women's clothing and wearing makeup, and the INS attorney is interested in whether this is an everyday practice for her.[31] The bodily practice of dressing as a woman and wearing makeup becomes fixed as part of one's essential gendered identity only when it occurs every day. In their respective decisions, both the immigration judge and the Board of Immigration Appeals (BIA) comment on Hernandez-Montiel's inability to remember if she was wearing women's clothing on a specific day when she was arrested in 1994. The fact that she cannot remember what she was wearing on a particular day two years prior to her immigration court hearing is used as evidence by both the immigration judge and the BIA to argue that her "assumed female persona" is not immutable or fundamental to her identity.[32]

For both affirmative and defensive asylum applications, if the immigration judge denies the applicant's petition, the asylum seeker has the option of appealing the decision with the BIA, within thirty days of the immigration judge's order of removal (with the accompanying fee).[33] The BIA is the highest administrative body for interpreting and applying immigration laws in the United States and currently consists of twenty-two permanent members and five temporary members who are appointed by the Attorney General.[34] For the majority of the cases it decides, the BIA does not hold courtroom proceedings, but rather reviews appeals on paper.[35] As a result of the "streamlining" of the BIA under George W. Bush, designed to increase the efficiency of the BIA decision-making process, the BIA may affirm the immigration judge's ruling without opinion or with only a one paragraph summary decision.[36]

If an asylum applicant loses an appeal before the BIA, the applicant can file a petition for review with the U.S. Circuit Court of Appeals.[37] It is difficult to win an appeal at the federal court level because the standard for appeal is the "substantial evidence test," which means that the federal court cannot replace the judgment of the BIA and/or the immigration judge with its own judgment. The circuit courts have limited jurisdiction in the sense that they can only review certain questions; circuit court decisions tend to focus on whether the right legal standard was applied. The circuit courts cannot grant asylum or withholding of removal or CAT protection but can only remand the case back to the immigration judge to reconsider. If the substantial evidence presented in the case supports the decision that is being appealed, the federal court must uphold the decision of the lower court.[38] Cases are usually decided by panels of three judges who represent the court. The court will not accept any additional evidence and it decides the case based on the briefs submitted by the attorneys for each side and on the oral arguments, if permitted.[39]

As my discussion in this section demonstrates, the procedure of applying for asylum functions as a process of legal subjection for trans asylum seekers through their abstraction and increased distance from their cases at each stage. To some extent, this is how the law works for everyone as it produces a disembodied legal subject, yet there is a tension between this legal process and how asylum claims for trans subjects are firmly grounded in their bodies in significant ways. Trans asylum applicants must argue that their sexual and gender identities are immutable and that their bodies serve as evidence of those identities. At the starting point, whether it is in an interview with an asylum officer or in a courtroom in front of an immigration judge, the applicant is physically present and has a voice, even if she has to articulate herself in prescribed terms. As her claim moves through the appeals process, the applicant herself is left behind. She is not present when a member on the BIA considers her claim and she is not present when a three-member panel of circuit court judges hears her case. Yet despite the law's insistence on increasing abstraction and the physical absence of applicants in the later stages of their cases, the sexed, raced, and gendered bodies of the trans asylum seekers reappear throughout the legal process and disrupt the process of legal representation. Trans bodies and bodily gestures are evaluated when asylum officers and immigration judges assess credibility, for example, and, as I show in the next section, fetishized constructions of racialized trans bodies inform the adjudicators' conclusions and circulate throughout written court decisions. Like other gendered, racialized, and marginalized subjects of the law, trans asylum seekers reveal the contradictions within liberal human rights law, which is premised on assumptions of universality and disembodied subjectivity.

Discourses of Immutability in the Category of "Particular Social Group"

Circuit court decisions like *Hernandez-Montiel v. INS* are the final product of this legal procedure of applying for asylum. Published circuit court decisions hold precedent for future asylum cases.[40] As such, they play a major role in the formation of asylum case law, and they are usually the point of entry for legal scholars and practitioners into particular legal questions. In this section, I draw on Bruno Latour's work to theorize circuit court decisions as "immutable mobiles," which can help us understand how these decisions circulate and shape asylum case law. I then explore how discourses of immutability structure the category of "particular social group" and discuss how to make sense of Hernandez-Montiel's classification as a "gay man with a female sexual identity" by the Ninth Circuit Court of Appeals.

Latour's analysis of the process of inscription within scientific inquiry offers insight into the relationship between the text of the court decision and the applicant.[41] Latour describes how the process of inscription, in which three-dimensional objects of inquiry are translated into two-dimensional figures and graphs on paper, displaces and dispatches the "original" object so that the inscription assumes the central place of importance.[42] Latour describes this translation as an extraction process through which complex phenomena are "made *flat*" and become both immutable and mobile as inscriptions.[43] The inscription, which is what Latour calls an "immutable mobile," only becomes valuable through the process of displacement from the initial object of study: "[w]ithout the displacement, the inscription is worthless."[44] Circuit court decisions illustrate Latour's contention that inscriptions and their mobilizations are key to understanding the power relations between objects and their written representations, and are a means through which institutions generate authoritative discourses about subjects. As "immutable mobiles," circuit court decisions—and the legal documents that inform them—displace the asylum seeker through the inscription process and then circulate as precedent to determine subsequent legal questions related to the asylum process.

In conjunction with the form and circulation of circuit court decisions as "immutable mobiles," discourses of immutability also condition the production of trans asylum seekers as legal subjects within these texts. Immutability is a central category within asylum cases due to the definition of "particular social group" within asylum case law which was developed in *In re Acosta*.[45] In this 1985 case, the BIA examined the category of "social group" in detail and developed an approach that continues to influence asylum claims based on social group today. The BIA described a particular social group as a group of persons who "share a common, immutable characteristic. The shared characteristic might be an innate one such as sex, color, or kinship ties, or in some circumstances it might be a shared past experience such as former military leadership or land ownership."[46] Only shared and unchangeable characteristics that form a fundamental part of an individual's identity or conscience are considered to constitute that individual as a member of a particular social group. In *In re Acosta*, the BIA noted that the definition of particular social group needs to be determined on a case-by-case basis and that, importantly, social group claims are not distinct from claims on the other four protected grounds, which can also be seen as being based on fundamental or immutable characteristics. The BIA thus suggested that claims based on particular social group must be approached analogously to the other grounds for asylum (race, religion, nationality, and political opinion) in order for the refugee definition to be consistent and rigorous.[47]

Because *In re Acosta* defined "particular social group" in terms of immutability, trans asylum seekers have to posit their sexual and gender identities as essential and fixed, even as their sexed and gendered embodiment may be shifting. It is particularly ironic and painful that trans asylum seekers must present their genders and sexual identities as immutable when the basis of their asylum claims is precisely that they have experienced persecution as a result of their changing sexes and genders. Hernandez-Montiel's successful asylum claim at the Ninth Circuit Court was based on her characterization as a "gay man with a female sexual identity." According to Robert Gerber, Hernandez-Montiel's attorney, fifteen-year-old Hernandez-Montiel had approached him and identified as gay, as having been on hormones, and as wanting to have surgery to become a woman. From conversations with his client, Gerber had originally developed the case for immigration court based on homosexuality and transsexuality; he made the same arguments before the BIA on appeal. However, he changed his legal strategy to that of sexual identity for the appeal at the Ninth Circuit Court, after consulting with some gay and lesbian rights groups.[48] In part, the change in legal strategy was successful because "sexual identity" had been previously established as an immutable characteristic in *In re Toboso-Alfonso* (1990).[49]

Hernandez-Montiel v. INS set an important precedent for the recognition of transgender identity as a grounds for asylum, even though it relies on the language of "sexual identity" rather than explicitly recognizing Hernandez-Montiel as trans.[50] In *Hernandez-Montiel v. INS*, the Ninth Circuit Court justices refuse to take up the medicalized language of "transsexual" even though the case materials offer it: in a footnote, the court decision notes that "In addition to being a gay man with a female sexuality identity, Geovanni's brief states that he 'may be considered a transsexual.'"[51] This footnote concludes with the statement that "We need not consider in this case whether transsexuals constitute a particular social group." Some of the court's reluctance to engage with this question may be due to the distinctions between procedural due process and substantive rights, and the court's ability to review the latter.[52] The final section of this chapter discusses the tensions between the procedural and the substantive in the constitution of legal subjects in more detail.

Given that *Hernandez-Montiel v. INS* is a precedential case for trans asylum seekers, it is notable that the language of "transsexual" or "transgender" is not taken up by the court. While the court's resistance to deciding whether "transsexual" constitutes a particular social group may be attributed to the limits on its ability to decide those kinds of substantive issues, the treatment of "transsexual" in the case tells us something beyond the question of judicial review. The Ninth Circuit Court's refusal to recognize transsexual as a specific legal category points to the U.S. state's investment in particular constructions of citizen and nation. After *Hernandez-Montiel v. INS*, there have been successful asylum cases in which applicants have represented themselves as transgender, but it was not until 2015 that the Ninth Circuit Court published an affirmative decision in which the petitioner was identified by the court as a transgender woman.[53] As I note above, the BIA is extremely selective about what cases it publishes as precedent. The Ninth Circuit Court also has a strict set of criteria for publishing its opinions and similarly only publishes a relatively small number of its decisions.[54] Publication can be seen as a defensive strategy used by the state to protect itself from further claims against it. The selectiveness of the BIA and the Ninth Circuit Court in publishing cases, combined with the fact that many successful asylum cases are decided by immigration officials and do not go to court, contributes to the lack of legal precedent in asylum case law that recognizes "transsexual" or "transgender" as a particular social group. The publication of precedential cases also makes clear how the mechanism of the law itself plays a central role in the transformation of the law, that is, the publication of cases is a calculated and strategic process for reshaping the practice of law.[55] Published decisions function as forms of "immutable mobiles" in the sense that they circulate to establish precedent and consistency for subsequent cases. Yet in doing so, they also prescribe the degree and nature of change allowed in the law, dictating how and how much the law can change (for example, to incorporate subjects who have been previously marginalized). The mutability of the law in these moments contrasts sharply with the immutability assigned to trans asylum seekers and their countries of origin.

The Ninth Circuit Court's refusal to consider whether "transsexual" constitutes a particular social group in *Hernandez-Montiel v. INS* also highlights the investment of state institutions in rigid and normalized binary gender categories. In her analysis of *Hernandez-Montiel v. INS,* Sara L. McKinnon argues along these lines, writing that the Ninth Circuit's insistence on Hernandez-Montiel as a male-assigned subject upholds the separation of sex/sexuality and gender in asylum case law and relies on a "one-sex, one-gender logic."[56] She continues, "When male-assigned applicants claim asylum for reasons involving what could be described as their gender identity and expression, their claims must be read through sexuality so as not to challenge the undergirding, naturalized logic of male as the immutable sex for which asylum (and arguably the nation) was originally intended."[57] While I agree with McKinnon's description of the way that gender identity is read through sexuality in *Hernandez-Montiel v. INS*, I disagree with her argument that gender was absent in the case and that trans women asylum applicants are successful because they can fit into the male-assigned subject box as neutral and appropriate subjects for the U.S. nation.[58]

Instead, I argue that the formulation of gender and sexuality in cases like *Hernandez-Montiel v. INS* actually offers some productive ways to think about the categories of "transsexual" and "transgender" in the law. Despite its shortcomings as a precedent-setting case for trans asylum seekers in terms of the court's refusal to consider "transsexual" as a particular social group, *Hernandez-Montiel v. INS* does acknowledge the links between sexuality and (trans)gender identity. Many trans people do not experience sexuality and gender identity as mutually exclusive and/or contradictory categories.[59] Yet definitions of transgender developed within academic scholarship, as well as within public policy and social services, tend to stabilize and homogenize dominant notions of transgender to the exclusion of other gender and sexual identities. Somewhat paradoxically, *Hernandez-Montiel v. INS* troubles these theorizations of transgender within the United States and highlights how the category of transgender is produced as a category of knowledge and management in legal and social realms.[60] Legal scholar Joseph Landau highlights this potential of the case in his discussion of *Hernandez-Montiel v. INS* and *Reyes-Reyes v. Ashcroft,* a 2004 case in which the asylum applicant is also referred to as a "homosexual male with a female sexual identity."[61] He argues that the court's decision not to refer to the plaintiffs as transgender could also be read more generously as a legal strategy that strives to be as expansive as possible, in order to define gender and sexual identity for the delimitation of particular social group categories that can incorporate trans-identified asylum seekers. Landau points out that in both these cases, the Ninth Circuit relied on a person's self-definition as an accurate reflection of gender identity rather than establishing a definitive standard for membership in the particular social group. Therefore, he contends that these two cases "highlight a greater respect for the manifold ways in which transgender identity is expressed."[62] While these two cases show how dominant legal paradigms fail to account for the category of transgender, that failure also highlights the limitations of the category of transgender itself (as well as the medicalized category of transsexuality) and the disciplining work that legal categories of "transgender" do to produce legible transgender subjects.[63]

The larger political and economic context of asylum law and the interests of the courts also influence the legal strategies that guide the formation of particular social groups. The courts tend to develop elaborate definitions of the particular social group category for each asylum case that are specific to that individual in that country in that historical moment. In order to narrow the proposed social group, the BIA and the courts often develop artificial, convoluted categories that produce distorted discussions of who gets to be protected from harm as well as what this harm is. This seems to be in response to the floodgates argument that is often made about asylum, in particular, about asylum claims based on gender and sexuality.[64] The courts and the BIA are concerned with what they perceive to be a potential problem of oppressed women and queer and trans people from all over the world trying to seek asylum in the United States; therefore, they define persecution and particular social group very narrowly in decisions about gender-related and sexuality-related claims.[65]

Gender, Sexuality, and Culture as Immutable

Much of the critical discussion of *Hernandez-Montiel v. INS* by legal scholars has focused on the role of immutability in the court decision. But focusing only on immutability can become a trap in legal reasoning because it reduces understandings of subjectivity to the terms of essential qualities.[66] In this section, I use the lens of mobility to think through the dominant discourse of immutability, and the established categories upon which it is grounded, in order to illustrate the other forms of legibility that operate in these legal texts. I focus primarily on the Ninth Circuit Court decision in *Hernandez-Montiel v. INS,* but I also discuss Geovanni Hernandez-Montiel's immigration court hearing and the testimony of the expert witness, Thomas M. Davies. Discourses of immutability also govern the role of expert witness testimony and the U.S. Department of State's country condition reports in trans asylum cases. Asylum procedure not only constructs gender and sexual identity as immutable but also constructs the applicants' cultures and their countries of origin as immutable through the conflation of violence and culture. Discourses of immutability serve an immobilizing function, stabilizing the otherwise messy mutual articulation of racial, cultural, and national identities with sexual and gender identity. In these court cases, immobility works on multiple levels—the level of the individual's identity, the level of the individual's relationship to her culture and country of origin, and the level of knowledge production itself—in the process of constructing the trans asylum seeker as a legible legal subject.

A close reading of the background section of *Hernandez-Montiel v. INS* underscores how discourses of immutability produce asylum seekers as legible and recognizable subjects in circuit court decisions. The "factual background" section is the first section of the circuit court decision and provides a narrative of Hernandez-Montiel's experiences of persecution and identity as evidence for her claim for membership in the particular social group of "gay men with female sexual identities" in Mexico. This narrative produces Hernandez-Montiel along two registers—gender/sexual identity and persecution/bodily violence—that proceed along parallel lines but come together to solidify the subject. Like the rest of the court decision, this section is written in the impersonal, formal voice of the circuit court judge writing the decision, which stands in stark contrast to the violent events and moments it presents. The story told in this section is the story of Hernandez-Montiel's life reduced to discrete and particular moments of violence and damage, so that the brief and partial glimpse of the person at the center of the case is related through the lenses of violence, trauma, and persecution. The background section of the court decision functions as a repository for the applicant's history of persecution.

The first sentence in the factual background section quotes Hernandez-Montiel's testimony about realizing an attraction to people of the same sex at age eight and then states that "[a]t the age of 12, Geovanni began dressing and behaving as a woman."[67] By beginning with this statement, the decision affirms the immutability of Hernandez-Montiel's gender and sexual identity, realized at a young age. This statement also treats gender as self-evident. The meaning of "dressing and behaving as a woman" is presumed to be apparent and universal. The court decision then recounts how Hernandez-Montiel experienced "reprimands" and disciplining from family members and school officials for what they perceived to be her "sexual orientation."

After a paragraph about Hernandez-Montiel's experiences with family and school officials, the background section dedicates three paragraphs to a discussion of the violence and harassment Hernandez-Montiel was subjected to by Mexican police officers. The decision describes how she was detained and "even strip-searched" by police on many occasions for walking down the street or hanging out with "other boys perceived to be gay."[68] Hernandez-Montiel and a friend were arrested twice in 1992, and "the police told them that it was illegal for homosexuals to walk down the street and for men to dress like women" even though the police did not charge them with any crime.[69] In addition to establishing police misconduct and abuse for the purposes of confirming past persecution, this passage reinforces the categorization of Hernandez-Montiel through the rubrics of homosexuality and female gender presentation and behavior, in order to substantiate the construction of her as a "gay male with female sexual identity."

The decision also includes a detailed description of how Hernandez-Montiel, at age fourteen, was sexually assaulted and raped on two separate occasions by police officers. These details further substantiate Hernandez-Montiel's claim of past persecution, but they also construct her as a victim. As I discuss in the next chapter, this is typical of asylum claims since asylum law incentivizes a victimization frame. While the section on "factual background" begins with an assertion of Hernandez-Montiel's self-identification, it proceeds to document how the perpetrators of the abuse perceived her in terms of gender and sexuality. Consequently, Hernandez-Montiel becomes visible and legible in this decision through the gaze of others. The circuit court judges never see Hernandez-Montiel in person, only through the paper inscriptions that have displaced her and through the voice of her attorney, Robert Gerber.

The discussion of Hernandez-Montiel's identity and persecution needs to be understood in relation to the representation of Mexico, since the legal argument that her gender—articulated through the language of sexual identity—is immutable depends on the simultaneous construction of "Mexican culture" and national identity as unchanging. Michelle A. McKinley discusses this in terms of how the administrative state "both operationalizes and naturalizes 'culture.'"[70] She argues that the articulation of culture within asylum cases has implications for the construction of citizenship. Judges, officials, and other bureaucrats are "largely removed from the loftier conversations about rights and citizenship that occur among academic political philosophers, yet their decisions are critical to enforcing decisions about refugee and asylum status, and by extension, the effective enjoyment of citizenship."[71] Expert witness testimony plays a vital role in substantiating a trans asylum seeker's claim for membership in a particular social group and claim of persecution, and it does so by embedding the testimony of the asylum applicant in the larger circulation of validated knowledge about the culture and society of the applicant's country of origin.[72] The authority of the expert witness can participate in the displacement of the asylum applicant's testimony and presence in her own case. In Hernandez-Montiel's immigration court hearing in 1996, the expert witness, Thomas M. Davies, was called to the stand to give his testimony before Hernandez-Montiel. Although this was due to Davies's limited time schedule—Gerber states in the hearing that he would normally call the respondent to the stand first—this order meant that in the court proceedings, Davies's testimony functioned as the initial framing for the case and for Hernandez-Montiel's testimony.[73] The "expertise" of Thomas M. Davies comes from his educational history and his academic position as a professor of history and director of the Center for Latin American Studies at San Diego State University.[74] Davies's testimony mediates the relationship between Hernandez-Montiel and "Mexican culture" by representing Mexico as a violent and oppressive place for queer and trans people. Asylum law requires that the applicant show that her country of origin as a whole is an unsafe place for her as a member of a particular social group, not just that she has experienced violence by individual actors.

It is this requirement of systematic persecution that illustrates how the asylum process reproduces dominant forms of U.S. nationalism and imperialism, in ways that parallel Chandra Talpade Mohanty's analysis of the construction of the "Third World woman" as a singular, monolithic subject in texts by Western feminists.[75] The asylum process calls for the denigration of an asylum seeker's country of origin as violent and oppressive, always in relation to the construction of the United States as a free, democratic, and superior civilized country.[76] In his analysis of *Hernandez-Montiel v. INS*, Lionel Cantú Jr. notes that Davies's expert witness testimony contributes to what he calls the "othering" of Mexico and the positioning of the United States as the only place in which Hernandez-Montiel can be her "true self."[77] *Hernandez-Montiel v. INS* serves as a site for the (re)production of nationalist ideologies about both Mexico and the United States, in which "Mexican culture" becomes the traumatizing agent that immobilizes and constrains Hernandez-Montiel's expression of gender and sexual identity. Héctor Carrillo problematizes these racialized representations of the United States and Mexico that rely on a romanticized view of the United States because they go against recent sociological research on sexuality in Mexico that suggests that there has been significant social change in relation to sexuality and homosexuality over the last three decades.[78]

In Hernandez-Montiel's immigration court hearing, Davies testifies to the difference of homosexuality in Latin America compared to Western Europe and the United States, due to the strict demarcation of "the role of the male" as opposed to that of the "female" in same-sex acts. He states that the Mexican police especially target those "homosexual males that are dressed or acting out the feminine role," more than those who act out the male role.[79] Later in his testimony, Davies further reifies this difference by stating that in his opinion, the homosexuals who act out a feminine role constitute "a separate social entity within Latin American society and in this case within the nation of Mexico."[80] In addition to representing Mexico as homophobic and sexist, Davies represents Mexican (homo)sexual identities as fixed and static, since he stresses the connection between sexual acts and gender identity—that is, being a bottom, the receptive partner, comes to determine a female gender identity. This formulation relies on and reproduces a culturally specific alignment of sex acts, sexuality, and gender identity, in which receptivity equals passivity equals female, consequently denying the complex and myriad relationships among these aspects of a person's acts, desires, and identity. Furthermore, although this works in Hernandez-Montiel's case, the conflation of "passive" and feminine sets a problematic standard that might make it difficult for others to obtain asylum, since the court ruled that Hernandez-Montiel "manifests his sexual orientation by adopting gendered traits characteristically associated with women."[81] In other words, the construction of Hernandez-Montiel as a "gay man with a female sexual identity" supports dominant representations of gay men as feminine in appearance and behavior, so that gay men and trans people who don't look "gay" or "feminine" enough may face skepticism from asylum officers and immigration court judges.[82] Latin American studies scholars have critiqued this construction of Mexican masculinity, which structures and limits academic interpretations of gendered homosexuality in terms of *activos* and *passivos* in Mexico, and in Latin America more generally.[83] The gendering of violence in Davies's testimony may also have implications for the use of *Hernandez-Montiel v. INS* for asylum cases involving transgender men, since the discursive casting of "a gay man with a female sexual identity" emphasizes the misogyny of "Mexican culture."

In addition to showing how arguments for the immutability of gender and sexual identities rely on the construction of cultural and national identities as immutable, Davies's testimony highlights the implication of these identities in the political and economic processes of the nation-state and points to how transnational economic policies impact and shape processes of asylum in the United States. Davies argues that the impending collapse of the Mexican economy will most likely increase violence against homosexuals and other marginalized groups in Mexico.[84] The INS attorney arguing against Hernandez-Montiel's claim expresses skepticism about the connection between the devaluation of the peso and increased persecution of homosexuals, but neither the INS attorney nor Davies acknowledge the role the United States plays in the stability of the Mexican economy through economic policies like the North American Free Trade Agreement (NAFTA) and others. While the passage of NAFTA in 1994, for example, benefited large agribusiness corporations in the participating countries, it also led to an increase in Mexico's poverty rate from 52 percent to 69 percent over two years, displaced approximately fifteen million farmers in Mexico, and heightened unemployment in Mexico's urban centers, resulting in increased undocumented migration to the United States.[85] Juana María Rodríguez notes that historically, individuals who come from countries that have an antagonistic relationship with the United States tend to be granted asylum more often than individuals who try to emigrate from countries that are supported militarily, politically, or economically by the United States.[86] Mexicans in particular are viewed with suspicion by asylum officials due to anxieties about the Mexico-U.S. border and due to the fears about masses of undocumented Mexicans migrating to the United States. Moreover, the fact that most of the published circuit court cases that involve trans asylum seekers are from Latin American migrants supports Cantú Jr.'s observation that "the exigencies of U.S. relations with Latin America clearly shaped the politics of gay asylum" within the United States more generally.[87]

In this part of the chapter, I have engaged in a close reading of the *Hernandez-Montiel v. INS* decision and the expert witness testimony in her immigration court hearing to examine the role of immutability in asylum process. The attention given to the details of terror experienced by Hernandez-Montiel from family members and police officers illustrate how discourses of violence and abuse become the primary register through which she emerges as a gendered and racialized embodied subject. These discourses are intertwined with—and dependent upon—discourses of culture and nation as immutable. In the following and final section of the chapter, I turn to questions of legal procedure in *Hernandez-Montiel v. INS*, which also play a central role in the construction of Hernandez-Montiel as a legal subject.

Substance and Process in Asylum Case Law

In this section, I read the tensions between the substantive and the procedural in circuit court decisions to show how the applicant's gendered, sexualized, and racialized body informs the entire circuit court decision even as the narration of Hernandez-Montiel's body and her experiences of bodily violence are largely confined to the front end of the document in the initial "factual background" section. Following the standard legal template of published circuit court decisions, this first "factual background" section is followed by a section that discusses the procedural background and history of the case, a section in which the circuit court establishes its jurisdiction over the central questions of the case, a discussion section in which the court evaluates the legal grounds of each of the claims made by the petitioner,[88] and a conclusion section that states the court's decision on the appeal. These latter sections of the published decision become more concerned with legal questions of jurisdiction and precedent rather than with the substantive facts of the case, and the subject of the case tends to recede in the discussions of legal procedure. Drawing on legal scholars who discuss the tensions between substance and procedure in litigation, I argue that despite the lessening of attention to the applicant herself, the focus on procedure, and the specific procedural questions with which the circuit courts are concerned, play a key role in the constitution of the trans asylum seeker as a legal subject.

Legal scholars Hiroshi Motomura and Jenny S. Martinez question the presumed distinction between procedural due process and substantive rights.[89] Claims rooted in procedural due process concern the *way* in which claims are heard, whereas substantive claims argue for certain substantive rights due as a matter of constitutional law. Substantive rights include constitutional rights, like the right to free speech, free association, and equal protection, as well as rights known as "substantive due process" rights that are based on the due process clause, such as the right to privacy. Procedural due process, in contrast, involves claims that are limited to procedure, usually the right to notice and fair hearing. While both Martinez's and Motomura's arguments are more limited in scope than mine, they provide a useful starting point from which to develop my analysis of the broader distinction between legal process and the substance of an individual's rights and claims. Motomura notes that there is a long history of debates over the distinction between procedural and substantive, a distinction that has "proved to be elusive (and perhaps illusory) in the numerous areas of law in which it has acquired rhetorical significance."[90] He contends that in specific areas of immigration law, procedural due process serves as a surrogate for substantive judicial review.[91] In immigration cases, arguments attempting to claim substantive rights have largely floundered, but those that are styled as claims about process have proven more effective. Similarly, Martinez argues that these two categories are intertwined, such that procedural rules can advance substantive claims but can also become a way of avoiding substantive questions.[92] In her critique of the procedural focus of "war on terror" cases that deal with Guantánamo detainees, Martinez argues that while a procedural focus is not completely undesirable, "it is also important to remember that, whatever its systemic virtues, the focus on process rather than substance comes at a human cost."[93] For example, in the case of litigation in the "war on terror," she argues that these procedural rulings have important implications for substantive rights.

Firstly, by delaying the final resolution of rights claims, the courts allow for serious violations of human rights to continue for years. Secondly, the procedural approaches foreclose "many rights-based challenges without actually considering the merits of those challenges."[94]

Like Martinez, I am also concerned with the human cost that results from the extensive focus on procedure in circuit court decisions, which often means that the substantive question of whether an asylum applicant will and should receive protection and legal status from the United States is frequently deferred and avoided in the published decisions of the circuit courts.[95] My focus on how the emphasis on the procedural works to constitute the trans asylum seeker as a legal subject provides another vantage point for considering the human cost of the asylum process, since the process of becoming a legal subject correlates to the asylum seeker's increasing abstraction in her case. Tracing the procedural history of the case shows how Hernandez-Montiel's racial, sexual, and gender embodiment plays a central role in the immigration court proceedings and in the BIA decision, even as it tends to disappear in the final circuit court decision. That is, the legal process constitutes Hernandez-Montiel as a subject whose asylum claim is grounded in her bodily experiences of gendered and sexual persecution, yet her embodied subjectivity is then largely absented from most of the discussion in the final circuit court decision.

Hernandez-Montiel's attorney, Robert Gerber, developed the initial case for the immigration court and the BIA based on the grounds of homosexuality and transsexuality. Professor Thomas M. Davies was the sole expert witness, and Davies's testimony was unrebutted in immigration court.[96] For the immigration court hearing, Hernandez-Montiel wore makeup and dressed in women's clothes and was asked by both Gerber and the INS attorney whether this was how Hernandez-Montiel normally presented herself in both Mexico and the United States. The attorney for the INS also asked Hernandez-Montiel about the charges on which she had appeared in juvenile court, as well as whether Hernandez-Montiel had ever been arrested for prostitution or possession of cocaine and drug trafficking. Because Gerber did not know what kind of evidence the persecution had (if any), he advised Hernandez-Montiel to take the Fifth Amendment right against self-incrimination.[97] In his written decision, Kenneth Bagley, the immigration judge, indicated that he held the invocation of the Fifth Amendment against Hernandez-Montiel, even though he did find Hernandez-Montiel's testimony credible. Bagley's stance on this point reinforces the arbitrariness of asylum, since asylum statute makes a grant of asylum an exercise of discretion on the part of the asylum adjudicator.[98] Bagley ruled that Hernandez-Montiel failed to prove past persecution or a well-founded fear of future persecution on account of membership in a particular social group.[99]

Gerber characterized these questions about drug use and sex work as irrelevant and invasive,[100] but I see these questions as integral to the way that asylum adjudicators like the immigration judge and the attorney for the INS understand and make sense of trans and queer migrants, especially those from Latin America. Migrants like Hernandez-Montiel become legible through overdetermined discourses of criminality and sexual deviation, so it is not surprising that the attorney for the INS attempted to imply that Hernandez-Montiel was a drug-using sex worker, even though there was no evidence and no legal finding by the immigration judge on this issue. These representations also reverberate throughout the appeals process, most notably in the BIA decision, and show how trans asylum seekers' bodies are constantly present in the decision-making process, even when they themselves are not. The production and circulation of these stigmatizing imaginaries about trans women's migrant bodies shape how immigration judges evaluate asylum applicants when they are physically present in the courtroom and become embedded into the decisions made by asylum adjudicators, which then continue to influence the case throughout the appeals process when subsequent adjudicators do not see or speak to the applicant directly.

The BIA denied Gerber's request for an oral argument and dismissed Hernandez-Montiel's appeal for asylum as well as for voluntary departure. Like the immigration judge, the BIA found Hernandez-Montiel's testimony credible, but also like the immigration judge, argued that Hernandez-Montiel did not meet the burden of proof for establishing that the abuse suffered was on account of membership in the particular social group of "homosexual males who dress as females." The BIA decision mentions the sexual assaults by Mexican police officers that Hernandez-Montiel experienced on two separate occasions as well as the attack by a group of men on the street, which left Hernandez-Montiel hospitalized. But the written decision focuses on the incidents when Hernandez-Montiel was stopped on the street by police officers who told her that it was illegal to dress as a woman or for homosexuals to walk on the street. After enumerating these incidents (but not the ones that involved actual physical and sexual violence), the BIA decision states "[t]he tenor of the respondent's claim is that he was mistreated because of the way he was dressed (*as a male prostitute*) and not because he is a homosexual" (my emphasis).[101]

Since there was no legal finding by the immigration judge on this issue, this statement reveals the homophobic, transphobic, and sexist assumptions made by Fred W. Vacca, the BIA member who authored the decision.[102] More importantly, this statement exemplifies the ways that the body of the asylum applicant informs the asylum process. Hernandez-Montiel exists for Vacca and the other BIA members on paper in court documents and legal briefs, in a mug shot, a set of fingerprints, and the biometrical data gathered by the border patrol agents. As inscriptions that become "immutable mobiles," these empirical data become the only representations of Hernandez-Montiel for the BIA members, and therefore become all of Hernandez-Montiel. Latour notes that people in power put faith into inscriptions' representations of phenomena: "They will never see more of the phenomena than what they can build through these many immutable mobiles."[103] I would add that cultural discourses of race, sexuality, and gender inform asylum adjudicators' interpretation of these flattened inscriptions. It is not surprising that Vacca translates this data into the racialized figure of a "male prostitute" for whom "mistreatment" by police is presumably to be expected. This is the figure that haunts the BIA decision, the figure whose fleshy racialized and sexualized embodiment is present in the room in Falls Church, Virginia, where the three BIA members deliberate Hernandez-Montiel's appeal while Hernandez-Montiel waits across the country in San Diego.[104] The BIA decision also echoes the immigration judge's argument—along with his misogyny and transphobia—that dressing as a woman is not an immutable characteristic, and the BIA therefore finds Hernandez-Montiel did not establish adequate grounds for a grant of asylum: "the respondent's mistreatment arose from his conduct (which is not immutable), thus the rape by the policemen, and the attack by a mob of gay bashers are not necessarily persecution, even if the Mexican authorities give low priority to protection of gays."[105]

The immigration court and BIA decisions, in which questions of Hernandez-Montiel's racial, sexual, and gender embodiment are central, form the backdrop of the Ninth Circuit Court decision in *Hernandez-Montiel v. INS*. Robert Gerber was surprised at the hostile and homophobic tone of the BIA decision; in order to prepare for the circuit court appeal, he distributed the BIA decision to lesbian and gay rights groups, and formed a defense team who issued an amicus brief. With the input of this defense team, Gerber reformulated his approach to one of "sexual identity," which made it easier for Hernandez-Montiel in terms of evidence and captured the interplay between her gender presentation, gender identity, and sexuality. This approach, which broadened the appeal beyond the categories of homosexuality and transsexuality, was successful.[106] The Ninth Circuit Court granted Hernandez-Montiel's request for review and remanded the case back to the BIA with specific instructions to grant withholding of removal of deportation and to present the case to the Attorney General for a grant of asylum.[107] In its written decision, the Ninth Circuit Court concluded that the BIA decision was "fatally flawed as a matter of law and is not supported by substantial evidence."[108] The final outcome of the case, upon remand to the BIA, was a double grant of withholding of removal and of asylum for Hernandez-Montiel.[109]

Circuit court decisions about asylum claims begin with a specific "background section" that presents the applicant's personal history and experiences of persecution, and then continue with sections about jurisdiction, correct legal standards, and other procedural issues. This background section serves to contain and bracket off the messiness of the applicant's embodiment from the procedural questions of the case, that is, bracket off the ways that the applicant's gender, sexuality, and race structure her positionality and experiences in her country of origin. Motomura and Martinez argue that courts use the procedural to both advance and avoid the substance of certain legal questions. Building on their analyses—and deploying a broader notion of "substance"—I argue that the dominance of the procedural in circuit court decisions for cases about trans asylum also plays a role in the production of the trans asylum seeker as a legal subject. The primary way this happens is through the disappearing of the applicant from her own case, so that the asylum seeker becomes a disembodied, abstracted legal subject. This is most obviously demonstrated by the physical absence of the applicant who does not appear before the circuit court judges in person. This abstraction is significant given that trans asylum claims are based on the experiences of violence and persecution trans migrants have experienced as a consequence of their embodiment, namely, their gender and sexuality.

Less obviously, the relative obscurity of the substantive final outcome of the case also contributes to the disappearance of the applicant. While the outcomes of precedential asylum cases at the circuit court level are published and accessible, the final substantive outcomes of those cases—whether the applicants received a grant of asylum, withholding of removal, or protection under CAT upon remand—are not. It is difficult to track down the final outcome of a "successful" case that has been remanded either by the BIA (back to an immigration judge) or by a circuit court of appeals (back to the BIA), because those final outcomes are not usually published. Immigration attorneys may announce their successful cases on listservs and LGBT legal advocacy groups—such as Immigration Equality and the National Center for Lesbian Rights—may compile databases of cases as a resource for attorneys.[110] But, to the best of my knowledge, a comprehensive and easily accessible listing of successful asylum cases (at all levels) involving queer and trans applicants does not exist for non-attorneys. Published court decisions are the most accessible to law students, attorneys, and practitioners (and within the legal framework, these are the most important decisions because they establish precedent). Yet these decisions do not mention the final outcome of the case, what the decision actually means materially for the asylum applicant. The obscurity of the substantive final outcome and the restricted ability of the circuit courts to decide only procedural questions converge to increase the remoteness of the trans applicant to her own asylum case proceedings.

This is most ironically and starkly illustrated in the proceedings of *Hernandez-Montiel v. INS*. According to Gerber, after the BIA denied the appeal in 1998 (which was two years after her immigration court hearing), Hernandez-Montiel disappeared, and Gerber lost contact with his client. After doing some research, Gerber found that he had implied permission from Hernandez-Montiel to continue with the case since it would be in his client's best interest. When he won the case at the Ninth Circuit in 2000, Gerber had to hire a private investigator to find Hernandez-Montiel, who had moved to Los Angeles during the two years since the BIA decision, and tell her that the case had been successful and that she had received a grant of asylum. Gerber made several television and radio program appearances after his success at the Ninth Circuit Court.[111] The celebrity and increased visibility that Gerber enjoyed as a result of the case—while admittedly not undeserved—stands in stark contrast to Hernandez-Montiel's disappearance, which was presumably partially in response to fear of deportation after the BIA's denial of appeal.[112] The fact that Gerber had to hire a private investigator to track down his own client to deliver the news that the case had resulted in a legal status for her reveals the ways that these court cases are less about the applicants themselves and more about the intricate and complicated power relations and struggles over jurisdiction amongst different government administrative and judicial bodies.[113] Legal process, therefore, entails movement for law and procedure but not necessarily for the subject.[114] The subject who is ostensibly at the center of the case becomes immobilized and absented as the case progresses, as the advancement of the case through the BIA and the circuit court of appeals means that the process becomes more about precedent and procedure than about the "substance" of the case, the actual applicant.

The process through which the trans asylum seeker emerges as a legible legal subject relies on the removal of the asylum seeker as an embodied individual from her case, that is, on the sidelining of her embodied experiences of her gender and sexuality. It is important to note that I am not arguing that making the applicant's body more central in the case would make a difference in the legal reasoning or outcome, and I am not necessarily arguing that this should happen. Rather, my focus is on how the disappearance of the asylum seeker in the process of legal subjection says more about the relationships between various administrative and judicial bodies and about the place of asylum law and procedure in U.S. inter/national politics. The abstraction required in the process of legal subjection—that all subjects experience—stems from the foundation of the law on the theory of liberalism, which assumes and produces a disembodied and unmarked individual. In order for an individual to be inscribed as a legible legal subject, the marked body of the individual must recede, if not be absented completely. Yet my analysis of the process by which trans individuals become legal subjects reveals how asylum law and procedure is haunted by the particular racialized, gendered, and sexualized embodiment of the asylum seeker. This is exemplified in the final written court decision of *Hernandez-Montiel v. INS* by the Ninth Circuit Court, in which the particulars of Hernandez-Montiel's identity and personal history are largely relegated to the first section of the court decision; the subsequent sections of the court decision are the ones in which the central legal questions of the case are outlined and decided. My reading of *Hernandez-Montiel v. INS* highlights the fictions and contradictions of liberalism and its assumption of universal personhood. The movement of the asylum seeker in and out of her case, and her ultimate disappearance as the condition of legal legibility, shows how the subject's embodiment does inform and structure the legal process. Furthermore, this movement demonstrates how the subject herself becomes (only) the means through which procedure and precedent are decided by the courts. The next chapter takes up these questions of subject formation under liberalism through an analysis of asylum declarations as a genre that produces a national subject of trauma.

2

Desiring the Nation

Transgender Trauma in Asylum Declarations

I dreamed that one day I would be able to leave to another place where people wouldn't offend me, make fun of me and abuse me, but I had no idea where to go or how to get there.

–Declaration of Claudia, January 2006, paragraph 26

As a transgender youth, I know that there are no resources or support for people like myself in my country. In this country I have an opportunity to do something with my life and live it the way that I was meant to as the woman that I am.

–Declaration of Ana, no date, paragraph 30

The first quote in the epigraph above comes from the declaration of Claudia, a trans woman from Guatemala applying for asylum in the United States, who voices her desire to be in another place where she can live without fear and mistreatment.[1] Her asylum declaration details the years of physical and sexual violence that she survived at the hands of family members, peers, and police officers who abused her as a young child from age five onward. She migrated to the United States at age twelve with her mother, joining her brothers and father, where she continued to experience violence from her father. After reporting her abuse to a teacher, her parents lost custody and she entered the foster system at age thirteen. As a teenager in San Francisco Claudia was able to access counseling, medication for her epilepsy, and start hormone therapy. She applied for asylum in 2006 when she was twenty-two, writing "Here in San Francisco, I still receive verbal abuse from some people, but at least is [sic] not much compared to what I went through. At least here I am safe."[2]

The second quote by Ana, also from Guatemala, also expresses her appreciation for the life that is possible for her in the United States. After enduring

harassment and violence in Guatemala for her femininity and narrowly escaping being killed by a violent mob in her hometown, Ana migrated to the United
States at age seventeen. In San Francisco she connected with El/La Para Trans-
Latinas, a community organization for Spanish-speaking trans women from Central and South America. She met other transgender women and was able to
access hormone therapy. She writes, "Although the time I have been in the US
has not been easy for me, I have found myself feeling safe which is something I
don't think I could ever be in my home country."[3] Ana's asylum declaration integrates her narrative of transition and becoming a woman with a narrative of
safety and opportunity in the United States. Both of these trans women were successful in receiving a grant of asylum, with legal assistance by pro bono attorneys and the National Center for Lesbian Rights in San Francisco.

Together, the two statements in the epigraph exemplify the different relationships trans asylum seekers have to mobility. Asylum seekers are figured
simultaneously as traumatized victims who are forced to flee their countries
of origin *and* as self-actualized agents who have made deliberate decisions to
migrate to the United States. Asylum law confines the conception of the self to
a liberal rights-bearing subject, one who is free of all ambiguity and marked
by stasis and teleological self-sameness. For trans migrants to the United
States, this legal subject neatly sutures the discourse of the asylum seeker as a
victim of persecution and suffering with the discourse of the transgender person as a self-actualizing subject who becomes what she has always been. Yet
the genre of declarations also make room for the expression of desires that
push against the disembodied subject of liberalism on which asylum law is
founded.

While the previous chapter focused on precedential asylum case law and
the Ninth Circuit Court of Appeals decision *Hernandez-Montiel v. INS*[4] to argue
that these cases produce a coherent legible legal subject made possible by the
disappearance of the asylum seeker as embodied subject, this chapter turns to
another legal document integral to asylum applications: the asylum declaration.
Declarations are the personal narratives written by asylum seekers that detail
the applicants' experiences of persecution in their countries of origin and the
reasons they fear returning. I argue that asylum declarations allow for the articulation of the excesses of legal subjectivity and provide alternatives for the construction of the trans asylum seeker in asylum case law. My analysis builds on
Michel Foucault's account of confession to understand how the asylum declaration functions as an incitement to discourse in which the applicant presents herself to the U.S. state. The asylum seeker is required to recount her life story in a
specific narrative form that is shaped by discourses of trauma and that constructs her as what Elizabeth Povinelli calls an "autological subject," the self-
made subject of liberalism, who is oppressed by a genealogical society.[5]

Understanding asylum declarations as a particular genre makes clear how these texts prescribe asylum applicants narrowly as liberal subjects of trauma and as desiring national subjects. However, declarations by trans migrants also push against this generic formulation to assert other desires and forms of sociality. Through close readings of asylum declarations by trans Latina migrants, I argue that the genre of asylum declarations allows for affirmations of family and community, and for the articulation of love, pleasure, and other kinds of embodied sensations and emotions that exceed the narrow legal subjectivity required by the genre. These desires introduce what Alexei Yurchak terms "minute internal displacements"[6] in the dominant discourse of asylum. Declarations by trans migrants strategically deploy nationalist desire in ways that displace and contest the prescribed boundaries of the traumatized trans asylum seeker. The expression of other forms of desire functions as minute displacements that challenge the discourses of generosity and exceptionalism undergirding the U.S. asylum regime. Yet as I discuss at the end of the chapter, the representation of trans Latinas as desiring subjects can also be appropriated by racist anti-immigrant discourses to construct these asylum seekers as undeserving criminal immigrants.

My archive in this chapter consists of legal documents, including legal briefs, asylum declarations, expert witness testimony, and court decisions, related to twenty-four trans asylum cases from the first decade of the twenty-first century. My analysis focuses on the asylum declarations I was able to obtain for twenty of those twenty-four cases. I received these legal documents from individual immigration attorneys working in California and from national LGBT immigration organizations who represent trans asylum seekers. It is very difficult to win an asylum case without legal representation, and most asylum seekers who do not have attorneys are not successful.[7] Immigration legal advocacy organizations that work with LGBTQ immigrants tend to have asylum programs that help queer and trans asylum seekers in their application processes, and connect them with pro bono lawyers to represent their cases. These organizations will often do outreach with LGBT community groups to connect to undocumented trans migrants who may not know much about their options for legal status. Many law schools also have asylum clinics that provide legal representation and support for asylum applicants, and of course private immigration attorneys across the United States will take on asylum cases.

In 2009, I reached out to several national and local San Francisco Bay Area immigration organizations that work on LGBT asylum cases: the Heartland Alliance's National Immigrant Justice Center in Chicago, the National Center for Lesbian Rights (NCLR) in San Francisco, the Lawyers' Committee for Civil Rights of the San Francisco Bay Area, and Immigration Equality in New York City. The National Immigrant Justice Center and the Lawyers' Committee for Civil Rights did not share case files with me and instead provided names of attorneys who had worked on trans asylum cases. A legal intern at Immigration Equality shared redacted legal briefs from four asylum cases involving trans women but was not willing to send me the actual asylum declarations related to those cases, citing confidentiality. I had the most success with the NCLR, due to a personal connection from a friend who had received asylum a few years earlier and had been represented pro bono by the NCLR. The NCLR shared thirteen asylum declarations with me, eleven of which were from applicants who had been granted asylum or withholding of removal and two of which were from applicants whose cases were still pending at that time. Of the individual attorneys I contacted, three were willing to talk with me and share their case files; I received an additional seven asylum declarations from these attorneys who were all based in California at the time.

These twenty asylum declarations were all written between 2006 and 2009, and are all from trans applicants from Central and South America. Fifteen of the applicants are from Mexico, two are from Guatemala, one is from El Salvador, one is from Peru, and one is from Costa Rica. All but one are written by trans women; the applicant from Peru identifies as a trans man. The combination of neoliberal economic globalization in the Americas and more restrictive immigration laws in the United States at the end of the twentieth century mean that Central and South American migrants have less access to legal immigration to the United States, which makes asylum a key strategy for migration. The majority of the declarations in this chapter come from asylum applicants who filed their cases in California. The fact that these declarations are all from Central and South American migrants most likely reflects migration trends within the Americas, which are tied to the history of economic exploitation through free trade agreements with the United States and to the longer histories of U.S. foreign policy and military intervention in Central America. *TransVisible: Transgender Latina Immigrants in U.S. Society*, a report by the TransLatin@ Coalition, found that the majority of trans Latina immigrants that they surveyed migrated to the United States to escape violence and persecution as well as economic marginalization.[8] Martha Balaguera's research on the embodied experiences of *chicas trans* migrating from Central America through Mexico to the United States found similar reasons for migration.[9] As I discuss in more detail in the Introduction, the overrepresentation of trans Latinas in my archive may contribute to the invisibility of other trans migrants, especially in the larger context of public and legal discourses on immigration in the United States that already tend to center on the U.S.–Mexico border and on Central and South American migrants. In this chapter, I am attentive to how the content of my archive of asylum declarations shapes my claims about trans asylum seekers and asylum declarations.

Before turning to my close readings of these declarations and their strategic deployments of desire, the next section of the chapter situates my theorization of trauma as a social and cultural discourse and shows how the asylum
declaration functions as an incitement to discourse. The subsequent sections
explore how the genre of the asylum declaration requires trans migrants to narrate the self through experiences of trauma and persecution, establish a coherent "I" in relation to that trauma, and position themselves as autological subjects
who are escaping the constraints of their genealogical societies. After this analysis of the prescribed parameters of the asylum declaration, I show how trans
migrants strategically mobilize expressions of desire to complicate the figure of
the normative and nationalist trans asylum seeker. The final section of the chapter illustrates how the representation of trans Latina desires can also be taken
up by anti-immigrant discourses.

Trauma and the Incitement to Discourse in Asylum Declarations

My analysis of trauma in asylum declarations develops from Ann Cvetkovich's
positioning of trauma as "experiences of socially situated political violence" that
complicate distinctions between physic and social sources of pain.[10] Rather than
thinking about trauma through pathologizing medical and psychiatric discourses, Cvetkovich treats trauma "as a social and cultural discourse that
emerges in response to the demands of grappling with the psychic consequences
of historical events."[11] This approach allows her to make clear connections
between politics and emotion as she thinks about how accounts of trauma in
the ordinary and the everyday—as opposed to the national and the catastrophic—
can be a foundation for creating queer counterpublics. While my focus is not
the creation of public cultures, Cvetkovich's exploration of trauma as a productive force of "felt experiences that can be mobilized in a range of directions"[12]
informs my reading of asylum declarations. Alice Miller, a legal scholar and advocate, similarly contends that discourses of trauma and violence come to constitute the identity of the asylum seeker, since asylum cases depend on (the
production of) a violated and persecuted sexualized, gendered, and racialized
subject. This subject, in turn, is substantiated by a violated and traumatized
body, since asylum advocacy relies on the "*embodiment of harm* in the stories of
specific individuals facing abuse."[13] Asylum law incites a discourse of trauma
from asylum seekers, but that trauma cannot be marshaled solely for the purposes of constructing the United States as beneficial savior of persecuted individuals. This chapter argues that the trauma solicited from trans asylum seekers
in their declarations moves in unpredictable directions, and can resist or
displace hegemonic narratives of the U.S. nation and the construction of trans
asylum seekers as properly desiring national(ist) subjects. Thinking about

trauma as a structure of feeling that "characterizes the lived experience of capitalism"[14] refuses individualizing explanations of trauma and helps situate the violence experienced by trans asylum seekers in a larger structural political and economic framework. Although the genre of the asylum declaration requires trans asylum seekers to narrate their experiences of persecution through the narrow lens of gender and sexual violence in their countries of origin, thinking about what counts as trauma for the law highlights how this gender and sexual violence cannot be divorced from the racialized effects of neoliberal capitalism and how these kinds of violence occur both in asylum seekers' countries of origin and in the United States.

Theorizing trauma as a structure of feeling departs from the pathologization of trauma in some psychological literature. Cvetkovich argues that these discussions of trauma tend to convert social problems into medical ones, and rely on medical discourses and diagnoses like PTSD to identify and verify the sources and symptoms of trauma.[15] Medical discourses about trauma do play a role in the production of trans asylum seekers as traumatized subjects, since asylum seekers often undergo medical evaluations as verification of their accounts of abuse and persecution. While these medical reports constitute an important component of their applications, I want to think about how the performance of trauma in declarations brings together intersecting modalities of subjectivity—psychiatric and medical, but also legal and social—to produce the trans asylum seeker as a particular national subject. And given the book's focus on relations of im/mobility, I track how the performance of trauma both moves across different spaces and also facilitates the physical movement of trans asylum seekers across national borders.

In the last chapter, I drew on Foucault's analysis of confession as a particular form of power-knowledge that produces the "truth" of sex and the subject to think about the relations of power that structure the asylum seeker's interview with an asylum officer. Foucault's argument about confession also provides a useful starting point to think about how the asylum declaration functions as an incitement to discourse. In the first volume of *The History of Sexuality*, Foucault notes that beginning in Europe in the Middle Ages, confession developed as a ritual for the production of truth within the religious and civic spheres, in which the individual was called upon to vouch for her or himself rather than relying on others to do so.[16] Confession functioned as the primary technique for producing truth and was a key site in which disciplinary power worked to engender the subject: "the truthful confession was inscribed at the heart of the procedures of individualization by power."[17] Peter Brooks makes a similar argument in the context of legal confessions. In his analysis of confession in law and literature, he contends that confession is intrinsic to modern selfhood.[18]

The asylum declaration, like the confession, works as an injunction to tell a life story and occurs within a power relationship between the individual and a set of larger institutions and actors. And like confession, declarations do not reveal the truth of the subject but are performative in that they produce this truth and the subject they are narrating. As Foucault notes, "[t]he truth did not reside solely in the subject who, by confessing, would reveal it wholly formed. It was constituted in two stages: present but incomplete, blind to itself, in the one who spoke, it could only reach completion in the one who assimilated and recorded it."[19] The production of truth through confession requires two parties and is produced in their interactions. A similar mode of production occurs in the writing of asylum declarations, although the process of writing happens in multiple stages and is more collaborative, extending beyond the two subjects of the Foucaultian scene of confession. This process is sometimes detailed in the declaration itself. For example, the second paragraph of the declaration of Ines, a transgender woman from Mexico, describes the complicated process of translation and authorship that produced her declaration: "My attorney and the staff at the Transgender Law Center in San Francisco, CA helped me to prepare this declaration. After three interviews with my attorney, this document was written in English. It was then read back to me in Spanish by the volunteer translator in this case. With her help, I made corrections to the document. The final document was then orally translated for me in Spanish and it is a true and accurate account of my experience."[20] Even if the applicant writes her declaration herself, the document will be edited and developed in partnership with her legal advisors, a partnership shaped by complex power relations between the applicant, interpreter, and attorney.[21] The involvement of LGBT and immigrant justice nongovernmental organizations (NGOs) also plays a significant role in the construction of the asylum applicant's narrative, as Siobhán McGuirk shows in her research on how specialist NGOs reproduce statist logics in their client selection and procedures.[22] Despite this collaborative process of production, the finished document needs to claim a forceful authenticity and transparency of experience meant to convey the unique authorial voice of the subject. The declaration is usually the most influential component of the larger application for asylum, although expert witness testimonies sometimes carry more weight, as I mention in chapter I.

Like the confession, which operates as a "ritual in which the truth is corroborated by the obstacles and resistances it has had to surmount in order to be formulated,"[23] asylum declarations are narratives that account for the "obstacles" an individual encounters in the discovery of her "authentic" self. The authenticity of self, expressed in the declaration, is corroborated by the body, which is often invoked as evidence of persecution through descriptions of scars, broken bones, and other injuries. The body acts as witness to trauma, mediated by medical declarations[24] and supported by country condition reports and expert testimony. However, the applicant's body and her testimony are still often considered to be secondary forms of evidence. Carol Bohmer and Amy Shuman describe the asylum process as one that produces "epistemologies of ignorance" in which the asylum applicant herself is seen as ignorant and not reliable. Due to the criminalization of asylum seekers as fraudulent, expert witness testimony is therefore seen as more credible.[25]

The persecution and violence that an applicant has experienced, therefore, become the external "obstacles" to the development and articulation of the applicant's trans identity. Simultaneously, the trans asylum applicant's body must also serve as evidence of their transness. Sometimes this is reinforced by expert witness testimonies and reports. For example, a licensed social worker who conducted a psychological evaluation of Gloria, an asylum seeker from Mexico, noted in her report that Gloria's "hands were well manicured and her face was groomed consistent with a woman's."[26] Similarly, Dr. Debra Rodman, an expert witness in the asylum case for Rosa, a trans woman from Costa Rico, wrote that Rosa is "immediately identifiable as a transsexual" based on her voice and appearance.[27]

Confession operates on a presumption of guilt, and contemporary asylum procedures also treat the asylum seeker as guilty. Gregor Noll contends that the heritage of confession, repentance, and absolution that shape asylum procedures in the European Union constructs the asylum seeker as a "sinner-perpetrator" rather than as a "victim of human rights violations."[28] While the history of confession in the United States, especially in relation to Catholicism, differs from that of Europe's, the construction of the asylum seeker as "sinner-perpetrator" resonates in the U.S. context, given the heightened national hysteria around immigration more generally and the circulation of discourses of fraudulent asylum seekers. The accusations of fraud that infuse news media representations of asylum seekers take on a deeper resonance for trans asylum seekers since they converge with other discourses that circulate around trans subjects, such as the transphobic claim that trans people are "deceiving" people with their gender presentations,[29] and with racist discourses that circulate around Latinx migrants constructing Latin Americans as threats to the U.S. nation.

Two news articles, published in the same time period as most of the declarations I examine in this chapter, provide contrasting examples of the figure of the fraudulent asylum seeker. In June 2011, the *New York Times* ran an article focused on the manufacture of false asylum claims and "asylum schemes."[30] Although author Sam Dolnick notes that "of course, thousands of those claims are legitimate," the main thrust of the article is that many migrants to the United States fabricate stories of persecution in order to apply for asylum and that a "shadowy industry" thrives in many immigrant communities to help migrants develop convincing and successful, but false, asylum claims. The image of asylum seekers that emerges from this article is one of large numbers of immigrants "who are desperate to settle here for other reasons" and who take advantage of an easily exploitable immigration system to fraudulently obtain legal documents. A few weeks later in 2011, the *New Yorker* published an article by Suketu Mehta on the embellishment and falsification of asylum claims by asylum seekers and asylum "coaches." Mehta more thoroughly contextualizes the difficulties of applying for asylum, given the "current political climate in a country [that] is not favorable for asylum seekers,"[31] and notes that more and more intense narratives become necessary since asylum officers become resistant to stories of persecution that sound too similar to all the other stories of persecution they have heard. Mehta also takes care to show how the asylum seekers he interviewed all had valid claims for asylum but had felt pressure to develop more violent and dramatic stories to have a more persuasive application (e.g., telling accounts of rape and sexual assault instead of "just" threats and beating). He pointedly represents these particular asylum seekers as hard-working, productive immigrants who do not rely on state services or public assistance to survive. While Mehta's portrayal of asylum seekers acknowledges the structural and legal barriers to an asylum claim, both Mehta's and Dolnick's articles illustrate how discourses of fraud circulate around and stick to asylum seekers.[32]

The determination of an asylum seeker's narrative and identity as credible marks the transition from being a potentially fraudulent "sinner-perpetrator" to being a victim of persecution. This moment of state recognition turns on the extent to which the asylum seeker's performative narration of persecution is convincing and therefore credible. Noll's analysis of asylum in relation to confession also emphasizes that "the asylum procedure is premised on an inexplicable element of grace."[33] Because a grant of asylum is discretionary, not a right to be automatically granted by an asylum officer or immigration judge, the asylum seeker relies on the asylum adjudicator's goodwill to listen to her story and grant her asylum. The discretionary quality of asylum—asylum as an act of "grace of forgiveness"—explains the unevenness of asylum grants across the different asylum offices and federal courts of appeals in the United States.[34] The shift from being treated as a guilty and potentially fraudulent migrant to becoming a victim of human rights violations relies on relations of mobility that ultimately neutralize the political agency of the asylum seeker.[35] As a subject with the political agency to cross national borders, the asylum seeker is initially a "subject of security," but is quickly immobilized as an "object of security" for the state through the discourses of victimization that structure asylum.[36] This immobilization materializes in the incarceration of many asylum seekers for months or years in immigration detention facilities as they await the outcome of their cases. More recently, the U.S. government has preemptively immobilized asylum seekers and other migrants even before they have a chance to present a legal claim. As part of the Trump administration's attack on Latin American migrants, many Latinx migrants were prevented from entering the U.S. border through Trump's "Remain in Mexico" policy and through his administration's use of the COVID-19 global pandemic to effectively close the U.S.–Mexico border to asylum seekers in 2020. While the Biden administration has tried to end the "Remain in Mexico" policy,[37] it has continued to enforce Title 42, part of the 1944 Public Health Service Act that the Trump administration invoked as a pretext for the summary exclusion of newly arrived migrants who are deported before being able to exercise their right to apply for asylum.[38] Understanding the asylum seeker as initially assuming the role of "sinner-perpetrator," a role that is also shaped by the racialization of Latinx migrants, highlights the intimate relationship between the asylum system in the United States and the immigration detention system. The state actors and institutions that administer asylum treat the narratives of asylum seekers with suspicion, while asylum seekers themselves are criminalized through the requirement of mandatory detention.

Declarations as a Genre of Trauma and Desire

Asylum declarations narrate the self through experiences of trauma and persecution. This mode of self-presentation is replicated in the briefs and court decisions I discuss in chapter 1, since declarations form the basis of attorney briefs that are submitted to asylum officers and immigration judges, which in turn are used by circuit court of appeals judges to write their final decisions on cases. Unlike briefs and court decisions, which present the asylum seeker's narrative in the third person, asylum declarations are written in the first person. Declarations deploy a conversational tone intended to closely approximate the applicant's *voice* as opposed to an attorney's, in order to sound like the narrative of a unique individual and not a standardized account of persecution. There is a tension between the prescribed nature of the declarations and the need to perform naturalness, immediacy, and transparency. This performance is also complicated by the time of the asylum application process, which can stretch out over months or years. The immediacy and urgency of the temporal moment of the declaration must be sustained over the course of the asylum claim.

The first few paragraphs of an asylum declaration provide the applicant's name, birthplace, date of birth and given name, age, and state that the applicant is filing the declaration in support for asylum. In these paragraphs, the asylum seeker also explains the basis of the claim. For example, one declaration states, "I am making a claim for asylum in the United States because I have experienced violence and discrimination in Mexico from private citizens and government officials because I am a transgender woman who is often mistaken for a gay man."[39] The slippage between gay and transgender allows applicants to advance parallel arguments for their claim of asylum. Asylum seekers need to make themselves legible as both/either gay and transgender, because if their claim for being transgender is not accepted by the asylum officer or immigration judge, they can still argue for being (perceived as) a gay man. The claim to both gay and transgender in these declarations introduces a tension within the subject they produce. Even as there is a need to express a stable, coherent identity to the asylum official, the structure of asylum law allows for the presentation of different aspects of identity. The law also highlights how individuals are subject to harassment and assault based on appearance and perception, so that a trans woman may be mistaken for a feminine gay man and a trans man may be mistaken for a butch lesbian. Furthermore, it acknowledges, as I discuss in relation to Hernandez-Montiel in chapter 1, how many trans people do not experience gender and sexuality as completely separate components of their identities.[40] Even as the theory of asylum law rests upon liberal ideals of a bounded, internally consistent subject, the application and practice of the law by attorneys and asylum seekers disrupt this notion of the liberal subject and reveal it to be a fiction.

Asylum seekers whose applications are based on gender or sexual identity need to prove their identities are immutable, so the rest of the declaration works to establish their trans identities as essential and fixed, even as their sexed and gendered embodiment may be shifting. As is the case in Hernandez-Montiel's declaration, these narratives proceed chronologically and tend to develop a plot with a beginning, in which the individual discovers her trans identity; a middle, in which she is subjected to constant harassment and varying degrees of physical, emotional, and sexual abuse and violence from peers, family, and authorities; the climax, in which the applicant usually experiences a particularly severe incident of sexual or physical brutality that prompts her decision to migrate to the United States; and a closing statement in which she avows the necessity of staying in the United States in order to be safe.[41] The conventions of the asylum declaration constitute a genre that attests to the perseverance and persistence of one's true self; the resilience of self under oppression and violence; and ultimately, an appeal for the rescue of this core self by the United States.[42]

The narratives in the declarations advance as life stories but also tend to circle back upon themselves through repetitions of violence, which has specific consequences for trans asylum seekers. Experiences of trauma are nodal points that hold the narratives together, establishing rhythms of fear that threaten to overwhelm the subjects of the declarations as they are narrated and produced in the texts. The declarations always make clear that the applicants experience this violence because of their trans identities through a careful detailing of the hate speech and verbal abuse that often accompanies physical and sexual assaults. All applicants who use "particular social group" as the basis of their asylum cases are required to establish a nexus between their identity and the persecution they have experienced. Partial life stories become accounts of whole selves that are formed through violence. For trans asylum seekers, however, this process of subjectivity becomes especially notable. Transgender identity overdetermines the subject produced by this narrative who then becomes only (all) transgender and, paradoxically, is constituted through the negation of self-hood. David Valentine has also noted the centrality of violence to the articulation of the category of transgender in the United States. Social service agencies and transgender advocates frequently use "violence against transgender people" as a strategy to draw attention to the lives of gender-variant people. The unintended effect of this strategy is that violence becomes constitutive of the category of transgender, since the complexity of individuals' self-identifications and their social realities are reduced to their experience as "transgender," an experience that is constructed as necessarily and inherently violent.[43] In asylum declarations, trans subjectivity becomes inextricable from the violence directed at it. These legal discourses reinforce the larger cultural discourses about trans vulnerability and trans death that tend to dominate political conversations about trans experiences.[44]

Asylum declarations mandate an abstraction of self in which the complexity of the subject is evacuated so that she is reduced to her trauma as a transgender-identified subject. This is precisely the process that Judith Butler details in their analysis of how identities within liberalism are formed on the basis of injured identities. The process of subject formation means that "[t]he more specific identities become, the more totalized an identity becomes by that specificity."[45] The asylum subject becomes the ideal wounded liberal subject who seeks sanctuary and recognition from the state. In their ethnographic research with asylum applicants, Amy Shuman and Carol Bohmer found that portraying oneself as "a victim, without dignity, is the necessary price of asylum."[46] Asylum seekers have to reveal their scars and other bodily and psychological evidence of torture to medical doctors and social workers, who perform physical and psychological evaluations, as well as to asylum officers and immigration judges who hear their claims, in order to make a compelling case for persecution. The distillation of the identities of trans asylum seekers in these declarations illustrates "the movement by which a juridical apparatus produces the field of possible political subjects."[47] The conventions of the declaration's narrative form are necessary for the production of a subject who is legible to asylum adjudicators and other state actors.

The first lines of asylum declarations demonstrate their generic conventions. Beginning with either "My name is ___" or "I, ___, declare," declarations posit a liberal individual subject who can name herself and who can assert an "I," who can present herself as a stable subject in order to narrate her story and function as a witness to a linear timeline of the development of that self-same "I." In this respect, asylum declarations exemplify C. B. Macpherson's notion of "possessive individualism."[48] By claiming herself and her capacity to tell her story to the state in her declaration, the asylum seeker becomes recognizable as a potential future citizen-subject who can be endowed with rights. If the trans asylum seeker does not have the capacity to narrate her experiences of trauma in the form of an asylum declaration, she will not be able to make herself recognizable to asylum adjudicators. U.S. asylum law dictates notions of temporality that do not acknowledge the ways persecution becomes embodied and continues to affect a person's life.[49] This temporality of the subject is what allows applicants to posit themselves as autonomous subjects who are ready and able to function in the United States as productive and useful citizens, despite having endured persecution and trauma that threatened to fracture their sense of self. Trans asylum seekers are faced with the double bind of positing a whole self-same identity while simultaneously arguing that identity is constituted through its external negation by others. The law resolves this issue by making a temporal argument about the self. Asylum law situates trauma and persecution as a discrete temporal moment rather than as an experience that marks individuals and that is relived at different points in one's life. This temporal argument obscures how the asylum process itself reproduces trauma by requiring asylum seekers to repeatedly retell their stories to different actors as well as requiring mandatory detention, which further traumatizes asylum seekers.[50]

The tension between past trauma and present-day stability often manifests in how many asylum seekers have to account for missing the one-year deadline for applying for asylum, which was mandated by the Illegal Immigration Reform and Immigrant Responsibility Act of 1996.[51] Many asylum seekers do not make this deadline because they do not know that they have the option to apply for asylum, they lack the legal resources needed, and they are suffering from trauma. Their attorneys must argue for a "reasonable exception" to the one-year deadline.[52] Often this "exception" takes the form of mental and physical illness, such as depression, alcoholism, and HIV status. Although the law's allowance for a "reasonable exception" can be seen as an admission of the persistence of trauma from experiences of persecution, the one-year deadline also makes it clear that the law will only recognize individuals as potential rights-bearing subjects once they have achieved a certain degree of stability. The asylum case of Carolina, an asylum seeker from Mexico who identifies as gay and transgender, exemplifies this balance between trauma and stability. Carolina entered the United States for the first time in 1984 at age nineteen and moved to Oakland, but she went back to Mexico several times over the next seven years to visit ailing parents. On these trips, Carolina experienced severe abuse and violence from local and federal police officers, and fled Mexico permanently in 1991. Her declaration details many years of instability—hospitalizations, arrests, and imprisonment—while living in the United States, due to a history of drug use, bipolar disorder, and HIV-positive status. Carolina was able to expunge her record of criminal convictions in 2008, and because none of those convictions were for an aggravated felony, she was able to file an affirmative asylum application in July 2009 and subsequently received a grant of asylum. Despite having lived undocumented in the United States for twenty-five years, Carolina was able to argue that bipolar disorder and HIV-positive status constituted a reasonable exception to the one-year filing deadline. The second to last paragraph of Carolina's declaration attests to the level of stability and coherency required by asylum law: "Today I am still in the CONRAP Independent Living Program at a group house at 19th and Judah in San Francisco. I receive treatment for my bipolar disorder as well as HIV. Monday through Friday every week I have a full schedule of psychotherapy, counseling and language classes from 10:00 a.m. to 2:00 p.m. At night I also attend Narcotics Anonymous and a LGBT-focused Alcoholics Anonymous program. On Saturdays I volunteer at the Open Hand HIV support program, helping to distribute groceries to Open Hand beneficiaries. This routine has helped give me the structure and goal-oriented perspective that has brought me to a place where I have hopes and dreams for the future."[53]

Even when asylum applicants do not have to make an argument for missing the one-year filing deadline, their asylum declarations and applications still exemplify the fragile balance between being traumatized "enough" by persecution and being "whole" enough to argue for themselves, which is often supported by assertions of their potential to become upstanding national subjects. The institution of asylum requires a certain amount of mental and emotional integrity, namely, the ability to narrate one's trauma in detail in the context of the articulation of a trans identity. The parameters of the declaration narrative, and of dominant nationalist U.S. ideologies, also encourage asylum seekers to gesture toward their potential as future citizens; this often manifests in statements about working hard, wanting an education or a steady job, and becoming a productive individual. Many applicants mention their social workers, psychotherapists, counselors, support groups, doctors, and Alcoholics Anonymous and Narcotics Anonymous meetings in their declarations. A declaration by Bárbara, a transgender woman from Mexico, speaks to the balance between trauma and wholeness. As a result of the physical and sexual violence she experienced at the hands of Mexican police officers and others, including family members, she had been diagnosed with posttraumatic stress disorder as well as panic disorder with agoraphobia and depression. Her declaration states, "Since coming to San Francisco, for the first time in my life I have experienced a life free of persecution and harassment because of my gender identity. I have built (and continue to build) a network of caring and supportive friends who, together with the doctors and social workers that I see regularly, are helping me deal with the legacy of violence and persecution that I experienced in Mexico."[54] This statement asserts a self who has the capacity to thrive and recover from trauma, yet pointedly shows how healing from persecution is a difficult and ongoing process. Including details about doctors and social workers also exhibits faith in the United States and in the resources it offers. At the same time, however, some declarations reveal the gaps between the promise of the United States and the reality that the asylum seekers face as trans migrants. Verónica writes, "I continue to struggle with anxiety and depression, especially on days I have nothing to eat. But to think of returning to my country is worse. I know that wouldn't be the right thing to do for me. I trust this country's laws and hope they have compassion in my case. All I ask is an opportunity to start my life again and leave behind the painful experiences I've lived through in my life."[55] Her acknowledgment that she struggles with anxiety and depression, "especially on days I have nothing to eat," reflects the difficulties faced by undocumented trans migrants. Verónica experiences some of the same challenges in the United States as she did in Mexico in terms of being able to provide for her basic survival.

Another trans woman from Mexico, Patricia, underscores how the narrative conventions of the asylum declaration weave together trauma, victimhood, and performances of citizenship. After documenting the persecution she experienced in Mexico because of her "transsexual status," Patricia's declaration describes her first attempt to enter the United States in March 2006 with a fake green card, during which U.S. immigration officials apprehended her, detained her overnight, and then made her sign an order of removal. In her declaration, she apologizes for entering the United States without documents and states that she regrets her actions. This apology is even more striking given the abuse and mistreatment she experienced at the hands of U.S. asylum officials, who violated asylum procedures by not asking her why she was trying to leave Mexico and by forcing her to sign an order of removal in English without translating it for her. They also humiliated and intimidated her by making her undress completely to 'prove' her gender while making transphobic jokes and remarks. The immigration officers put her in a cell by herself but in the building where migrants who were assigned male at birth were housed, so she was subjected to sexual comments by those migrants. These actions constitute specific forms of transphobic violence as the declaration points out: "The immigration officials never interviewed me or asked me any questions. They were upset with me because I had the fake green card, and because I am transsexual, and they did not give me a chance to explain why I had to leave Mexico."[56] After being returned to Mexico where she experienced more sexual assaults and indifference from police officers, Patricia tried to enter the United States again with another fake green card in August 2006 and managed to pass inspection at the border. This admission is followed by another apology: "I am sorry that I entered the United States illegally. I did this only because I was so afraid that I would be killed in Mexico. By applying for asylum, I hope that I can make things right, and live in the United States legally."[57] While documentation of illegal actions by U.S. immigration officials is not rare in asylum declarations, the inclusion of this woman's apologies and expressions of regret are unusual but strategic, since they help to position her as a properly grateful and respectful future citizen.[58]

Patricia's apologies illustrate how the logics of sin and forgiveness that structure the asylum system configure a grant of asylum as an act of grace, not a human right. This has significant implications for the production of the liberal subject in the asylum declaration and for reproduction of nationalist ideologies through asylum law. The liberal subject of trauma in the asylum declaration is produced alongside the construction of the United States as a compassionate and welcoming nation, in stark contrast to the construction of the applicant's country of origin. In the previous chapter I discuss how expert witness testimony in *Hernandez-Montiel v. INS* constructed Mexico as a homogenous sexist, homophobic, and transphobic space. This is the discourse required from expert witness statements.[59] The asylum declarations I discuss in this chapter also contribute to these nation-building projects through the voice of the asylum applicant. Statements of appreciation and gratitude for a possible grant of asylum participate in the operation of liberal discourses that profess an attachment to freedom even as they normalize forms of violence and war, what Mimi Thi Nguyen calls "the gift of freedom" under liberalism.[60] Nguyen explains that "the gift of freedom emerges as a site at which modern governmentality and its politics of life (and death) unfolds as a universal history of the human, and the figuration of debt surfaces as those imperial remains that preclude the subject of freedom from being able to escape a colonial order of things."[61] The statements of regret and apology of Patricia, the Mexican asylum applicant I discuss above, demonstrate how asylum becomes problematically represented as a gift to the asylum applicant. Like the refugee, the asylum applicant's acceptance of the gift of freedom means she also accepts a debt: "the conditional recognition of racial, colonial subjectivity."[62]

Even as these declarations position the asylum applicants' countries of origin as sites of violence, they also tend to decontextualize persecution so that the violence experienced by the applicant becomes the result of individualized actions, obscuring the larger structural oppressions that play a role in the persecution. Because this decontextualization stems from the contradictions inherent in liberalism, the individualization of persecution within asylum claims operates simultaneously with the nationalist discourses I discuss in the previous chapter. Both are constitutive of the institution of asylum. There exists a tension between the requirement of membership in a particular social group, which implies recognition of a larger community and ties to other individuals, and the requirement of "a well-founded fear" of persecution as a specific individual.[63]

The universal personhood assumed by liberalism sees human rights violations as deviations from the status quo, since the normal citizen-state relationship assumed by U.S. law is the relationship between an individual who gains rights via membership in the nation-state and a state that is supposed to protect those rights.[64] Asylum law both recognizes difference by offering sanctuary to marginalized individuals yet also denies difference through its assumptions of universal personhood and experience, and thus continues the exclusions produced by liberalism.[65] In this way, the law contributes to the violence that caused the individual to seek asylum in the first place, by exceptionalizing and individualizing persecution that is often a daily reality for subordinated groups who are marked as different from the hegemonic racialized, gendered, and sexed citizen prioritized and normalized by the state in other countries and in the United States. This process is constitutive of human rights discourse which functions as a mode of governmentality to produce both particular and universal subjects. As a "regime of truth" based on racialized and gendered systems of knowledge, human rights regimes are most often applied in a global arena and not in a domestic context.[66] The United States frequently deploys human rights discourses in the service of U.S. empire, to condemn foreign governments and to justify military interventions. This is what Nguyen means when she posits "the gift of freedom" as a central tenet of liberal war and empire. Yet the U.S. government refuses to acknowledge that conditions of poverty, lack of access to clean water, police violence, or mass incarceration within the United States constitute human rights violations domestically. U.S. asylum law configures the persecution asylum seekers experience in their countries of origin as human rights violations, but ignores the violence and oppression that trans migrants often live with *in* the United States.[67]

The Autological Subject and Tropes of Mobility

By obscuring both the violence of subjection and the everyday violence perpetrated by various state institutions, asylum declarations represent subject formation as a process of liberation and autonomy. For example, Verónica ends her declaration with the statement, "My hope is to stay here and be able to live as the individual I have become."[68] The phrasing of "the individual I have become" invokes what Povinelli calls the "autological subject," the self-made subject of liberalism. The genre of asylum declarations requires asylum applicants to position themselves as this kind of liberal subject, a subject who develops from the "discourses, practices and fantasies about self-making, self-sovereignty, and the value of individual freedom associated with the Enlightenment project of contractual constitutional democracy and capitalism."[69] The autological subject exists in relation to the "genealogical society," which Povinelli describes as the "discourses, practices and fantasies about the social constraints placed on the autological subject by various kinds of inheritances."[70] Asylum applicants must position their families, communities, and cultures as those "inheritances" that have prevented them from becoming their authentic selves and from obtaining autonomy and freedom. Most of the declarations in my archive recount how early

childhood expressions of sexual and gender nonconformity were met with abuse
and rejection from family members. Many applicants experienced sexual abuse
and violence at the hands of relatives. For example, Gloria endured regular
instances of rape and sexual abuse from boys in her neighborhood as well as
from male family members, starting at age five. She writes that when her mom
found out, her mom beat her and blamed her for allowing those abuses to happen to her.[71] The declarations in my archive also detail experiences of violence
and abuse from teachers, employers, and the police, all of which are well-
documented in human rights reports and in the scholarship on trans asylum
seekers from Central and South America.[72] The recounting of these experiences
of violence and discrimination in asylum declarations discursively produces
Mexico and other Latin American countries as extremely transphobic, as the
genealogical societies that these trans women must leave. The asylum system
also functions as a process of racialization for asylum applicants, who must position themselves against their cultures and countries of origin and orient themselves toward the United States, ignoring the pervasive transphobic violence and
discrimination that also exists in the United States.[73] McKinley emphasizes this
aspect of the asylum process: "The asylum context brooks no ambivalent attachments: the realist logic is that people persecuted in one country seeking the
protection of another simply do not deserve that protection if they demonstrate
allegiance to the county (read: culture/religion) from which they flee. Protection
is extended in exchange for *total* cultural repudiation."[74] This framing makes
possible the articulation of the trans Latina asylum applicant as a liberal subject rejecting the inheritances of her genealogical society.

Povinelli's theorization of liberal subjecthood provides a useful frame for
thinking about how relations of mobility constitute the condition of possibility
for the construction of trans migrants as self-sovereign subjects who have fled
the social constraints of their countries of origin. In asylum declarations, trans
asylum seekers reproduce these discourses when they represent themselves as
liberal individuals whose self-actualization was made possible in the United
States. Since "transsexuality itself is already marked by a discourse encouraging
self-transformation and emphasizing the productive capacities of the individual,"[75] trans asylum seekers effectively bring together dominant discourses of
transgender subjectivity and discourses of the autological subject, highlighting the grounding of both in the time and space of liberalism. Verónica's plea to
continue to "live as the individual I have become" also draws on the dominant
transgender narrative of becoming one's true self, which turns on a tension
between "becoming" and "already being."[76] As I discuss in the introduction, the
sexed and gendered changes that characterize trans identities are often imagined
in terms of movement; in transgender narratives, this "becoming" what you
already "are" relies on tropes of travel and mobility. Trans asylum narratives
articulate these tropes of travel in relation to gender identity differently than

traditional travel narratives by more privileged trans subjects, complicating the construction of a gendered body as home and revealing how class, race, and nation shape narratives of a gendered self in relation to mobility. In his analysis of the persistent trope of "safe return" in transgender travel narratives, Aren Z. Aizura notes that many trans narratives by Western trans women mark the return home from gender affirmation surgery as the turning point of their gender transitions, such that transitioning enables a metaphorical "coming home" to one's body that coincides with a literal return to one's home after surgery.[77] This representation of transsexuality depends on a home-elsewhere distinction that develops from Euro-American colonial travel narratives.[78] Aizura argues that the travel narrative of out and return—traveling for surgery and returning to a home and to a normatively gendered body—contains "the temporal moment of gendered indeterminacy within a spatialized elsewhere."[79]

Trans asylum declarations offer a different trans travel narrative. While trans asylum seekers do frame their migration to the United States as being motivated by their trans identity formation, their travel does not spatially contain the "moment of gendered indeterminacy" since the return home is foreclosed by the very act of applying for asylum. Furthermore, many Latinx trans asylum applicants cross the southern border of the United States multiple times before applying for asylum. Many of the declarations in my archive mention returning to a country of origin in order to visit family members who were sick or dying, or because they wanted to try again to see if life would be liveable in their communities of origin, or because they were deported from the United States. The narrative of out and return as a founding narrative of transsexual recognition applies only to those trans subjects privileged enough to have a safe home to which to return. In contrast, the trans asylum seeker must disavow her country of origin as a desirable and safe home and position the United States as a national space of self-actualization that holds the promise of a "return" to a gendered self. Yet the operation of colonial narratives of travel is still evident. The country of origin operates as the spatialized elsewhere of gendered indeterminacy in which the asylum seeker is not recognized as her authentic self, and the United States becomes the space in which the asylum seeker will be fully recognized as the woman she has become. This is the liberal promise of asylum, even though the language of the law may not confer this gendered recognition, as Hernandez-Montiel's legibility as a "gay man with a female sexual identity," rather than as a trans woman, demonstrates.

Asylum declarations mobilize the rhetoric of the autological subject oppressed by a genealogical society in their countries of origin to explain why the applicant should be granted asylum and allowed to remain in the United States. Many of the declarations in my archive end with statements about deportation being a death sentence. After detailing the history of horrific sexual violence she experienced from her brothers, teachers, and police officers in her declaration, Sofía writes, "I cannot go back to Mexico. I would rather kill myself than return there. Unfortunately in my country, the violence and discrimination against people like me continues. I read it in the news, see it on the internet and hear from transgender individuals that I know. Transgender individuals continue to get raped, tortured and killed. They continue to be abused by the police and by society. That is why I rather die than face a future there."[80] Statements like these position the United States as the only place in which the asylum applicant has a livable future. For example, Martina's declaration asserts, "If I had to go back, I would never go out with other gay or transgendered people. I would be without my liberty to live the way I am."[81] Drawing upon the language of dominant U.S. ideologies of freedom and liberty, Martina rhetorically situates herself in relation to the values of the U.S. nation; she insists upon her "right" to stay and live freely, while simultaneously positioning the United States as a place that guarantees those rights. Furthermore, she goes on to state, "Here, I have the support of friends and medical providers. I am not judged for my condition [her AIDS status] and people are helping me become healthy. I know I can be productive, healthy, and safe in the United States, and fear only abuse, harassment, and inevitable death awaits me in Mexico."[82] Similarly, Ines reproduces the self-making project integral to the construct of the "American Dream" when she maintains that "[t]his country has given me back my life, and I would like the opportunity to give back to it" and asserts "I wanted to come here to be who I am, to be a woman, and I think that I have succeeded in part."[83] These strategic deployments of U.S. nationalist discourses position asylum seekers as proper U.S. national subjects.

Desiring Subjects: Displacing Nationalist Sentiment

So far, this chapter has argued that asylum declarations construct trans Latinas as liberal subjects escaping the constraints of their cultures / countries of origin, while producing discourses of democracy that leave unacknowledged the violence that also exists in the United States and obscuring the ways this rhetoric justifies U.S. aggression and imperialism abroad. Therefore, it is easy to read these declarations as complicit with hegemonic U.S. ideologies, as narratives that simply reproduce—albeit strategically and purposefully—celebratory imaginings of the United States as the most democratic, free, and liberated country in the world. The success of asylum cases for trans people paradoxically depends on the omission of trans-related violence in the United States, which needs to be represented as a safe space. The inverse is also true. The passage of gay and trans rights or antidiscrimination legislation in asylum seekers' countries of origin may make it difficult for those asylum seekers to win their cases, even though that legislation may not produce changes in the lived experiences of trans and queer people.[84] These two political projects—offering a sanctuary to persecuted

trans individuals from other countries, and discounting violence directed at
trans people in the United States—are not contradictory within the framework
determined by the state. This is because the institution of asylum plays a key
role in a larger, biopolitical project through which the state guarantees the per-
petration of violence as a way to manage marginalized populations in the United
States while still asserting itself as a beneficial actor in international politics.[85]

Although asylum declarations do function within the economies of power
relations that shape asylum and immigration policy in the United States, moving beyond frameworks of complicity and consent reveals other ways of understanding the subjects produced in the declarations. Reading asylum declarations
as only reproducing narratives of oppression and subjection means accepting
those ideologies as wholly determinant of subject production, and ignoring the
articulation of other desires that are not solely nationalist desires. The declarations in my archive do more than what they are intended to do, and theorizing
those excesses makes it possible to see the subjects produced in the texts differently.[86] In this section of the chapter, I examine how the generic conventions of
the declarations allow for the expression of desires that are not mandated by the
genre and that complicate the required construction of the liberal subject. This
is significant for trans asylum applicants whose legal subjectivities are overdetermined by discourses of trauma and violation such that gender nonconformity
becomes only a source of pain and violence. Paying attention to the expression
of desires that exceed the requisite nationalist desire for the United States reveals
how trans asylum declarations mark the construction of the credible and legible transgender asylum applicant as what Fadi Saleh terms "a temporary subject
position" and push against the limits of that construction.[87]

Although he is writing about a very different context, Yurchak's theorization of agentival capacity is helpful in understanding the role of the performative in the articulation of desire in asylum declarations. In his historical
ethnography of the late-socialist period in the Soviet Union, Yurchak discusses
youth and party meetings in which the "performative reproduction of the form
of rituals and speech acts actually *enabled* the emergence of diverse, multiple,
and unpredictable meanings in everyday life, including those that did not correspond to the constative meanings of authoritative discourse."[88] Drawing on
Judith Butler's and Saba Mahmood's accounts of power and agency, he contends
that agentival capacity can be about "introducing minute internal displacements
and mutations into the discursive regime in which they are articulated."[89] Yurchak's "minute internal displacements" offer a provocative lens to reframe the
question of complicity and how the performance of a traumatized subjectivity
may enable unpredictable meanings and interpretations. The declarations of
trans Latina asylum applicants create meanings of family, community, and
recognition that challenge the restrictive terms of the asylum narrative, even
as they perform and adhere to that narrative. Yurchak explains that minute

displacements "do not have to contradict the political and ethical parameters of a system and, more importantly, may even allow one to preserve the possibilities, promises, positive ideals, and ethical values of the system while avoiding the negative and oppressive constraints within which these are articulated."[90] We can start to see this in two ways in the declarations in my archive, namely, in the expression of desire and in the affirmation of family and of trans communities.

I have noted already that many of these declarations express the normative immigrant desire for "freedom" and "liberty" in the United States. The professions of nationalist desire align with how, as Lauren Berlant argues, the Reaganite right succeeded in making "citizenship into a category of feeling irrelevant to practices of hegemony or sociality in everyday life."[91] This push to privatize citizenship means that dominant expressions of nationalism are seen as detached from racial, social, and economic inequalities, which radically reshaped both dominant accounts of U.S. citizenship and the U.S. nation.[92] As political identification with the state decreased, affective identification with the nation became more prevalent. Trans asylum seekers mobilize these discourses of "passionate attachment" to the nation to position themselves as properly desiring subjects and future citizens. It is important to note that the state also functions as a site of affective power in the production of citizenship, as Siobhan Somerville discusses in her work on histories of naturalization. She asks about the extent to which "the construction of a desiring immigrant obscure[s] the ways that the state itself, through immigration and naturalization policy, sets the terms of this imagined love, actively distinguishing between which immigrants' desire will be returned and which will be left unrequited?"[93] This question also animates my larger project, as each chapter maps out how the incorporation of the category of transgender allows state institutions to differentially include and exclude trans migrants. The immigrant desires of a smaller number of trans asylum seekers are returned by the state in the form of a grant of asylum or withholding of removal, compared to the larger numbers of trans migrants who are detained and deported by the state.

Although the narratives in these declarations make clear the asylum seekers' "passionate attachment" to the nation, they also suggest other kinds of desires that cannot be reduced to desire for the United States, such as the desire for belonging, for feeling comfortable in one's body, for community, and for recognition. I do not want to argue that desire always constitutes a resistant excess, but rather that the performance of nationalist desire in these texts may make possible the articulation of other desires that are not solely about the veneration of the United States. That is, I am interested in thinking about the possibilities for what Yurchak discusses as the contingent relationship between the performative and the constative, two dimensions of speech and discourse.[94] The relative importance of each dimension may shift historically, but they are indivisible and mutually productive. While the literal meaning of a statement or act—its constative dimension—may become less relevant, the performative dimension may expand such that the reproduction of a form of discourse can allow for the emergence of new and unpredictable meanings.[95] In the context of asylum declarations, the performance of national desire allows for the unexpected expression of other desires. Some of these desires are about everyday life, such as the pleasures that many of these trans women experienced when they were very young and played with other girls, dressed up in girls' clothing, or did their hair and nails.[96] While invocation of these kinds of pleasures in declarations may be formally intended to "produce *felt* sensations of recognizable authenticity" as part of the applicants' effort for recognition and credibility by asylum adjudicators,[97] these quotidian acts also index the embodied pleasures of gender expression and bodily autonomy, including the ability to move and inhabit one's body in particular ways.

Other desires include the desire for love, often connected to leaving home and finding validation as a result of migration. For example, in the closing paragraph of her declaration, Luisa proclaims, "In the U.S., I will be able to find the right person who will love and respect me, someone who will not be ashamed of having a romantic relationship with me. I can be proud of myself. I will be able to be proud of my love."[98] Throughout her declaration, she makes strong statements about how life for her is not livable in Mexico and how it is much better in the United States, yet this last statement does more than just recite nationalist tropes. Here Luisa asserts her desire for love and intimacy, for pleasure, her claim to be loveable. These kinds of sentiments are rare in asylum declarations, which are supposed to focus narrowly on experiences of persecution. In their ethnographic research on asylum in the United States, Shuman and Bohmer found that some asylum seekers wanted to emphasize their loyalty to their countries of origin or wanted to think about their lives before persecution. They note that "the narrative elements that might be extraneous to the B.C.I.S. [Bureau of Citizenship and Immigration Services] decision process are often significant for the claimant's sense of self."[99] The expression of pleasure and desire gestures to other aspects of self and subjectivity that exceed the narrow confines of the legal conception of the asylum seeker. These details are not required and may even be considered not relevant by asylum adjudicators, given the generic conventions of the asylum declaration.[100]

Affirmations of family and community in declarations are a second mode through which the performance of a traumatized trans subjectivity introduces "minute internal displacements" into the dominant discursive regime of asylum. I want to consider the extended version of Ines's quote at the end of the previous section, which I first read as reinforcing the dominant nationalist ideology of the "American Dream." In the last paragraph of her declaration, Ines states, "This country has given me back my life, and I would like the opportunity to give back to it. I cannot return to Mexico, even though it kills me to be separated from my family. It's not their fault that I had to leave. My sister, Estrella, always tells me that I cannot go back, because I will be killed. My mother said people like me die there all the time, and she said that she did not want to lose another daughter. I wanted to come here to be who I am, to be a woman, and I think I have succeeded in part."[101] In this statement, Ines performs the obligatory narrative of the persecution she experienced, and would experience again, in Mexico as a trans-identified person. But her performance displaces this violence in significant ways. While her declaration as a whole reproduces the binary of an oppressive Mexico versus a free America, these concluding sentences attempt to disrupt that absolute binary by asserting her love for her family and their support. This is particularly noteworthy since earlier in her declaration Ines describes how her mother used to beat her every day when she was younger to force her to learn to be a man. The avowal of love for family marks a slippage in the suturing of the narrative of an autological subject oppressed by her genealogical society, and it pushes against the racist and colonialist conflation of family, culture, and country in the establishment of well-founded fear for the purposes of asylum law.

Furthermore, the two uses of "kill" in this statement are striking: deploying the same word to convey both the emotional pain she feels being separated from her family in the United States *and* the physical destruction she would be subject to in Mexico, Ines posits an equivalence between the suffering she experiences in each country. In doing so, she pushes back against what Cvetkovich refers to as the "amnesiac powers" of national trauma culture, which frequently uses one trauma story to cover up another.[102] The story of her persecution in Mexico does not completely cover the story of her hardship in the United States— being separated from her family, and her experiences of domestic abuse and fear of the police in the United States. Invoking her mother's "expert" testimony about how "people like me die there all the time" allows Ines to insist upon her mother's recognition of her as a loved and valued daughter, which interrupts the totalizing and denigrating construction of Mexico that is produced in the declaration as a whole. Emphasizing the losses associated with migration and family separation also disrupts the narrative of liberty tied to asylum.

Ines mentions the support she received from other trans women in Mexico, describing how she would hang out with a group of trans girls at a park in her town. Despite police attempts to regulate their mobility and access to public space, they continued to meet: "We liked to talk about when we could all wear our real clothes—ladies' clothes. The police came by often, and we would scatter, running in all directions. They did not catch me. But we kept coming back to see each other, because we were a family."[103] Other declarations also insist on the importance of communities and chosen families, both in countries of origin and in the United States.[104] For example, Ana, who I cited in the epigraph, ends her asylum declaration by discussing the value of the trans community she found with El/La Para Translatinas in San Francisco.[105] Granted, narratives of community can reinforce nationalist sentiments.[106] As Anne-Marie D'Aoust argues, expressions of migrant love are often still inscribed within narratives of the nationalist nuclear family.[107] But the articulations of desire for family and community within these asylum declarations nevertheless highlight forms of queer and trans relationality that fall off the "genealogical grid" of heteronormativity,[108] and therefore introduce minute displacements that intervene in the normative logics of the nation.

Excessive Desires: The Politics of Representation

The strategic uses of desire in these asylum declarations push back against the genre's more reductive requirement of a traumatized subject to insist upon other aspects of self and subjectivity. But the representation of trans asylum seekers as desiring subjects also can be taken up in order to undermine asylum claims and the process of asylum itself. This final section shifts from my broader critique of desire and mobility to zoom in on a particular set of events in San Francisco that illustrate the movement and mobilization of representations of trans asylum seekers beyond the legal realm. On November 26, 2008, the SF Weekly, a free alternative weekly newspaper with a centrist political perspective, ran a cover story titled "Border Crossers" written by Lauren Smiley. As one of the few mainstream news media stories specifically on trans asylum seekers at that time, Smiley's article marks the moment in the early twenty-first century when it becomes clear that many trans Latinas are seeking asylum in the United States and that many of those women are going to California to file their applications and find a larger trans Latina community. Her article exemplifies an anti-immigrant response that depicts trans Latina asylum seekers as excessively desiring subjects. This cover story in the SF Weekly—and the responses it elicited from the trans migrant community in San Francisco—serve as a microcosm of the cultural discourses that circulate nationally to create the larger context in which grants of asylum for trans asylum seekers are determined.

The cover of this issue of SF Weekly is dominated by a photograph of a Latina with long hair and heavy eye makeup who appears to be naked under the large American flag she holds up to her breasts. Shot from below and set against a white background, the woman poses in tall stilettos and looks down at the viewer. Drawing on racialized stereotypes of trans Latinas as overly sexualized prostitutes, the image conflates sexual desire and nationalist desire to map them both onto the body of the trans Latina in the photograph. The accompanying text reads, "Border Crossers. Transsexuals from Latin America find it easy to get asylum in the U.S.—even if they have extensive criminal records." Even before turning to the article itself, the cover image and text presents trans Latina asylum seekers as undeserving criminals who are cheating the immigration system to gain legal status in the United States, mobilizing what Natalia Molina terms "racial scripts" about Latinx migrants that have been used effectively in California in particular to advance anti-immigrant sentiment and legislation.[109]

The opening paragraphs of Smiley's cover story describe the trans women she interviewed for the article in sensationalistic language that reproduces racist and misogynistic narratives about trans Latinas. She portrays trans Latinas who work as sex workers in crude, objectifying, and transphobic ways, describing one woman as having "all the porn-worthy ass a backroom peddler of industrial-grade collagen could inject."[110] Calling them "vanity-stricken," Smiley consistently refers to the women as "hookers" throughout her article and notes that "transgender hookers aren't the type of ladies you would imagine Uncle Sam would want to be seen in public with, let alone endorse to stay in the country."[111] The slideshow of photographs running alongside the article—which includes shots of one of the women at her job in a strip club and one woman working the street, with the caption "Ana hooks while she waits for asylum"—reinforces the easy slippage between trans Latina and "hooker." While she notes that three of the trans women she spoke with said that they did sex work because they couldn't find other work due to discrimination, overall, her article presents a decontextualized account of trans Latina asylum seekers. She integrates detailed accounts of her interviewees' experiences with drug use and sex work into a discussion of the asylum process, accompanied by quotes from immigration attorneys who discuss their successes obtaining asylum or other protection (withholding of removal or protection under the U.N. Convention Against Torture) for their trans clients who have criminal records. Smiley includes multiple quotes by Dan Stein, president of the Federation for American Immigration Reform (FAIR), but fails to mention that FAIR is a right-wing anti-immigration organization that the Southern Poverty Law Center lists as a hate group because of its ties to the white supremacist movement in the United States.[112]

Smiley's article elicited widespread outrage from trans and immigration rights advocates nationwide, trans health and medical care providers, public health and HIV/AIDS organizations, and members of the trans community in the SF Bay Area, many of whom wrote lengthy letters to SF Weekly challenging her characterization of trans Latina asylum seekers and the asylum process.[113] Smiley dismisses these critiques of her article by stating that the focus of her article was not on the obstacles trans women face in San Francisco, but on "a previously unreported aspect of the asylum system."[114] Responding to an op-ed in the SF Guardian criticizing "Border Crossers," Smiley writes that "the root issue is the people who have won protection from the U.S. government on humanitarian grounds, and who have broken and/or continue to break the law."[115] By divorcing this "root issue" from the larger structural oppressions and violence that trans Latina immigrants (and other trans migrants) face and by characterizing the "law" as a neutral and fair instrument of governance that affects all populations equally, Smiley perpetuates racist, sexist, and criminalizing narratives about trans Latinas. She also raises the specter of the false asylum claim that is referenced in the two journalistic accounts I discuss at the beginning of this chapter.

Her article exemplifies the high stakes of writing about asylum and the politics of representation of trans migrants, as it reveals how anti-immigrant discourses can take up nuanced arguments about trans asylum and use them against trans asylum seekers. One of the letters protesting the article was coauthored by a group of immigration attorneys and advocates from across the United States who Smiley had interviewed: "We all spoke with Smiley at length, and are outraged at the misrepresentation of what we said. Rather than present a balanced picture of the incredible hurdles transgender asylum seekers face in proving their cases, Smiley unfairly painted them as criminals and prostitutes who are essentially given a free pass to immigration in the United States. This could not be further from the truth."[116] The collective reaction to Smiley's article also makes clear the prescribed boundaries for a politics of response. In order to challenge Smiley's depiction of trans Latinas as yet another group of immigrants who are cheating the system, the letter writers need to reinscribe the suffering and trauma that trans asylum seekers experience in their countries of origin and in the United States. The letters emphasize the difficulty of obtaining asylum in the United States, detail trans migrants' mental and physical health issues, discuss employment and educational discrimination, and describe the forms of violence and poverty faced by many trans migrants. While the accounts of the obstacles trans migrants experience and the ways they are criminalized are decidedly not exaggerated, as I discuss in chapter 4 in relation to immigration detention, these responses to Smiley's article illustrate how the discourse of asylum requires that the trans asylum seeker be a subject of trauma. One of the letters to *SF Weekly* attempts to disrupt this discourse through the assertion of trans people as good productive citizens. The Transgender Advisory Group (TAG) writes that "Beyond Smiley's ignorant and negative portrayals of transgender people, there are exciting and positive aspects of the community we have much to celebrate about. In recent years, transgender people have slowly made their way into mainstream media, have become leaders and advocates for the community, contributed immensely to the socio and political LGBT consciousness, and have much to boast about local transgender services and program [sic] that models [sic] San Francisco as one of the most transgender accepting metropolitan city [sic] in this nation."[117] These are indeed important accomplishments of the trans community, which has provided invaluable and much-needed resources for trans people in San Francisco. Yet this response also illustrates the limitations of a counterdiscourse, as TAG resists Smiley's representation of criminal trans Latinas by representing trans people as productive members of their communities. Their response still operates within the binary of deserving versus undeserving immigrant.

While the genre of asylum declarations requires trans migrants to represent themselves as traumatized but properly desiring national subjects, Smiley's representation depicts trans migrants as excessively desiring sex workers and criminals. Neither of these flattened representations does justice to the subjectivities or experiences of trans migrants. Alexandra Byerly, Program Coordinator and Health Educator at El/La Program Para Translatinas in San Francisco, highlights this in her letter to the editor. Byerly writes that she feels "our community has been betrayed by Lauren Smiley in her article," since Smiley "chose to sensationalize and abuse the people that trusted her with their stories" by presenting a partial view of the experiences of trans Latina migrants in San Francisco.[118] As a trans Latina who is able to respond to the representation of trans Latina asylum seekers in "Border Crossers," Byerly seeks to complicate Smiley's deployment of anti-immigrant discourses, although she does contribute to the discourses of trauma that characterize trans migrant subjectivity: "In my two years of experience as a program coordinator for the El/La Program, I have seen the hardship, the pain, and the suffering caused by the violence and rejection most of the Translatinas have endured in their home countries and in the U.S. as well." Yet the voice of Byerly and the invocation of El/La also counter both the violence of the law and legal representations and the violence of representations like Smiley's. El/La Para TransLatinas is a nonprofit HIV organization that provides personal and professional workshops, education, and leadership development for trans Latinas.[119] Led by trans Latinas, El/La operates as a space of affirmation, empowerment, and community for trans Latinas who experience discrimination, housing and employment insecurity, and everyday violence in San Francisco. El/La also works closely with the National Center for Lesbian Rights' asylum clinic in San Francisco to help many trans Latina asylum seekers write their asylum declarations and prepare their asylum cases. El/La constitutes a counterpublic to the representations of trans Latina asylum seekers in both Smiley's article and in the genre of asylum declarations. As a vital community resource, El/La offers space for a fuller and more complex articulation of what it means to be a trans migrant and asylum seeker in the United States. Despite their differences, the legal, journalistic, and community depictions of trans asylum seekers tend to mobilize the registers of desire and trauma to argue for the legitimacy of trans migrant subjectivity.

Conclusion

Theorizing the relations of im/mobility that structure asylum declarations on multiple levels reveals the ways that the profession of nationalist desire makes room for the expression of other kinds of desires and subjectivities by trans asylum seekers. These minute displacements complicate the legal construction of the trans asylum seeker as a legible subject, pushing against the colonialist discourses of generosity and exceptionalism that undergird the U.S. asylum system. Yet as the specific example of Lauren Smiley's article in the *SF Weekly* demonstrates, the representation of trans Latinas as desiring subjects can be easily appropriated by racist anti-immigrant discourses that depict asylum seekers as undeserving criminal immigrants. Asylum offers the promise of recognition and protection to those few trans migrants who can prove and perform the requisite trauma and fit into the established categories of gender and sexuality. While I do not want to disregard the legal protection offered by asylum, many trans migrants experience varying degrees of transphobic and racial violence and discrimination in the United States as well, even after they receive a grant of asylum and have a documented legal status and work permit. It is also important to remember that the mobility and status given through a grant of asylum to a relative few trans migrants in turn legitimates the mass detention and removal of other trans and non-trans migrants caught in the rapidly expanding U.S. immigration deportation system. This is why the expression of other desires in declarations point to how kinship—whether it develops through family, lovers, or intentional trans communities—offers trans migrants a space of belonging and community with far more potential than the promise of the United States as an inclusive space of national belonging.

While asylum functions as an exceptional form of entry into the nation-state that requires trans migrants to perform a traumatized subjectivity, marriage offers legitimation and normalization for other trans migrants to be socially and legally integrated into the national body politic. As a form of belonging historically tied to the nation-state, marriage determines social citizenship rights and is often elided with citizenship status. The next chapter turns to the intersection of marriage and immigration law to explore marriage as another means for trans migrants to access rights and recognition from the U.S. state, and to address key questions about trans citizenship as it is shaped through marriage, immigration, and neoliberalism.

3

Trans Citizenship

Marriage, Immigration, and Neoliberal Recognition

In 2005, the Board of Immigration Appeals (BIA) decided *In re Lovo*, a precedential decision that confirmed immigration benefits for marriages involving transgender spouses.[1] This case marks an important moment in the expansion of citizenship rights through marriage for trans subjects.[2] The case centered on Gia Teresa Lovo-Ciccone's marriage to José Mauricio Lovo-Lara, a citizen of El Salvador. Lovo-Ciccone, a U.S. citizen who was assigned male at birth in 1973, transitioned in 2001 when she had genital surgery and changed all of her identification documents to reflect her female identity. After her marriage in 2002, Lovo filed an instant visa petition on behalf of her husband. Her visa petition was denied in 2004 by the Nebraska Service Center, one of the U.S. Citizenship and Immigration Services's (USCIS's) field offices that process immigration applications and petitions, which argued that her marriage was not valid for the purposes of immigration, since it constituted a same-sex marriage. Lovo appealed the denial with the help of the American Civil Liberties Union's (ACLU's) Lesbian and Gay Rights Project, and the Board of Immigration Appeals (BIA) sustained her appeal and granted her husband a visa. *In re Lovo* established that as long as a marriage is valid where it is entered into, it should be valid for immigration purposes.

As a quotidian site of state regulation, marriage produces and disciplines racialized, sexualized, and gendered subjectivities in the construction of proper and deserving citizens. Alongside asylum and immigration detention, marriage operates as site for the differential inclusion of trans subjects. For trans subjects like Gia Teresa Lovo-Ciccone, marriage offers a transit to cultural and legal recognition as a normatively gendered heterosexual national subject. Feminist historians and legal scholars have shown how marriage supports constructions of U.S. citizenship, since it is implicated in property relations, racial hierarchies, immigration policy, and other projects determining national membership.[3]

Marriage determines the distribution of social citizenship rights by providing access to benefits like health care and by granting a sense of belonging and legitimacy.[4]

Examining *In re Lovo* raises key questions about trans citizenship as it is shaped through marriage, immigration, and neoliberalism.[5] This chapter traces the production of trans citizenship through marriage in the *In re Lovo* decision and its inclusion into LGBT legal advocacy and USCIS policy. The circulation and incorporation of *In re Lovo* illustrates how the process of normalizing and disciplining trans subjects is dispersed across different institutions and sites. In chapter 1, I used Bruno Latour's concept of "immutable mobiles" to think about court decisions as inscriptions that assume value and meaning once they are displaced from the trans subject who is at the center of the case.[6] *In re Lovo* functions similarly as an immutable mobile that is distinct from Lovo herself, who is flattened and frozen as a legal subject, even as the BIA decision circulates as a legal text that establishes precedent for subsequent cases and the continued development of law. The content of my archive determines the shape of my argument in this chapter. *In re Lovo* did not receive much coverage in the popular press, or even in the gay and lesbian press.[7] I know little about Lovo as an individual; my analysis focuses on how she emerges as a legal subject in the BIA decision and how the decision circulates in relation to other texts. The BIA also had access to Lovo only as she is represented in legal documents, since it reviews most of its appeals on paper and does not usually hold courtroom proceedings. This chapter contributes to the book's larger project of tracing the emergence of trans subjects as legal subjects in immigration law and policy. The process in which Lovo becomes a legal subject is one in which she also becomes a universalized trans subject. My analysis highlights how legal regulation works through the ways different legal documents and actors condition each other as well as the legal subjects they are intended to govern and produce. The law remakes itself through these interactions and revisions and through its movements across different sites and subjects. This chapter explores how marriage functions as a neoliberal technique of governance to discipline and incorporate trans subjects into proper citizenship, and how immigration law becomes a site through which this discipline and management is administered. Attending to the operation of immigration law and marriage law illustrates the limitations of seeking rights and recognition from state institutions for trans subjects.

I focus on *In re Lovo* as a central text because the case is precedent setting but also because marriage has a special status under immigration law. Marriages involving U.S. citizens have a favorable status, since they are not subject to visa quotas and can "forgive" some violations of immigration law to allow foreign nationals to apply for lawful permanent residency.[8] Marriage offers some immigrants privileged access to documented status and legal citizenship, even though legal citizenship itself does not protect immigrants of color and trans immigrants from racism, transphobia, and other forms of state-sponsored violence. While the treatment of marriage involving transgender spouses in immigration law is variable and changing, the specter of same-sex marriage shaped the legal reasoning about trans immigrant marriages at the time *In re Lovo* was decided. In 2005, the USCIS did not recognize same-sex marriages for immigration purposes; this chapter analyzes *In re Lovo* in that context. However, in June 2013, the U.S. Supreme Court's decision in *United States v. Windsor* held that section 3 of the Defense of Marriage Act (DOMA), which limited federal marriage recognition to different-sex couples, is unconstitutional.[9] This section of DOMA had prevented lawfully married lesbian and gay couples from obtaining lawful permanent residence through marriage.[10] *United States v. Windsor* allowed U.S. citizens and lawful permanent residents to submit green card petitions for their same-sex spouses, which theoretically opened up marriage for binational couples in which one or both partners are trans. In 2015, the U.S. Supreme Court decided *Obergefell v. Hodges*, which found that the Fourteenth Amendment guaranteed same-sex couples the fundamental right to marry.[11] Although the legal landscape of marriage law has changed significantly since 2005, *In re Lovo* is helpful for understanding the process of legal recognition and inclusion for trans people in the United States, and what is at stake in the incorporation of trans subjects as citizens through marriage.

Marriage is based in family law, which is governed by state law, but immigration law is governed solely by federal law. Marriages involving trans partners for the purposes of immigration highlight the unevenness of federal and state policies that regulate trans subjects and their shifting legal statuses. Before 2013, for marriages involving trans partners, the USCIS turned to the law of the state in which the marriage was entered into (or to the state in which the U.S. citizen spouse lives, if it is a foreign marriage). Both where trans people live *and* where trans people were born determined whether they could enter a heterosexual marriage. Most states do not have a statute about marriage rights for trans individuals, but some states' case law explicitly recognizes or denies such marriages. Courts in Kansas and Texas have ruled that trans women who have undergone genital surgery (and who have changed their birth certificates) are legally male for the purposes of marriage, and a court in Florida ruled that marriages in that state will be void if the sex assigned at birth of the two parties are the same, regardless of any subsequent surgeries.[12] In contrast, in New Jersey a court ruled in 1976 that a transsexual woman was legally female for the purposes of marriage.[13] Furthermore, some states require birth certificates to obtain marriage certificates, yet not all states allow for sex reclassification on birth certificates. Ohio, Tennessee, and Idaho prohibit amending birth certificates to more accurately reflect a trans person's sex/gender.[14] Of the remaining forty-seven states, twenty-eight authorize sex reclassification on birth certificates by statute or by administrative ruling. The other nineteen states have no written rules regarding sex designation change, but they do provide a change upon application.[15] Every state that allows for a change of sex designation on a birth certificate requires evidence of surgery, but the type of surgery and the type of evidence varies.[16] Thus, although *In re Lovo* ruled that a marriage is valid for immigration purposes, if it is valid in the state in which it was entered into, this ruling did not help all trans migrants. Since many of these policies are based on surgery requirements and most trans people do not have genital surgery, even those trans people living in states that allow for sex reclassification on birth certificates are unlikely to be able to do so.[17]

The unevenness of recognition and access that trans people have to marriage confirms the incoherence of the U.S. administrative state. Rather than a totalizing, consistent entity, the state is better understood as a set of practices that share certain logics about sex/gender but that diverge in terms of rules and the implementation of those rules with respect to trans people. These state practices tend to share a belief in binary sex/gender and in the capacity of a person to change sex/gender, and they require the medical and legal documentation of gender to be authorized and confirmed by experts. The differences and insistencies in how courts define legal sex in relation to marriage demonstrates that while state practices may share rationales and influence each other, they also vary widely in terms of requirements and implementation. Yet as Paisley Currah points out, contradictions do not undermine state policies: "it is a mistake to think these incongruities necessarily pose a problem either for the state or for the intractability of the organic 'common senses' of gender that make many transgender people strangers to the law."[18] Consequently, trans advocates should focus on how state institutions "*police* the relation between sex and gender," since that is the biggest obstacle to the project of trans rights.[19] Following Currah, this chapter focuses on how state institutions regulate the relationship between sex and gender in the administration of laws and policies around immigration and marriage for trans subjects.

This chapter contributes to the existing body of scholarship on marriage by feminist and queer theorists who have interrogated how marriage as a state institution produces and disciplines proper racial, sexual, and gendered subjects. While some attention has been given to trans marriage law—primarily by legal scholars—less attention has been given to trans subjects at the intersection of immigration law and marriage law.[20] My analysis unpacks the specific ways marriage law and immigration law work on trans subjects to produce them as trans citizens. In doing so, I explore how "trans" modifies "citizenship" as a political and legal status and as a cultural form of belonging as well as how "citizenship" modifies "trans" with different expectations from different trans subjects and different consequences for subjects' mobility.

In order to contextualize the emergence of the normative trans subject in *In re Lovo* in longer histories of U.S. immigration law's regulation of marriage, this chapter proceeds chronologically. The next section provides a brief historization of the federal immigration, marriage, and welfare legislation that constitutes the larger context for *In re Lovo*. I then turn to the case itself to explore how racialization and gender normalization condition the procedural history of the case and the final BIA decision. Trans legal advocacy organizations like Immigration Equality and the Transgender Law Center celebrated *In re Lovo* as a victory for trans people. I examine discussion of the case in the immigration attorney handbook, *Immigration Law and the Transgender Client*,[21] to show how LGBT legal advocacy organizations participate in the construction of a normative transgender subject. The final section of the chapter explores how *In re Lovo* was codified into USCIS policy. The inclusion of the *In re Lovo* decision into the USCIS *Adjudicator's Field Manual* (AFM) reveals how discourses of privacy structure state recognition of trans immigrants as liberal subjects through marriage.

Immigration Law and the Regulation of Marriage

Like miscegenation law, immigration law has played a key role in building the racial infrastructure of the administrative state by producing racist hierarchies that privileged those immigrants racialized as white.[22] The earliest federal legislation connecting immigrant citizenship to marriage was an act of Congress in 1855 that declared that any women of any nationality or origin who married an American man became a citizen of the United States, as long as she met naturalization requirements, which at the time meant being a "free white person." This act also stated that the child of an American man would be a U.S. citizen, regardless of whether the child was born in the United States or abroad. Nancy Cott notes that this act "expressed marital unity at the national level and signified the male citizen's prerogative of representation."[23] Other major federal immigration laws did not specifically focus on marriage as an institution, but because they regulated immigration in terms of racial categories and gender, they impacted the relationship between marriage and immigration. These laws limited immigration for those populations that were racialized as nonwhite.[24] While most of the immigration laws in the late nineteenth century and early twentieth century did not center on marriage, these immigration policies prioritized male immigrants whose choice of wives reflected the appropriate desires and models of consent that marriage signified for proper citizenship. These laws produced categories of race for state institutions, upheld racist hierarchies, and naturalized whiteness as a form of citizenship. The use of immigration law to regulate marriage along racial lines continues into the twenty-first century.[25]

The major federal legislation around marriage, welfare, and immigration in 1996 forms the backdrop for understanding the recognition of trans marriage in 2005. The same Congress that passed DOMA also passed major legislation around welfare and immigration reform, including the Personal Responsibility

and Work Opportunity Reconciliation Act (PRWORA),[26] the Anti-Terrorism and
Effective Death Penalty Act (AEDPA),[27] and the Illegal Immigration Reform and
Immigrant Responsibility Act (IIRIRA).[28] While only DOMA is cited explicitly in *In
re Lovo*, DOMA must be contextualized in relation to PRWORA and IIRIRA. Thinking across these different pieces of legislation helps us understand how state
logics of racialization and gender normalization structure marriage and immigration policy in the decade preceding the *In re Lovo* decision, which reflects and
upholds these logics by reconfiguring heterosexual marriage to include normative trans subjects. DOMA passed quickly through Congress with little discussion and large majorities in both houses, and was signed into law by President
Clinton.[29] Section 2 of DOMA mandated that no state would have to recognize a
same-sex marriage contracted in another state,[30] and section 3 explicitly defined
"marriage" and "spouse" in relation to the heteronormative sex/gender binary
for the purposes of federal law.[31] PRWORA, which was signed into law a month
before DOMA, also targets heteronormative marriage as a key mechanism for
state governance of particular racialized populations.[32] The Act frames the existence of poor single mothers on welfare as a crisis undermining the stability
and prosperity of the U.S. nation.[33] PRWORA privatizes poverty and promotes
marriage as a requirement for government support.[34] Support for PRWORA drew
upon racialized discourses about Black women and other women of color as "welfare queens," even though it had negative impacts on a wide range of women.[35]
The fact that DOMA and PRWORA were passed by the same Congress indicates
how the U.S. government continued to treat marriage as a racialized and economic condition for citizenship in the late twentieth century. DOMA restricts
marriage rights and benefits to heterosexual couples, and PRWORA withholds
basic civil rights from poor women if they are not married. Together, these acts
show how the neoliberal state can use marriage in a variety of ways to manage
different populations and life chances for marginalized groups.[36]

The section of PRWORA dealing with welfare benefits for immigrants also
reflects racist discourses about immigrants as burdens on the public benefits
system and restricts governmental assistance to documented immigrants who
are positioned as being responsible for their own personal well-being, a responsibility that should occur through self-sufficiency. Under neoliberal governmentality, social goods such as health care, education, and social welfare are
privatized and "lack of access has been redefined as an individual failing rather
than a reflection of systemic inequality."[37] PRWORA marks marriage and work
as the means to self-sufficiency, which marginalizes trans subjects who have
variable access to marriage and face difficulties obtaining employment due to
lack of accurate identification documents. As Dean Spade argues, inconsistent
administrative regulations governing gender make trans people especially vulnerable to economic instability, discrimination, and interpersonal and state violence. Not being able to get an accurate ID constrains access to social services

and employment for many trans people who often "experience a downward mobility in terms of wealth/income because of their trans identities."[38]

The concept of "immigrant responsibility" also animates the IIRIRA and AEDPA, which represent some of the most significant procedural and substantive changes in U.S. immigration law since the passage of the Johnson-Reed Act in 1924.[39] While the latter solidified the figure of the "illegal alien" in the twentieth century, the IIRIRA contributed to the construction of the "criminal alien" in the twenty-first century.[40] Lisa Marie Cacho notes that the 1996 immigration laws targeted immigrants of color with the presumption that "criminality for certain human beings is an interior attribute, inherent or irreversible."[41] Marriage is not discussed at length in the text of IIRIRA, unlike in PRWORA, but the legislation has implications for immigrant marriages. By narrowing the possibilities for entering and residing in the United States through the criminalization of immigration, the passage of IIRIRA meant that heterosexual marriage and family reunification became even more important, if also more restricted, paths to documented status for immigrants. Yet many trans migrants cannot access other avenues of family-based immigration because they frequently experience rejection by their birth families. And before *United States v. Windsor* (2013) and *Obergefell v. Hodges* (2015), marriage was often inaccessible to the majority of trans migrants who could not produce the medical evidence required to be eligible as a transitioned spouse in a heterosexual marriage.

Collectively, the immigration and welfare legislation in 1996 constitute part of the larger context for the *In re Lovo* decision. They demonstrate how marriage works as a regulatory state mechanism for maintenance of hierarchies of gender and race under heteropatriarchy and racial capitalism, by denying or granting social services and state support to different populations and by producing discourses of self-sufficiency, responsibility, and criminalization. *In re Lovo* represents a continuation of, rather than a break from, these logics. The precedential BIA decision illustrates how cultural discourses of neoliberalism shape the construction of trans citizenship through marriage by positing a racialized economic basis for deserving citizens.

In addition to this immigration and welfare legislation that regulates marriage, the history of immigration policies toward Salvadorans also informs the larger context in which *In re Lovo* is decided. Jose Mauricio Lovo-Lara's position as a Salvadoran immigrant becomes significant given the longer record of shifting U.S. immigration policies toward Salvadorans in the late twentieth century. The population of Salvadoran immigrants in the United States increased dramatically in the early 1980s as hundreds of thousands fled political violence and human rights violations from the Salvadoran civil war (1980–1992). Susan Bibler Coutin notes that the U.S. government initially characterized these migrants as economic immigrants rather than as victims of persecution, in part due to the U.S. government's support of and involvement in the Salvadoran government's war on guerilla insurgents in the 1980s.[42] The out-of-court settlement in the 1991 *American Baptist Churches v. Thornburgh*[43] case and the granting of Temporary Protected Status (TPS) under the 1990 Immigration Act[44] provided Salvadorans temporary legal status in the United States but rarely led to permanent residency. In the mid-1990s, Salvadoran activists, with the support of the Salvadoran government, pushed for exemptions from certain provisions of the IIRIRA. This led to the passage of the Nicaraguan Adjustment and Central American Relief Act in 1997[45] and to administrative concessions that enabled many Salvadoran asylum seekers to finally gain permanent residency.[46] Coutin remarks that "Salvadorans who, during the 1980s, had been regarded as undesirable and deserving of deportation came, in the late 1900s and early 2000s, to be defined as deserving immigrants, "people we knew" (to quote one asylum official interviewed), and future citizens."[47] While not specifically mentioned in the *In re Lovo* decision, the history of Salvadoran asylum seekers in the United States comprises part of the historical backdrop for the case, and for Jose Mauricio Lovo-Lara as a Salvadoran national petitioning for immigration through marriage.

More recently, Salvadorans and other Central American migrants were targeted by the Trump administration in its efforts to radically transform the U.S. immigration system. In addition to limiting legal immigration and increasing enforcement, the administration worked to narrow the pathways for humanitarian forms of relief, demonizing asylum seekers, refugees, and Temporary Protected Status (TPS) holders as burdens on social welfare programs and as threats to public safety. The administration moved to end TPS designations for nationals of six countries, including El Salvador.[48] The ending of TPS for Salvadorans was halted by a federal district court judge in October 2018, but this preliminary injunction was reversed by the Ninth Circuit Court in September 2020; this case may reach the U.S. Supreme Court.[49] It is unclear what will happen under the Biden administration, which has pledged to review TPS designations. During the first three years of the Trump administration, the Department of Homeland Security (DHS) and the Justice Department also enacted numerous policies and rulings to narrow asylum eligibility for large populations seeking protection in the United States, focused in a large part on Central and South Americans, and then used the COVID-19 pandemic in 2020 to effectively end asylum at the southern border.[50]

Federal Recognition of "Transsexual Marriage"

This section traces the procedural history of Gia Teresa Lovo-Ciccone's immigration visa petition for her husband, leading up to the precedential BIA decision in her favor in 2005. I show how the BIA responds to the potential threat trans marriage poses to heteronormativity and DOMA by incorporating "transsexual marriage" into the regulation of heterosexual marriage at the federal level.

Lovo-Ciccone filed a visa petition for her husband, Jose Mauricio Lovo-Lara, a citizen of El Salvador, in 2002. In support of her petition, Lovo-Ciccone submitted her new North Carolina birth certificate recognizing her as female; an affidavit from her physician confirming she had undergone genital surgery; a North Carolina name change court order; the North Carolina Registrar of Deeds marriage record recognizing her marriage to Lovo-Lara; and a North Carolina driver's license listing her current name and her female sex designation.[51] On August 3, 2004, the director of the Nebraska Service Center, one of the USCIS's field offices that process immigration applications and petitions, denied her visa petition.

For many years, immigration visa petitions like Lovo-Ciccone's were not treated differently from other marriage cases. But in 2002, the USCIS abruptly began to issue denials in all marriage-based petitions involving a trans spouse.[52] Given that this shift occurred near the beginning of the "war on terror," it is likely related to increased national security concerns post-9/11 which fixated on nonnormatively racialized and sexualized populations.[53] In his analysis of the "persistent relationship between the concept of national security and state regulation of transgressive gender," Toby Beauchamp argues that U.S. surveillance practices, in relationship to racism and border anxieties, construct gender nonconformity as inherently deceptive and threatening.[54] In 2004, two years after the USCIS started to deny these marriage petitions, William R. Yates, the Associate Director for Operations, issued a public memorandum to state USCIS policy on issues related to trans immigrant applicants.[55] The memo, dated April 16, 2004, was sent to all regional directors, service center directors, and district directors. Citing DOMA, the memo announced the USCIS would not recognize a marriage or an intended marriage in which either party claims to be transsexual, regardless of whether either individual has or is in the process of undergoing "sexual reassignment surgery."[56] It acknowledged that "neither the DOMA nor any other Federal statute addresses whether a marriage between (for example) a man and a person born a man who has undergone surgery to become a woman should be recognized for immigration purposes or considered invalid as a same-sex marriage."[57] This is the gap in federal statute that the Yates memo intended to address. The memo states that it is a response to the varying policies individual states have toward the issuance of new birth certificates for people who have undergone "sex reassignment surgery," which, in combination with the absence of federal regulations, "resulted in inconsistent adjudications within the INS and CIS offices involving transsexual applicants."[58]

The Yates memo thus reaffirmed the USCIS policy in the early 2000s that marriages in which one or both parties claim to be transsexual shall not be recognized for any immigration benefits, regardless of whether the transsexual spouse has or will surgically transition.[59] The memo outlines the process by which USCIS officers should use "objective indicators, and avoid imposing subjective assumptions or judgements" in order to ascertain whether an individual identifies as trans, including noticing that the application lists a previous name that is gendered differently from the name listed on other parts of the application.[60] In these instances, USCIS officers are instructed to request more evidence to establish the applicant's identity such as all birth certificates and court documentation of a legal name change. According to the Yates memo, if this information reveals the applicant or spouse to be trans, the visa petition will be denied.

In his denial of Lovo-Ciccone's visa petition in August 2004, the director of the Nebraska Service Center did not explicitly cite the Yates memo, although his denial followed the instructions provided in the memo.[61] Instead, the director cited DOMA to argue Congress had not addressed the issue of marriage in which one party has undergone "sex reassignment surgery" and claimed that there was no legal basis for the Nebraska Service Center to recognize a change of sex.[62] With the legal support of the ACLU's Lesbian and Gay Rights Project, Lovo-Ciccone appealed the decision at the BIA, which sustained her appeal and approved the visa petition in its May 18, 2005 decision.

The BIA disagreed with the Nebraska Service Center's interpretation of DOMA. The BIA argued because neither DOMA itself nor the congressional record leading up to the passage of the Act explicitly mentioned trans people or marriages involving trans people, it was clear that Congress intended DOMA to only prohibit same-sex marriage. Neither the Nebraska Service Center in its initial decision nor the DHS in the appeal claimed that the marriage was not valid under North Carolina law, which expressly prohibited marriages between individuals of the same sex.[63] Because North Carolina considers Lovo-Ciccone to be female and recognizes her marriage as a valid heterosexual marriage, the BIA found "the DOMA does not preclude our recognition of this marriage for the purposes of Federal law."[64] Instead, the BIA argued that the legal case centered on whether the marriage was valid under the Immigration and Nationality Act, which did not define the word "spouse" in terms of sex.[65] The BIA disagreed with the DHS counsel's argument that an individual's chromosomes or assigned sex at birth determines that individual's gender, and concluded that "for immigration purposes, we find it appropriate to determine an individual's gender based on the designation appearing on the current birth certificate issued to that person by the State in which he or she was born."[66]

In re Lovo contains the possible threat that trans marriage poses to heteronormativity by including it in the regulation of heterosexual marriage. The BIA decision counters the Yates memo and upholds DOMA. Recognizing Lovo-Ciccone's "transsexual marriage" as valid for the purpose of immigration benefits allows the BIA to suppress challenges to DOMA. Trans embodiment has the potential to complicate marriage and immigration law's management and normalization of racialized and gendered subjects. The BIA decision admits as much in a footnote that acknowledges the "anomalous results if we refuse to recognize a postoperative transsexual's change of sex and instead consider the person to be of the sex determined at birth in accordance with the DHS's suggestion."[67] The BIA's recognition of Lovo-Ciccone's marriage resolves this problem by demarcating the category of "transsexual" as legally and conceptually distinct from that of "lesbian" or "gay." By recognizing Lovo-Ciccone's marriage, the BIA expands and redefines heterosexuality to gender-normative and heteronormative "postoperative transsexuals" who seek state-sanctioned marriage. This conditional recognition of trans identity will only provide a limited number of trans migrants and migrant partners of trans people with legal documented status. Yet the significance of this BIA decision extends beyond its impact on a relatively small number of trans migrants, since it marks a moment in which legal institutions reproduce and reify medical and cultural discourses of sex, gender, and sexuality as distinct and definable normative categories.

The legal analysis in *In re Lovo* centers on the question of whether Lovo-Ciccone's marriage is valid for the purposes of immigration law, given that it was recognized as a valid heterosexual marriage under state law. The success of this case hinges on the fact that the trans spouse in this case is a U.S. citizen who was able to legally and surgically transition. In confirming the validity of Lovo-Ciccone's marriage for immigration purposes, *In re Lovo* confirms her as a normative heterosexual U.S. citizen who has the legal right to extend her citizenship benefits to petition for her husband's immigration visa. In other words, the case represents an instance in which a complex interplay of gender and racial logics enables the normalization of a trans citizen through marriage to a migrant. Lovo-Ciccone's citizenship as a heterosexual trans woman is recognized at the federal level alongside Lovo-Lara's legitimacy as a heterosexual non-trans Salvadoran immigrant and presumed future U.S. citizen. Even though the BIA decision does not reference race or racism explicitly, the case cannot be abstracted from the underlying context of racist anxieties about immigration and about the migration of Salvadorans and other Central Americans in particular, as I noted in the beginning of this chapter. In the era of race-neutral law, evidence of racialization rarely comes through the specific naming of race as an administrative category. Instead, racialization in law operates through routes of reference in multiple ways: through precedent, through the citation of other cases, through the citation of nationality. Jose Mauricio Lovo-Lara's name and nationality as "a native and citizen of El Salvador" are the only details given in the BIA decision. He is mentioned simply as the beneficiary of the visa petition, as the husband of Gia Teresa Lovo-Ciccone. His coding as normal and unremarkable, in relation to the relevant legal issues of the case, facilitates the recognition of Lovo-Ciccone's cultural and legal citizenship status at the federal level.

Incorporating and Normalizing Transgender

Legal advocates and organizations, such as Immigration Equality, the National Center for Transgender Equality (NCTE), and the Transgender Law Center, celebrated *In re Lovo* as a rare legal victory in a federal tribunal for trans people in the areas of marriage and immigration law. The authors of the attorney handbook and practitioner manual *Immigration Law and the Transgender Client* describe the BIA decision as a "shockingly favorable precedential decision."[68] This section of the chapter focuses on the discussion of *In re Lovo* in *Immigration Law and the Transgender Client* as a precedential case and its implications for trans people filing marriage-based visa petitions to illustrate how legal advocacy organizations contribute to the legibility of the category of transgender and to the production of the figure of the trans citizen.

Immigration Law and the Transgender Client was published in 2008 and coauthored by Victoria Neilson, legal director of Immigration Equality, a New York-based national LGBT immigration rights legal organization, and Kristina Wertz, legal director of the Transgender Law Center in San Francisco. Originally formed as the Lesbian and Gay Immigration Rights Task Force in 1994, Immigration Equality has become a prominent national legal advocacy organization focused on impact litigation and policy change, primarily for binational same-sex couples. Karma R. Chávez notes that Immigration Equality's focus on the rights of binational same-sex couples leading up to the 2013 *Windsor* U.S. Supreme Court decision meant that the organization's legal and policy agenda articulated the relationship between LGBT politics and immigration politics very narrowly, ignoring the concerns of the majority of queer and trans migrants for whom access to marriage was not a priority or a form of relief.[69] Immigration Equality also provides legal services for LGBT asylum seekers and more recently provides support and legal assistance to detained LGBTQ immigrants. The Transgender Law Center was founded in 2002 as a project of the National Center for Lesbian Rights, and became an independent nonprofit in 2004, focusing mainly on direct legal services for trans people in California. At the time of the publication of *Immigration Law and the Transgender Client* in 2008, the Transgender Law Center had expanded to have a national scope, advancing important impact litigation. The organization's focus and mission shifted in 2015 when Kris Hayashi became executive director and the Transgender Law Center began to explicitly center racial justice in its trans liberation work. While it continues to pursue impact litigation and argue for precedent-setting legal cases, the organization now also focuses on programs and community-building projects like Positively Trans, the Black LGBTQIA+ Migrant Project, and TLC@SONG, a national collaboration with Southerners on New Ground that engages in policy advocacy, public education, and movement building.

Bringing together transgender civil rights law and immigration law, *Immigration Law and the Transgender Client* was the first LGBT-themed book published by the American Immigration Lawyers Association, a mainstream immigration bar association, and at the time became a valuable and much-needed resource for immigration attorneys representing trans clients. Arguably, the handbook also served as a guide for trans immigrants themselves trying to navigate the U.S. immigration system.[70] Directed at immigration attorneys who are not familiar with trans identities or legal issues, the handbook opens with a chapter on "Trans 101" and has chapters on immigration law basics, identity documents, marriage-based petitions, asylum, and detention. It provides analyses of existing case law, legal advice on how to construct successful cases, and practice tips for attorneys.

In the chapter on marriage-based petitions, the authors characterize *In re Lovo* as having "the perfect fact pattern for a positive decision" since the trans spouse was a U.S. citizen who had "undergone complete sex reassignment surgery" and whose state of residence allowed for the amendment of birth certificates for trans individuals.[71] Cases with other fact patterns might not be as successful. For example, *In re Lovo* was preceded by *In re Widener*, a nonprecedential BIA decision that involved the visa petition of Jacob Widener, a U.S. citizen living in South Carolina, for his wife, Esperanza Martinez Widener, a citizen of the Philippines who was assigned male at birth. What happened in this case was similar to what happened the following year in *In re Lovo*: the Nebraska Service Center denied Widener's petition on the grounds that his marriage did not meet the definition of marriage and spouse under DOMA. The BIA disagreed with the Service Center's denial of the visa petition. Because Esperanza Martinez had had genital surgery and legally changed her name and sex marker in the Philippines, the BIA concluded that Widener's marriage was an "opposite-sex marriage for purposes of section 7 of the DOMA" and vacated the denial of the visa.[72]

In re Widener is striking because it prefigures much of the legal reasoning in *In re Lovo* around DOMA and the legal recognition of gender transition. However, unlike in *In re Lovo*, the BIA did not reach a final decision on Widener's visa petition because South Carolina does not have a specific policy recognizing legal changes of sex by "post-operative transsexuals."[73] The BIA remanded the case back to the Nebraska Service Center for further consideration of whether South Carolina would recognize the marriage or whether it "has such a strong public policy against such marriages as would render the marriage invalid for immigration purposes."[74] This aspect of *In re Widener* illustrates the narrowness of the normative requirements for the legal recognition of trans migrants and the limits of the law reform strategies that *In re Lovo* represents. In addition to not helping trans migrants who live in U.S. states that do not recognize legal changes of sex/gender, *In re Lovo* is not a useful precedent for trans migrants who have not been able to access gender-affirming surgeries or who cannot provide documentation of a legal sex marker change in their countries of origin.

In their discussion of *In re Lovo,* the authors of *Immigration Law and the Transgender Client* acknowledge that other cases with different fact patterns will probably be more complicated and more difficult for attorneys to argue. Their explanation of how attorneys should use the BIA's legal analysis in *In re Lovo* to prepare cases exemplifies the handbook's role in the production of normative transgender subjects. For example, the chapter on marriage-based petitions contains a section called "Open Questions" that considers various scenarios that have not been explicitly addressed in the existing case law. One such "factual situation" is that of a lesbian-identified couple consisting of one partner who was assigned female at birth and one partner who was assigned male at birth and who identifies as female but who has not had surgery nor changed her sex/gender marker on her identity documents. This couple could get married as an "opposite sex couple" and obtain a marriage-based petition. The authors of the handbook state, however, that as "a matter of internal policy, some transgender rights organizations, including Immigration Equality and Transgender Law Center, will not generally accept cases such as this for representation," since these organizations would be in the "ethically difficult" position of advocating—alongside the DHS—that a trans individual who self-identifies as female should legally be considered male because she has not had surgery.[75]

This statement underscores how queer and trans advocacy organizations participate in the circumscription of the legal and social category of transgender as distinct from queer, lesbian, and gay. The authors of *Immigration Law and the Transgender Client* do acknowledge that immigration law is—at that moment in 2008—discriminatory toward same-sex relationships and the handbook provides a practice tip for private practitioners who may choose to take on these kinds of cases. But the refusal of Immigration Equality and the Transgender Law Center to represent a same-sex couple who could present themselves as a heterosexual couple because one or both of the partners has not had surgery reveals the handbook's emphasis on the specificity of transgender identity. *Immigration Law and the Transgender Client* is invested in maintaining the category of transgender as separate from homosexuality in part because the push for same-sex marriage by national lesbian and gay rights advocates in the 1990s and early 2000s caused trans marriages to be subject to more scrutiny than they were previously.[76] The legal demand for consistency and legibility from trans people is often divorced from trans people's self-identifications and the complexities of gendered embodiment in everyday life. Trans people who identify as queer, lesbian, gay, or bisexual may understand their gender and sexuality as intimately interconnected, particularly trans and gender variant migrants from non-Western cultures whose local epistemologies of gender and sexuality do not conform to normative constructions of transgender and lesbian/gay in the United States.[77] Furthermore, as Aren Z. Aizura notes, the handbook's emphasis on transgender as signaling consistency across "social, bodily, and administrative gender" ignores the lived realities of many trans people for whom it might not be possible or practical to change their administrative gender.[78]

Understandably, Immigration Equality and the Transgender Law Center are trying to help as many trans people in immigration marriage cases as possible by providing guidance on how to build the strongest cases most likely to result in immigrant visas for clients. Yet *Immigration Law and the Transgender Client* also contributes to the regulation of the category of transgender and to the production of normative and legible trans legal subjects. Legibility here is premised on administrative visibility. Aizura argues that the "transgender client" emerging from the handbook is distinguished both by her willingness to be administratively visible as transgender and by her capacity to negotiate the law as an entrepreneurial neoliberal subject.[79] The authors' focus on case law and legal reform through the creation of favorable precedent means that political, legal, and social change is represented as the responsibility of individuals.[80] The handbook, and immigration marriage law more broadly, reward self-sufficient trans individuals who have access to legal resources and who are able to present themselves in accordance with racialized, gendered, and sexualized norms and narratives.

The emphasis on self-sufficiency and adherence to norms in this context is similar to the autological subject of asylum declarations. As I discussed in the previous chapter, trans asylum seekers must present themselves as self-made, albeit traumatized, national subjects to fit prescribed parameters, even though the process of asylum is difficult to navigate without legal aid, and most applicants need an attorney to be successful in their cases. While trans migrants seeking marriage-based immigration visas also have to express nationalist desires for normative U.S. citizenship, they do not have to position themselves as liberal subjects in relation to oppressive genealogical societies like asylum applicants. Instead, the institution of marriage and coupled relationships function as technologies for fostering good neoliberal citizenship for both immigrants and U.S. citizens.[81] As an economic institution, marriage-based immigration means that the U.S. citizen assumes privatized financial responsibility to vouch for and support the migrant spouse.[82] The requirement of a legally recognized change of sex/gender makes marriage-based immigration inaccessible to low-income trans migrants who cannot afford hormonal, surgical, and legal transition. As Olga Tomchin argues in her review of marriage-based immigration for trans people, regulations around legal sex categorization and marriage "primarily benefit trans* people who are privileged based on race, class, and immigration status, and are not responsive to the lived realities of many low-income, undocumented trans women of color who stand to gain the most from legal status through marriage-based immigration."[83] The differences between the construction of the trans asylum seeker and the trans migrant applying for a marriage-based immigrant visa reflects the ways that class and racial stratification structure trans migrants' access to legal status. It also highlights the limits of relying on legal rights-based strategies for trans political projects that ignore broader biopolitical analyses of structural inequality.

For example, legal recognition for trans people through both marriage and asylum is contingent upon location and one's access to mobility. *Immigration Law and the Transgender Client* addresses this problem when the authors note that some states, like Florida, explicitly prohibit the recognition of trans marriages.[84] The solution recommended is one of physical relocation: "If at all possible, the couple should move to a state that will either recognize their marriage or, at a minimum, not prohibit their marriage."[85] While marriage-based immigration makes possible migration to the United States for some trans people, the various convergences of federal laws around immigration and state laws around marriage and legal sex/gender changes may also compel involuntary migrations and movements from one state to another. Geographical mobility conditions the shifting legal statuses that often accompanies the embodied movements of transition for trans migrants. In instances in which the couple are already married in a jurisdiction like Florida that will not recognize the marriage, *Immigration Law and the Transgender Client* suggests that the couple declare their marriage void and then get married again in another state. While the authors admit to the difficulty of this option, they stress that it may be the best course of action: "Although this sounds like a great many hurdles to jump through, it is far more likely to yield a favorable result than applying for immigration benefits based on the marriage in a state that does not recognize the marriage."[86] This proposed solution presumed a certain degree of mobility that is premised on socioeconomic status, employment opportunities, and lack of family obligations, and marks the ways that marriage-based immigration functions as a form of differential inclusion for normative trans citizens.

Codifying *In re Lovo* in USCIS policy

In 2009, USCIS amended the AFM to reflect the BIA's ruling in *In re Lovo*. At the time, the AFM was the binding guide for all USCIS staff administering immigration procedures.[87] When the AFM was revised with respect to the *In re Lovo* decision, USCIS added that the transgender spouse must have had "sex reassignment surgery" for the marriage to be recognized. This additional surgery requirement was eliminated in 2012, after extensive lobbying by national transgender legal advocacy organizations like the NCTE and Immigration Equality. The USCIS issued a policy memorandum on April 13, 2012, entitled "Adjudication of Immigration Benefits for Transgender Individuals" (April 2012 Policy Memo), which superseded its previous policies.[88] This policy memo set guidelines both for a change of sex/gender on immigration documents and for immigration visa petitions in marriages involving trans spouses. It revised the AFM so surgery is not required to change the sex/gender designation on immigration documents, and therefore realigned USCIS policy with *In re Lovo*. This final section of the chapter focuses on the April 2012 Policy Memo to highlight the continued centrality of medicalization for trans rights and recognitions, and the ways that discourses of privacy obscure the perpetuation of state violence toward trans migrants.

The medicalization of trans bodies continues to inform federal policies around marriage-based immigration for trans migrants, despite the removal of the additional surgery requirement. Historically medical discourses of sex have structured laws around legal sex/gender change, and the legal reasoning governing trans people's legal change of sex often invokes heteronormative standards, namely the possibility of heterosexual penis-in-vagina intercourse.[89] The April 2012 Policy Memo's statement that the federal government will not require "sex reassignment surgery" for a legal change of sex/gender on immigration documents is remarkable for this reason, although of course many federal and state agencies still maintain genital surgery as a standard. The April 2012 Policy Memo notes that "Not all states or foreign jurisdictions that recognize a legal change of gender require the completion of gender reassignment surgery before an individual can legally change his or her gender," and goes on to state these new USCIS guidelines are intended to reflect "the broader range of clinical treatments that can result in a legal change of gender under the law of the relevant jurisdiction."[90] Modeled after the U.S. State Department's updated passport policy, which also does not require surgery, the April 2012 Policy Memo allows a licensed physician (a doctor of medicine or a doctor of osteopathy) to medically certify the change of sex. A trans individual needs to present either medical certification of change of sex/gender from a licensed physician or present an amended birth certificate, passport, or court order recognizing the new gender. This policy contributes to the standardization of federal policies around identity documents for trans subjects. Yet by acknowledging the variety of state practices and policies that exist for a legal sex/gender change, the memo itself admits to the difficulty of demarcating the category of "transgender" in any clearly defined manner.

A striking feature of the April 2012 Policy Memo is how it purports to offer privacy to trans migrants. The memo claims that because proof of "sex reassignment surgery" is not required for a change of gender on immigration documents, evidence of such surgery will not be required, and even "if such surgery has taken place, a statement to that effect in the medical certification is sufficient to establish the fact. USCIS will not ask for records relating to any such surgery."[91] This statement stands in stark contrast to *In re Lovo* and the other unpublished BIA decisions that preceded it, in which the trans spouses were often asked to provide extensive documentation of their transition-related medical and surgical histories. The BIA decisions themselves often recounted the details of these surgeries when they decided the validity of marriages as heterosexual. While the BIA's decision in *In re Lovo* notes only that Gia Teresa Lovo-Lovo had provided a physician's statement that she had had "sex reassignment surgery," *In re Widener*, the unpublished BIA decision that I discussed previously, narrates a high level of medical detail. The trans migrant in that case, Esperanza Martinez Widener, had surgically and legally transitioned in the Philippines, which required her to stand in front of the Regional Trial Court of Manila and describe the various medical procedures and surgeries she had undergone. She also had to be physically examined by a medical practitioner and a plastic surgeon who presented testimony to the court about the details of her external genitalia, confirming its "femaleness," and the fact that she was not capable of pregnancy. These Manila court proceedings were included in the record that the BIA examined, and the BIA reproduced those details in its own decision. The visibility required for legal recognition often extends to the most intimate aspects of trans migrants' bodies.

The April 2012 Policy Memo notes that the USCIS will not ask for more documentation of medical transition if the jurisdiction in which the marriage took place recognizes the marriage as a valid heterosexual marriage. However, if the jurisdiction in which the marriage took place prohibits or has specific requirements for a legal change of sex/gender for the purposes of marriage, then the trans spouse must demonstrate that she or he has met those jurisdictional requirements, presumably by providing the USCIS with further documentation of surgery and/or medical procedures.[92] The memo invokes discourses of privacy in this section when it states that "medical certification of gender transition" from a licensed physician is sufficient to document gender change: "If the physician certifies the gender transition, USCIS will not 'go behind' the certificate by asking for specific information about the individual's treatment."[93]

The NCTE and Immigration Equality highlighted the extension of privacy to trans migrants in their joint press release celebrating the AFM revisions. Entitled "Victory for Trans Immigration Documents and Marriage Benefits: NCTE and Immigration Equality Applaud President Obama for Taking Important Action," the press release explains the revisions to the *Adjudicator's Field Manual*. It quotes NCTE Policy Counsel Harper Jean Tobin: "Today's announcement is another example of the Obama Administration's long-term commitment to equality. These revisions mean that trans people and their families can obtain accurate identification while maintaining their privacy. It'll also reduce bureaucratic delays, intrusive questions, and wrongful denials of immigration benefits."[94]

Given that trans people are frequently denied privacy and are routinely asked to provide details about their sex and gender embodiment, often in violent and exploitative ways, it is true that not being forced to detail one's medical history to immigration officials in order to have one's marriage recognized is an improvement. Yet NCTE and Immigration Equality's valorization of privacy for trans migrants who are applying for marriage-based immigration status exemplifies how liberal discourses of privacy converge with neoliberal processes of privatization. The histories of gay and lesbian organizing for same-sex marriage and military service have shown how the "right to privacy" is often invoked by racially and economically privileged lesbian and gay activists. These efforts to gain access to forms of state recognition ignore the impact of neoliberal economic policies that defund and privatize social services, public education, affordable housing, and health care to the detriment of the majority of queer and trans people. A privatized lesbian and gay identity further marginalizes queer and trans people who do not conform to the expectations of homo- and trans-normativity. Discourses of individual privacy work together with processes of privatization to produce more privileged trans subjects as entrepreneurial, responsible self-sufficient citizen-subjects, while less privileged subjects are denied access to those same rights and resources.

Tobin's comment highlights the irony of framing the gaining of rights and state recognition for trans people in terms of privacy, since state institutions granting privacy to some trans people, like Gia Teresa Lovo-Lovo, through marriage, also require other trans people to relinquish their privacy completely. The granting of privacy for trans migrants and trans spouses of U.S. citizens must be contextualized in a broader understanding of privacy as racialized and classed. Trans migrants incarcerated in immigration jails and prisons, homeless trans people, and trans people on welfare have little to no access to privacy in order to receive services they need to survive. And as I discuss in the next chapter, discourses of privacy are frequently co-opted by state institutions to justify forms of state violence like immigration detention.

By characterizing these policy revisions as "another example of the Obama Administration's long-term commitment to equality," Tobin's comments frame the USCIS policy change as another step to the full inclusion of trans migrants and their families. The press release ends with a call to end "the discriminatory Defense of Marriage Act;" this call fails to recognize that marriage will always serve as a form of differential inclusion for relatively few trans and queer migrants. The incorporation of certain trans subjects may shift the lines around citizenship but still depends on a normative sex/gender and on normative economic participation. The fragility of these kinds of legal victories was made even more clear post-Obama when the Trump administration rolled back numerous gains for queer and trans people while simultaneously expanding punitive immigration enforcement and policing and closing national borders. Instead of advocating for a politics of privacy, trans immigration politics need to focus on broader issues of economic and racial justice, and the development of a humane and equitable immigration system for longer-term social, political, and economic change.

This chapter has centered the BIA decision of *In re Lovo* to explore how the incorporation of trans marriage into immigration law offers legal status and national belonging to those trans migrants who can meet the normative sex/gender and socioeconomic requirements. While Gia Teresa Lovo-Ciccone is not a migrant herself, the recognition of her marriage for the purposes of an immigration visa for her husband conferred cultural citizenship onto her as a normatively gendered heterosexual trans woman. The circulation and implementation of *In re Lovo* demonstrates how the inclusion and legal recognition of relatively few trans migrants is premised on state logics that mark other trans migrants as excludable and disposable, which the next chapter explores in relation to federal immigration detention policies.

4

Transfer Points

Trans Migrants and Immigration Detention

In 2007, Victoria Arellano, a twenty-three-year-old transgender woman from Mexico, died from complications from AIDS while in a U.S. Immigration and Customs Enforcement (ICE) federal immigration detention facility. Arellano was in good health before she was detained at the San Pedro Service Processing center in south Los Angeles pending her deportation proceedings.[1] While in detention, medical staff denied Arellano access to her regular prescriptions for antibiotics and antiretroviral medications, causing her health to quickly deteriorate. Although she and her fellow detained migrants made numerous requests for medical attention, Arellano did not receive appropriate or timely medical treatment. She died eight weeks after entering detention.

In the weeks after her death, Victoria Arellano's story circulated widely in news media.[2] Hers was one of the first stories of trans death within an ICE facility to receive national publicity.[3] Many trans, human rights, and immigration advocacy groups also took up Arellano's story to raise attention to the mass detention of immigrants, the conditions of ICE detention facilities, HIV/AIDS care, and LGBT rights.[4] This outcry built upon June 2007 investigative reports in both the *New York Times* and *Washington Post* that at least sixty-two deaths had occurred in immigration detention facilities since 2004.[5] Arellano's death also prompted congressional Democrat Zoe Lofgren (California) to hold a congressional hearing on medical care in immigration detention in early October 2007.[6]

The accounts of Arellano's weeks in detention describe in graphic detail the medical neglect and humiliating treatment she received from guards and medical staff as well as the slow progression of her illness and the moment of her death. The realist representation of Arellano's death is intended to engage the reader on a visceral and emotional level, inciting indignation and horror. Graphic descriptions are supposed to function as evidence of the inhumanity of the immigration detention system in the United States, but the recitation of these

details maintains the spectacle of violence in ways that can as easily immobilize the reader as they can motivate the reader to action.[7] The discursive reproduction of violence and death in detention reinforces the spectacle of the trans
body, a body already considered to be spectacular, increasing the distance
between the reader and the detained and violated trans subject. The detailed
accounts of Arellano's death also freeze her in that moment, creating what
C. Riley Snorton and Jin Haritaworn refer to as the "trans of color afterlife."[8] Arellano becomes a figure that can be easily circulated and mobilized for various
political ends without connecting the reader to the systems that caused her
detention and death.[9] Like the asylum declarations discussed in chapter 2, the
accounts of Arellano's death often produce Arellano's trans subjectivity as wholly
determined by violence; she becomes the universal trans subject notable and
newsworthy only in the moment of injury and death.[10] These accounts present
immigration detention facilities as exceptional sites of violence rather than as
institutions that are continuous with other forms of transphobic violence outside
of detention facilities. Such accounts also ignore the ways that criminalization,
racialization, and administrative violence produce the space of detention for
trans migrants.

Arellano's story—and the response by the media, advocacy organizations,
and governmental bodies—captures the central threads of this chapter.[11] Her
death starkly illustrates how gender violence intersects with immigration detention and how racialization and criminalization make trans migrants vulnerable
to state violence. Yet rather than focus on Arellano or on the many other stories
of abuse and neglect of detained trans migrants, this chapter shifts the focus
from the spectacle of the brutalized and vulnerable trans feminine body to the
spectacle of the state itself. This move helps us think through the ways that state
institutions respond to critiques of their own violence by incorporating discourses of the vulnerable trans subject. This chapter takes as its central text
ICE's *Performance-Based National Detention Standards 2011* (PBNDS 2011) to interrogate the role of mandatory detention in the U.S. immigration regime.[12] My
focus on immigration detention continues the larger project's investigation of
how relations of mobility and immobility mediate trans migrants' differential
access to legal and cultural citizenship in the United States. I track how the
PBNDS operate as a reformist reform that legitimate the continued incarceration and deportation of trans migrants.[13] ICE's recognition of the vulnerability
of trans migrants in detention facilities in the PBNDS 2011 naturalizes the deportability and immobilization of these migrants in detention.

Immigration detention facilities are a key type of what Mimi Sheller and
John Urry call "transfer points"—immobile and immobilizing spaces that structure mobility. All mobilities are attached to immobile structures, since "extensive
systems of immobility" make possible movement.[14] Chapters 1 and 2 demonstrate
that asylum provides trans migrants with a conditional form of entry into the

U.S. nation-state. This chapter argues that detention functions as a corresponding form of displacement and detainment to the promise of asylum.[15] Far from being each other's opposite, asylum constitutes detention as integral to the U.S. immigration regime's regulation of noncitizens. Because trans immigrants are disproportionately detained and deported, immigration detention facilities operate as transfer points that mediate access to the nation for many trans migrants, not just trans asylum seekers. Mobility and immobility are not a matter of unequal distribution across different populations, but rather the mobility of some subjects is tied to the immobility of others. Tim Cresswell contends that in the United States, "mobility as a right—as a geographical indicator of *freedom*—has most forcefully intertwined with the very notion of what it is to be a national *citizen*."[16] The denial and restriction of mobility therefore marks some subjects as not having access to full citizenship.[17] While Cresswell contrasts the "good" mobility of the citizen to the "bad" mobility of the noncitizen, citizen mobility is also stratified through racial, class, sexual, and gender hierarchies. For example, Black and Latinx citizen mobilities are frequently restricted, and their policing through the criminal legal system authorizes the policing of migrants through the U.S. immigration regime. The mobility of normative and privileged citizens relies on the immobility of noncitizens, like trans migrants in immigration detention as well as on the immobility of racialized subjects who are denied access to full legal and cultural citizenship. These relationships do not operate through the logic of exclusion: undocumented immigrants, noncitizens deemed "deportable," and citizens of color are the others that function as the condition of normative citizenship.[18] The regulation of mobility is central to the production of state power and the assertion of state sovereignty.[19] The U.S. state naturalizes the imprisonment of immigrants in detention facilities as a legitimate exercise of state power,[20] contributing to the criminalization of asylum seekers as well as other migrants.

This chapter examines how the category of "transgender" becomes incorporated into immigration detention regulations through the PBNDS 2011. Investigating this process of incorporation works to denaturalize immigration detention as a necessary "organizational structure to administer the entry and deportation of foreigners,"[21] and instead shows how the incarceration of noncitizens contributes to the construction of the space of the nation and the normative citizen. Focusing on the treatment of transgender migrants in the PBNDS offers a productive vantage point for understanding how state institutions respond to activist and legal critiques of state violence. It also raises questions about the complicated relationship of trans advocacy organizations to the immigration enforcement and the criminal punishment systems. My close reading of the detention standards in this chapter argues that the incorporation of transgender functions as a reformist reform that helps ICE better manage trans migrants in detention facilities. The PBNDS's recognition of the particular vulnerabilities of detained trans migrants perpetuates the invisibility of immigration detention as a system of mass incarceration founded on forms of gender, sexual, and racial violence. The abuse, isolation, and neglect that migrants experience in immigration detention facilities results in extreme mental and physical harm, including death and deportation. As a reformist reform, the supposedly more humane management of transgender migrants outlined in the PBNDS 2011 further criminalizes trans migrants and legitimates the continued expansion of the U.S. immigration detention system as a response to undocumented immigration. The incorporation of transgender into the PBNDS reveals the necessity of an abolitionist framework for challenging the violence of the U.S. immigration system, one that would concentrate on the abolitionist steps needed to address the immediate conditions and concerns of detained migrants while pushing for the elimination of the immigration detention system as a whole.

This chapter begins with a brief discussion of how trans migrants have been impacted by the criminalization of immigration law over the past few decades, followed by a section on the process through which transgender was included in the publication of the PBNDS 2011. I then turn to a close reading of the sections of the standards that mention transgender—classification and housing, search procedures, and medical care—to show how the PBNDS rely on state logics of safety to justify the incarceration of trans migrants. The final section of the chapter problematizes the role of LGBT nongovernmental organizations (NGOs) in the promulgation of the PBNDS and explores how the standards themselves can help us think about abolition as a political project.

Criminalization of (Trans) Migrants

The criminalization of trans migrants in the PBNDS is continuous with longer histories of the criminalization of immigrants in the United States. The rapid expansion of immigration detention over the last twenty years reflects the development of what Jonathan Xavier Inda and Julie A. Dowling call the neoliberal logic of governing immigration through crime.[22] The neoliberal emphasis on individual responsibility draws a marked racialized distinction between the proper citizen (a subject position that is itself raced and classed as white and middle class) and the deviant noncitizen: "Whereas the government of the 'responsible' has largely taken place through the mechanisms of the market and outside the formal political apparatus, the regulation of the deviant anti-citizen has increasingly occurred through the widening reach of the repressive arms of the state."[23] This has most strikingly occurred through the various ways that ICE has partnered with local and state law enforcement agencies, which have become more involved in policing immigration through programs like the Criminal Alien Program (CAP), Secure Communities, and the Delegation of Immigration Authority section 287(g).[24] The majority of immigrants caught by these programs are not individuals who have been convicted of serious criminal offenses, but rather individuals who have been arrested for offenses like minor traffic violations and possession of marijuana.[25]

In addition to these programs designed to identify "criminal aliens," the Department of Homeland Security (DHS) has also intensified the criminal prosecution of immigration-related conduct such as entry without inspection. Crossing the border without proper documents used to be treated as an administrative infraction that was grounds for deportation, but under DHS initiatives like "Operation Streamline," this is now punishable as a federal crime.[26] After these migrants serve their criminal sentences in prisons, they are placed in immigration detention proceedings and facilities pending their deportation. This policy is premised on the faulty assumption the threat of a criminal sentence and time in prison will function as deterrence for undocumented border crossers. Deterrence does not work as a state strategy to dissuade migrants who are fleeing violence and instability in their countries of origin; instead, it only serves to bolster the criminal punishment system.

The cumulative effect of these programs has been the transformation of the space of the nation into a carceral space for immigrants, in which trans migrants are particularly vulnerable. A "form of racial governance," immigration enforcement targets Latinx and Black migrants and conditions their everyday lives.[27] Mass deportation policy, as scholars like Nicholas de Genova and Tanya Maria Golash-Boza argue, is intended to make large populations of people deportable and vulnerable, to create the condition of deportability.[28] Trans migrants have been disproportionately affected by the criminalization of immigration law and policy,[29] and they are more vulnerable to being detained and/or deported as a result of the criminalization of trans people and the barriers that trans migrants face in gaining legal immigration status.[30]

For example, sex segregation structures many services and institutions on which low-income trans immigrants and trans people of color rely, and trans people "who have gender markers on records and ID that do not match their identity face major obstacles in accessing public bathrooms, drug treatment programs, homeless shelters, domestic violence shelters, foster care group homes, and hospitals."[31] Difficulty in accessing services means that trans people have increased likelihood of coming into contact with criminal punishment systems and that trans immigrants face higher risks of ending up in immigration detention. Trans people are frequently falsely arrested for lack of proper identity documents or for using the "wrong" bathroom, and trans women in particular are subject to police profiling as violent and as sex workers.[32] The Sylvia Rivera Law Project refers to the increased police scrutiny and surveillance that many trans women of color experience as the phenomenon of "walking while trans."[33] Lack of access to legal employment or education means that poor trans immigrants may need to resort to survival crimes such as sex work, drugs, and theft. While many of these offenses are minor enough that they usually do not result in much or any prison time, due to ICE's partnerships with local and state law enforcement agencies, these convictions still result in removal orders and mandatory detention for immigrants. Human Rights Watch found that almost half of the detained trans women they interviewed for a 2016 study were placed in detention facilities because of these kinds of low-level criminal convictions, including having false identification.[34] Dean Spade argues, "Trans and gender nonconforming people's experiences expose how population-management methods organized by race and gender produce structured harm and insecurity for people targeted by criminalization, immigration enforcement, and economic apartheid."[35] Together, these elements produce the condition of deportability for trans migrants and lead to their disproportionate detention. As the following sections show, the PBNDS continue to reproduce these carceral logics and naturalize immigration detention, revealing the necessity of an abolitionist approach to immigration enforcement for the protection and survival of trans migrants.

ICE's PBNDS 2011

The publication of the PBNDS 2011 was preceded by a report on the immigration detention system in 2009 by Dr. Dora Schriro. Janet Napolitano, then Homeland Security Secretary, commissioned Schriro to conduct an assessment of the immigration detention system, as part of the Obama administration's effort to transform it into a "truly civil detention system" and move away from dependency on the criminal justice system.[36] In October 2009 Schriro released her report, *Immigration Detention Overview and Recommendations*, which acknowledges the problems with ICE's system that human rights groups, investigative journalists, and congressional hearings had been documenting for many years prior.[37] This report stresses that one of the central issues with the immigration detention system develops from the adoption of the punitive framework of the criminal incarceration system, even though the administrative purpose of detention is to "hold, process, and prepare individuals for removal."[38]

Immigration detention is structured like criminal incarceration in part because the material infrastructure of the detention system is an extension of the criminal punishment system. Most of the facilities used by ICE to detain immigrants were built and operate as jails and prisons designed to incarcerate people awaiting trial and those who have been convicted for criminalized behavior. Immigration detention in the United States is a sprawling system that consists of three types of facilities: service processing centers that are operated by ICE, detention facilities that are run by private prison corporations contracting with ICE, and reserved bed space at state and county jails. In addition to the materiality of the architecture, the immigration detention system also imports logics of criminalization from its reliance on prison reform manuals. Schriro points out that the ICE detention standards are based on the correctional incarceration standards of the American Correctional Association and argues they are more restrictive and expensive than is necessary for detained migrants. She remarks in her report that the material conditions of detention facilities contribute to the criminalization of detained migrants, reinforcing the criminalization of undocumented immigrants, despite legal differences between immigration detention and criminal incarceration: "Immigration Detention and Criminal Incarceration detainees tend to be seen by the public as comparable, and both confined populations are typically managed in similar ways."[39]

Schriro's report emphasizes the differences between the immigrant detention population and the criminal incarceration population in an attempt to humanize detained migrants for her audience; however, this strategy contributes to false dichotomies and naturalizes the criminal punishment system as a response to social problems. Schriro writes, "The majority of the [detainee] population is motivated by the desire for repatriation or relief, and exercise exceptional restraint. According to reports provided by contract monitors and submitted by the field, relatively few detainees file grievances, fights are infrequent, and assaults on staff are even rarer."[40] Distinguishing detained migrants from those incarcerated in the criminal system in these kinds of behavioral terms leaves unquestioned the conditions of those who are incarcerated on criminal charges (which many migrants are prior to being transferred into ICE custody); by implication, the inhumane conditions in prisons are considered to be appropriate for people imprisoned for criminalized behavior. Activists and lawyers also often advocate for detained migrants by arguing that they are not criminals yet they have fewer rights than those in criminal detention. Spade notes that in addition to creating a deserving/undeserving framework that demonizes those locked up in prisons, this analogy creates divisions between those populations targeted by the immigration system and those targeted by the criminal system. It also perpetuates the idea that the criminal system is fair, which ultimately justifies the continued expansion of that system.[41] This analogy ignores how the immigration detention system is integrated into the prison system in material and structural ways, and how immigration detention is a key component of the larger deportation regime focused on the regulation of movement and border control. Despite Schriro's best efforts to recast detained migrants, the congressional hearing in the House of Representatives that followed the publication of her report demonstrated how the characterization of immigrants as law-breaking criminals continues to guide immigration discussions and policies. For example, congressional Republican Mark E. Souder (Indiana) repeatedly argued in this hearing that migrants should not be kept in facilities that are nicer than the jails and prisons in which U.S. citizens are held.[42] In addition to not recognizing how the immigration detention system is integrated into the prison system, Souder's comments illustrate the persistence of the conflation of undocumented immigrant with criminal.

Schriro's report ultimately takes a reformist approach to the problems plaguing the immigration detention system in the United States. Not surprisingly, rather than condemning the increase in the unnecessary detention of hundreds of thousands of immigrants, her official assessment locates the problem in the way the immigration detention system had expanded rapidly over the previous fifteen years without centralized planning and "without the benefit of tools for population forecasting, management, on-site management, and central procurement."[43] Schriro posits the development of comprehensive immigration standards as key to resolving these problems: "Establishing standards for Immigration Detention is our challenge and our opportunity."[44] She identifies seven components that ICE needs to address in order to "design a successful system of Immigration Detention": population management, alternatives to detention, detention management, programs management, medical care, special populations (which includes "families with minor children, females, the ill and infirm, asylum seekers, and vulnerable populations"), and accountability.[45] Here the problem is framed as the need for better regulation and protection of populations within immigration detention facilities, which intentionally justifies the continued existence of a sprawling and rapidly expanding system for jailing and deporting immigrants. In deploying such technocratic language for the biopolitical management of immigrants in detention, Schriro's report contributes to the naturalization of the caging of immigrants and supports the legitimacy of national detention standards.

Schriro does not mention transgender migrants in her report, although the reference to "vulnerable populations" gestures toward them. However, ICE's PBNDS 2011 includes transgender-specific provisions. Released in early 2012, the PBNDS is a 397-page document that responds to many of the issues Schriro raises in her assessment of the immigration detention system. The PBNDS establish nonbinding standards for the administration of immigration detention facilities in the United States.[46] The standards are recommendations only and may be implemented (or not) at the discretion of individual detention facilities. ICE Director John Morton writes in his preface to the standards that they are "drafted to include a range of compliance, from minimal to optional. As such, these standards can be implemented widely, while also forecasting our new direction and laying the groundwork for future changes."[47]

Despite Schriro's critiques of ICE's reliance on prison reform manuals, the PBNDS continue to be based on the American Correctional Association (ACA) Standards for people awaiting pre-trial detention.[48] Morton describes the publication of the new standards as "an important step in detention reform" that provide guidelines for the provision of care and services to detained migrants.[49] The Table of Contents of the PBNDS lists seven chapters: "Safety," "Security,"

"Order," "Care," "Activities," "Justice," and "Administration and Management."
Each chapter contains multiple sections that provide detailed guidelines for
managing migrants within immigration detention facilities.

The 2011 edition of the PBNDS updates the previous 2008 version and for
the first time mentions gay and transgender migrants, largely as a result of the
work of trans and queer immigration advocacy groups like the National Immigrant Justice Center, the National Center for Transgender Equality, and Immigration Equality. These three national organizations work toward legal and policy
protections for LGBT people and immigrants, through impact litigation, policy
changes, and direct legal services. These groups collaborated with ICE over the
course of several years to develop immigration detention standards that address
issues specific to LGBT migrants in the areas of placement and housing within
detention facilities, intake procedures, and search procedures.[50] For example,
the influence of trans advocacy organizations in the development of the PBNDS
2011 is apparent even in the definition of "transgender" in the glossary of the
standards, which reads, "Transgender people are those whose gender identity or
expression is different from their assigned sex at birth."[51] This definition is striking because it is a nonmedicalized definition that emphasizes self-determination,
something that is conspicuously absent in the materiality of incarceration. References to transgender migrants in the PBNDS 2011 occur in the sections related to
custody classification, admission and release, searches of detained migrants, and
medical care.[52] In the following pages, I read these sections of the PBNDS against
themselves to detail how the standards reveal the state's mechanisms of classification to be a cataloging of violence against trans migrants. The incorporation of
"transgender" as a category in the national detention standards helps us understand how state logics redefine "safety" in order to justify the incarceration of
trans migrants. Three main themes emerge out of these sections of the PBNDS:
the ways that discourses of risk contribute to the criminalization of transness, the
justification of surveillance through discourses of privacy, and the production of
vulnerability and death through the deprivation of health care. My reading of
the PBNDS illustrates the failure of reformist reforms as a remedy to anti-trans
violence. This makes clear the necessity of abolitionist approaches that identify
immigration detention facilities as sources of state violence regardless of how
"humane" and responsive they become and that work to dismantle the detention and deportation regime.

Classification and Housing: Criminalization through
Discourses of Risk and Vulnerability

Not surprisingly, one of the places that the PBNDS 2011 mentions transgender
migrants is in the section on custody classification and housing placement. Like
prisons, immigration detention facilities are sex-segregated, and this structure
makes them dangerous for trans migrants who are usually misclassified based

on external genitalia. Trans women may be housed with male detained migrants regardless of their gender presentations, and trans men may be housed with female detained migrants. When they are not housed with the general population, trans migrants may be placed in solitary confinement, usually termed "administrative segregation" and sometimes called "protective custody" units. Detention staff frequently place queer and trans migrants in solitary confinement because they are not willing to deal with their needs and treat solitary confinement as a place for vulnerable populations.[53] Policies for administrative segregation are often more arbitrary than those for disciplinary segregation. These policies and their phrasing reflect homophobic and transphobic attitudes about gender and sexuality. For example, some county jails that contract with ICE to house detained migrants have policies that call for the segregation of "obvious alternative lifestyle inmates" (Ventura County Jail in California), individuals with "overt homosexual tendencies" (Washoe County Jail in Nevada), and "gender challenged" individuals (Cobb County Jail in Georgia).[54] Many detention facilities justify the use of solitary confinement by highlighting the potential threat of particular populations to other migrants.[55]

In practice, solitary confinement is often discretionary and is used as a method of control and punishment for detained trans migrants.[56] As a tactic of immobilization and isolation, solitary confinement is deployed by detention staff to pressure detained migrants to accept deportation, even when they have valid legal claims for staying in the United States. The use of solitary confinement is often justified as a means to provide safety to trans migrants and other vulnerable populations. Gabriel Arkles notes that this rationale rests on two false assumptions: that isolation and control reduces violence and that violence experienced by detained trans migrants is perpetrated by other detained migrants. Not only does administrative segregation place trans migrants at the mercy of immigration detention guards and staff—who are responsible for most of the sexual, physical, and psychological violence experienced by trans migrants[57]— but administrative segregation means that trans migrants are isolated in small cells without access to recreation, freedom of movement, or other "privileges" that may be afforded to the general population of detained migrants.[58]

Section 2.2 of the PBNDS 2011, entitled "Custody Classification System," presents guidelines for the classification of transgender migrants. This section lays out a "formal classification process for managing and separating detainees based on verifiable and documented data."[59] The PBNDS naturalize the classification of detained migrants as self-evident in the descriptions of how migrants' classification as "low," "medium," or "high" custody determines their housing placement. The standards state that special consideration should be given to factors that make detained migrants more vulnerable to victimization or assault. Protected categories include those who are elderly, pregnant, physically or mentally disabled, ill, or victims of violence crimes like torture, abuse, and trafficking. They also include transgender migrants. When making classification and housing decisions for trans migrants, "staff shall consider the detainee's gender self-identification and as assessment of the effects of placement on the detainee's mental health and well-being;" this classification should be made in consultation with a medical or mental health professional.[60] The standards explicitly state that "Placement decisions should not be based solely on the identity documents or physical anatomy of the detainee, and a detainee's self-identification of his/her gender shall always be taken into consideration as well."[61]

The "ICE Custody Classification Worksheet" in Appendix 2.2A of the PBNDS details the process of classification. The first page of the form is dedicated to identifying particular vulnerabilities or special needs that a detained migrant might have. In "Part I. Basic Information," the migrant is marked according to the binary sex categories of "M" or "F," but in "Part 2. Special Vulnerabilities and Management Concerns," there is a box for "risk based on sexual orientation/ gender identity."[62] "Part 3. Custody Classification Worksheet" on the second and third pages of the form states that the migrant is to be classified in terms of her or his "offenses" in the following categories: "Severity of Charge/Conviction Associated with the ICE Encounter," "Single Most Serious Conviction in the Individual's Criminal History," "Additional Prior Convictions," "Supervision History" [refers to attempts at escaping a facility], "Security Threat Group," "History/Pattern of Violence (Two or more arrests)," and "Number of Sustained Disciplinary Infractions Involving Violence or Behavior Representing a Threat to the Facility."[63] The detained migrant receives a numerical score for each of these categories, which then add up to generate the "Total Custody Classification Score." This classification score is used to determine whether the detained migrant is "low," "medium," or "high" custody.[64]

The formal processes for classifying detained migrants in section 2.2 of the PBNDS 2011 rely on logics of crime and the management of risk. This is evident in how the standards sort migrants in terms of their vulnerabilities and their (potential) levels of violence, thus producing the category of violent detained migrants in relation to the category of vulnerable detained migrants. The production of these two categories together obscures the actual sources of violence in the immigration detention system, namely, the caging of migrants itself. The emphasis on the relationship of "violent" versus "vulnerable" ignores the fact that detention staff and guards perpetuate most of the sexual and physical violence experienced by detained trans migrants.[65]

These classification guidelines recommend a process for the housing placement of trans migrants that is virtually the complete opposite of how trans migrants are actually placed in detention facilities. The recommendation that detention staff should take into account a trans migrant's gender self-identification indexes the influence of trans immigrant advocacy organizations on the development of the PBNDS 2011 and marks how more progressive trans politics are taken up by the state to justify carceral practices. Adopting the language of self-determination, these standards assume a protective stance toward detained trans migrants who are categorized as vulnerable to violence and assault. The inclusion of a check box for "risk based on sexual orientation/gender identity" in Part 2 of the ICE Custody Classification Worksheet makes this clear. Nonnormative sexual and gender identities are collapsed with "risk," which both naturalizes queer and trans identities as deviant and forecloses the question of responsibility. This question on the worksheet sidelines the state's own role in producing vulnerability through these same mechanisms of incarceration and surveillance.

While the "Part 2. Special Vulnerabilities and Management Concerns" section of the classification worksheet does acknowledge to a certain degree the violence of the space of detention, it is followed by the section called "Part 3. Custody Classification Worksheet" that tabulates the criminal "offenses" of migrants into an overall "Total Custody Classification Score." The fact that the classification of the special vulnerabilities of detained migrants in Part 2 is coterminous with the classification of their criminal history shows how both operate according to the same logics of criminalization. Part 3 of the worksheet translates complicated individual histories of encounters with criminal punishment and immigration systems into simple numerical categories as part of the process through which individuals are produced and then confirmed as deportable. The numerical calculations de-personalize and de-policitize the process of classification and production of criminality, which is key to the justification of the system itself: "making taxonomies for those incarcerated assumes the rightness of labels, the categorical certainty of description."[66]

As a method of criminalization, the process of classification works to immobilize detained migrants through strategies of containment and management. The immobility of migrants contrasts with the mobility of the carceral logics that criminalize immigrants, carceral logics imported from the larger prison industrial complex.[67] The formality of classification functions as a supposedly objective measure that "allows officials to be unaccountable in the exercise of their power."[68] Colin Dayan explains, "The winnowing away of the substance of incarceration (what actually happens to the body and soul of a person in custody) in favor of an increasingly vague, if more adamant pragmatics of forms, rules, and labels, allows increasingly abnormal circumstances to be normalized while in prison."[69] This is precisely the work that the PBNDS do: they circulate as an abstract and nonbinding representation of the immigration detention system that acts as a proxy for the actual conditions of detention and the treatment of trans migrants. For example, in January 2013, ICE implemented the Risk Classification Assessment (RCA), which is used to generate recommendations for custody classification and for detention or release. The RCA actually conflicts with the special vulnerabilities sections of the PBNDS.[70] And even when the RCA tool recognizes the heightened risk LGBT migrants have in detention, it is frequently overruled by ICE officers who have the final determination of custody classifications. A 2015 report by the Center for American Progress found that despite the RCA tool recommending release for LGBT migrants 70 percent of the time, ICE officers overrode those recommendations and chose to detain LGBT migrants 68 percent of the time.[71]

The relations of mobility and immobility that structure immigration detention are also exemplified by the use of detained migrant transfers. For example, after Victoria Arellano's death in the San Pedro Service Processing Center, the migrants with whom she was detained were transferred to other detention facilities far across the country. Tom Jawatz, an immigration attorney with the American Civil Liberties Union (ACLU), emphasized this when he recounted the story of Arellano's death in a 2007 congressional hearing on medical care in immigration detention: "Such transfers have taken place following other deaths. They appear retaliatory, they hinder investigations, and they intimidate other detainees into silence."[72] The physical movement of Victoria Arellano's cellmates to other detention facilities after her death served to render them politically, psychologically, and emotionally immobile. A month after her death, thirty-nine migrants from Arellano's pod, including all the gay and transgender migrants, were transferred to detention facilities in Texas; the migrants who had spoken to reporters about Arellano's death were denied telephone access for two weeks.[73] Detained migrants are frequently transferred from one facility to another without warning, and like their custody classifications, transfers and placement decisions rest with individual ICE officers.[74] Due to lack of space in detention centers and the reliance of the immigration detention system on subcontracts with state jails and private prisons, detained migrants are shuffled amongst the hundreds of facilities in the United States.[75] These transfers have disastrous effects on migrants' immigration proceedings, since they make attorney-client relationships unworkable;[76] they separate detained migrants from the evidence they need to present in court; and they make family visits difficult or impossible.[77] The physical mobility of migrants amongst detention facilities affects their intersubjective mobility in terms of sustaining their relationships to their attorneys, friends, family, and community. Transfers also create problems for continuity of health care for HIV-positive migrants, especially when they are transferred to facilities without HIV/AIDS specialty care.[78] Transfers are tactics of an immigration detention system that utilizes different registers of im/mobility to discipline and manage detained migrants in ways that regularly result in death and deportation. The use of transfers exemplifies how detention officials control migrants' mobility to destroy relationships and activist organizing within and outside of detention facilities, to cause illness and death, and to make legal challenges to deportation impossible.

Search Procedures: Safety and Surveillance through
Discourses of Privacy and Visibility

The PBNDS 2011 also mention transgender migrants in the sections on strip searches, body cavity searches, and the collection of data related to the sex/gender of detained migrants. The first mention of "transgender" occurs in section 2.1, "Admission and Release," in the guidelines on strip searches. In many detention facilities, initial intake and processing procedures includes a strip search, which can occur in front of other staff and migrants and therefore out migrants as trans. While section 2.1 states that strip searches should not be routinely conducted on detained migrants, it notes that when strip searches are done, they should be performed by staff of the same gender as the migrant. In the case of a trans migrant, "special care should be taken to ensure that transgender detainees are searched in private. **Whenever possible, medical personnel shall be present to observe the strip search of a transgender detainee."[79] Section 2.10, "Searches of Detainees," contains similar guidelines for body-cavity searches of detained migrants, stipulating that "whenever possible, transgender detainees shall be permitted to choose the gender of the staff member conducting the body-cavity search."[80]

Even though the PBNDS state that detained migrants should not be regularly subjected to strip searches, human rights organizations and immigrant justice organizations have documented that strip searches are a frequent occurrence in immigration detention facilities where they are used as a form of gender and sexual violence to discipline and control detained migrants.[81] Many trans women asylum seekers are fleeing sexual and gender violence in their countries of origin; these women describe their experiences of strip searches and body cavity searches in immigration detention as especially traumatizing given that they are survivors of sexual assault.[82] The italicized recommendation that medical professionals witness strip searches of trans migrants positions doctors and nurses as guarantors of safety for those migrants classified as vulnerable. In addition to naturalizing strip searches as routine procedures, this recommendation bolsters the medicalization of transsexuality, despite the decreasing reliance of legal recognition of gender on medical definitions of sex.

The language of "choice" in these sections on strip searches and body-cavity searches masks the involuntariness of the searches themselves, which are used as violent, invasive, and traumatizing tools to subjugate migrants and to enforce gender normativity in detention facilities. These standards actually adopt the language of self-determination for trans migrants, in relation to choosing who performs the strip search, and suggest that the detained migrants have bodily autonomy and control over their own levels of safety while incarcerated. The incorporation of the language of choice and self-determination serves as another example of how state institutions take up trans activist discourses to fortify and legitimate forms of state violence against trans people. The recommendation that detained trans migrants be searched in "private" also obfuscates the fact that lack of privacy and constant surveillance are constitutive features and functions of detention. From an abolitionist perspective, the sections on searches in the PBNDS 2011 exemplify the limits of reformist reforms, and make legible state violence and hypocrisy. In revising the standards to account for trans migrants, ICE is forced to detail the exact forms of violence it enacts on an everyday basis. The institutionalization of strip search procedures for detained trans migrants in the PBNDS does not draw our attention away but instead highlights the normalization of this violence. These specific guidelines for detained trans migrants positions them as exceptional and especially vulnerable, which in turn reveals the underlying violence of immigration detention for all immigrants.

In June 2015, ICE released a memo entitled "Further Guidance Regarding the Care of Transgender Detainees" that provided guidelines for updating the data systems described in the PBNDS.[83] Like the standards, this memo is also not enforceable and explicitly forecloses the creation of rights for detained migrants.[84] The memo's updates include the addition of a "biological sex" category and a data field to record if a detained migrant identifies as transgender. The memo instructs detention facility staff to ask migrants during their initial processing if they self-identify as transgender and if they want to formally disclose their gender identity.[85] The memo specifies that information about a detained migrant's gender identity is "sensitive information" and should be kept private from other detained migrants or detention facility staff who do not have a need to know the information.[86] Similar to the provisions on strip searches and body-cavity searches in the PBNDS, the memo's guidelines frame the disclosure of gender identity in ICE custody as voluntary and as intended to ensure the safety of trans migrants. It bears repeating that this kind of framing obscures the actual material conditions of detention facilities, in which detained migrants have little to no privacy and are under constant surveillance. Trans women in particular are often especially visible as trans to other migrants and guards, as evidenced by the extensive documentation of sexual and physical violence against them as well as the common practice of placing trans women in administrative segregation, even though the June 2015 memo states that "placement into administrative segregation due to a detainee's identification as transgender should be used only as a last resort."[87]

As with the PBNDS 2011 sections on searches of detained migrants, the use of the language of self-identification, privacy, and safety in ICE's 2015 memo reflects the influence of LGBT NGOs. It also functions as the simultaneous acknowledgment and production of trans vulnerability. Being administratively visible as transgender is offered here as a form of protection by state institutions, belying the fact that this visibility occurs in the context of incarceration (and

that most violence and abuse experienced by detained trans migrants is perpetrated by detention facility staff). The recommendation of administrative visibility decontextualizes the meaning of safety. Safety in this instance is not safety
from state violence or safety from deportation. ICE's appropriation of discourses
of visibility, privacy, and safety works to justify and normalize the surveillance
and routine violation of the bodily autonomy of trans migrants in detention.

Medical Care: Producing Vulnerability and Death in Detention

As my opening discussion of Victoria Arellano's death in immigration detention
in 2007 illustrates, detained trans migrants are especially vulnerable due to
deprivation of medical care. The revised detention standards in the PBNDS 2011
acknowledge this through the inclusion of transgender-specific guidelines in the
section on medical care. Before I turn to this section of the PBNDS, I want to
discuss two congressional hearings on immigration detention leading up to the
publication of the PBNDS in 2012. These hearings clearly illustrate how the discursive construction of detained migrants as undeserving criminals is deployed
to excuse medical neglect and death in detention in order to naturalize the
detention and deportation regime. Two and a half months after Victoria Arellano's death in 2007, congressional Democrat Zoe Lofgren (California) chaired a
congressional hearing called "Detention and Removal: Immigrant Detainee
Medical Care" as a response to recent reports of deaths in ICE custody due to
lack of medical care. Lofgren argued that with the large increase in detained
migrants over the past decade, Congress needed to ensure that ICE was providing safe and humane conditions for migrants in their custody. She opened the
hearing with two stories of deaths from medical neglect in ICE custody: the story
of a detained migrant who died due to epilepsy complications, even though his
sister had tried to deliver his medications to him twice, and the story of Arellano's death. Lofgren declared that the purpose of the hearing was to determine
whether the medical care standards employed by ICE were satisfactory and
whether they were being implemented appropriately; she noted that preliminary
reviews revealed problems with both.[88]

    The witnesses in this hearing who argued for the adequacy of medical care
in detention mobilized discourses of migrant criminality grounded in the figure
of the "illegal alien." Mae M. Ngai traces how the figure of the "illegal alien" developed with the passage of the Johnson-Reed Act of 1924,[89] the first comprehensive
immigration restriction law that established a national origins quota system and
marked "the emergence of illegal immigration as the central problem in U.S.
immigration policy in the twentieth century."[90] Ngai argues that this legislation
"produced the illegal alien as a *new legal and political subject*, whose inclusion
within the nation was simultaneously a social reality and a legal impossibility—a
subject barred from citizenship and without rights."[91] This is the "impossible" legal and political subject that undergirds the anti-immigrant attitudes

rationalized by witnesses like Gary Mead, Assistant Director for Detention and Removal Operations (DRO) for U.S. Immigration and Customs Enforcement, and Timothy Shack, M.D., Medical Director of Immigrant Health Services.[92] Mead and Shack argued for the adequacy of medical care within detention centers by citing statistics about how much money is spent on medical care in terms of the number of medical visits completed, physical exams given, and prescriptions filled.[93] Mead ended his testimony by saying that over the last four years, one million people had passed through ICE custody, and there were (only) sixty-six reported deaths. The strategy of statistical comparison was also taken up by congressional Republican Steve King (Iowa) in his opening statement after Lofgren's, in which he claimed that despite the extensive media coverage of deaths in ICE custody, the death rate in detention centers was lower than those in prisons in the United States and that the current statistics did not show "an endemic flaw in the ICE health care."[94]

These comments—particularly King's comparison to deaths in prisons—are premised on the belief that the health care provided is good enough for immigrants who have broken the law by crossing the border unlawfully, by being undocumented, or by committing a criminal act. Steve King expressed similar virulently anti-immigrant attitudes in a second hearing on medical care in detention facilities eight months later in June 2008, when he sought to minimize the systemic problems with medical care for detained migrants. In that second hearing, King asked why American taxpayers should be responsible for "Rolls Royce-quality medical care for aliens who are doing everything in their power to stay detained and therefore avoid deportation," especially since he claimed that they "hold the keys to their own cells because immigration detainees can simply agree to their own deportation."[95] This statement naturalizes immigration detention as a necessary administrative response to the "problem" of unwanted immigration, as King reframes mandatory detention as a "choice" immigrants make. These comments also reveal how the figure of the "illegal alien" criminalizes immigrants to the extent to which they are "ineligible for personhood." Lisa Marie Cacho uses this concept to understand how certain populations are "subjected to laws but refused the legal means to contest those laws as well as denied both the political legitimacy and moral credibility necessary to question them."[96] King and other anti-immigrant politicians deploy racist arguments about illegality to justify the inhumane detention and deportation of immigrants.

The sections of the PBNDS 2011 on medical care clearly respond to the issues raised in these congressional hearings about the denial of adequate and timely medical care to detained migrants. For example, section 4.3, "Medical Care," states that all detained migrants who are diagnosed with HIV/AIDS should receive medical care as dictated by the national recommendations and guidelines of the U.S. Department of Health and Human Services, the Centers for

Disease Control and Prevention, and the Infectious Diseases Society of America, and that all Food and Drug Administration–approved medications should be accessible. Newly admitted migrants should be able to continue their treatments without interruption, and when released, they should be given a thirty-day supply of their medications.[97] For detained trans migrants, the standards note that their initial medical screening should "inquire into a transgender detainee's gender self-identification and history of transition-related care, when a detainee self-identifies as transgender."[98] The standards state that trans migrants should continue receiving hormone therapy if they were receiving it before being taken into ICE custody. Furthermore, "all transgender detainees shall have access to mental health care, and other transgender-related health care and medication based on medical need. Treatment shall follow accepted guidelines regarding medically necessary transition-related care."[99]

These guidelines around medical care are striking because they recommend a level of access to medical care that is far different from what many nonincarcerated trans people in the United States receive, let alone those who are in ICE custody.[100] Human rights reports published after the promulgation of the PBNDS 2011 continue to document widespread medical neglect that results in severe illness and death in detention. In immigration detention facilities, HIV-positive migrants are frequently segregated, isolated, and often denied antiretrovirals. Human Rights Watch notes that Arellano's death was extreme but not surprising, given ICE's systemic neglect of detained migrants with HIV/AIDS. Little has changed since 2007, as evidenced by the case of Roxsana Hernandez, a trans asylum seeker from Honduras who died after being detained for less than a month at the Cibola County Correctional Center in May 2018. Hernandez was physically assaulted while in detention and, like Arellano, was repeatedly denied access to the medical care and medications she requested.[101] ICE fails to collect basic health information to monitor detained migrants with HIV/AIDS, has substandard policies for HIV/AIDS care and services, and does not supervise the care that is delivered.[102] Immigration detention facilities fail to ensure the confidentiality of medical care and prescriptions for HIV-positive migrants. Medications—when they are administered—are often distributed publicly so prescriptions and medical records are visible to other detained migrants, stigmatizing trans and HIV-positive migrants and subjecting them to discrimination and harassment from other detained migrants and staff.[103]

Despite the guidelines in section 4.3 of the PBNDS 2011 about the continuation of hormone therapy to trans migrants who have been receiving hormone therapy before being detained, most detained trans migrants are denied hormone therapy. In order to legally obtain hormones—inside and outside—trans people need a doctor's prescription. But many trans people are unable to obtain a prescription for hormones, due to lack of health care and/or discrimination from health care providers and insurance companies, and have to resort to buying illicit hormones. This makes it impossible for them to continue hormone therapy in immigration detention. The deprivation of hormones has intense psychological and physiological effects, especially when an individual has been taking them for years. Refusing to administer hormones to detained trans migrants thus functions as a specific form of gender policing and punishment.[104] The medical neglect of trans migrants in immigration detention, as exemplified by the inadequacy of HIV/AIDS services and the denial of hormone therapy, signals the disposability of trans migrant lives both within immigration detention and outside detention.

Like the section of the PBNDS on strip searches, the standards outlining medical care for detained trans migrants frame the delivery of medical care in a manner that draws attention away from the fact that this medical care would be occurring in a detention environment. The provisions relating to HIV/AIDS medications and hormone therapy for detained trans migrants present the time and space of immigration detention in ways that are completely divorced from the realities of incarceration. The references to the continuation of HIV/AIDS medications, hormone therapy, mental health care and other transition-related care depict immigration detention as a space that provides life-sustaining and life-affirming care, when it is clearly the opposite. The spatial and temporal relations of immigration detention hinge on the incapacitation and suspension of migrants, as detention removes migrants from their lives and communities to place them in conditions that are designed to create deprivation and death.

Trans and immigrant justice activists have responded to the continued medical neglect of detained trans migrants by arguing that since ICE cannot adhere to its own standards, trans migrants and other vulnerable populations should not be detained at all. The more abolitionist organizations also call for the ending of immigration detention for all migrants, given the failures of ICE to provide safety and care. The political demand to "abolish ICE" also began to circulate more widely in early 2018 following increasing public awareness of the Trump administration's family separation policy and the caging of children and unaccompanied minors.[105]

In addition to these arguments, there might be the other ways that these standards could provide inroads for abolitionist approaches to the detention of trans migrants. Upon my first reading of this section of the PBNDS, I was struck by the fact that these standards on medical care for trans migrants are based on ideals that do not even exist in the worlds outside of detention. The standards outline basic guidelines for trans-related care within detention that are more robust and comprehensive that what most nonincarcerated trans people have access to. If ICE acknowledges that these are best practices for the delivery of medical care to trans populations, then these standards should operate as a starting point for the provision of health care for all trans people in the United States. In a way, the PBNDS 2011 could be mobilized by activists to represent the government's endorsement of a baseline of care for trans individuals, albeit one that should not occur in carceral settings. As prison abolitionists have long argued, state and federal governments should not waste resources to provide more robust health and medical care in prisons and detention centers, since this serves as a reformist reform that ultimately shores up the prison industrial complex.[106] Instead, an abolitionist perspective calls for the release of detained migrants and imprisoned people and for the investment of these resources in local community organizations that are better situated to provide for the health care needs of those people who are currently incarcerated.

Resisting Carceral Logics

My close reading of the PBNDS has shown how these standards use discourses of vulnerability to simultaneously intensify and legitimate state violence against detained trans migrants. The incorporation of transgender into the standards functions as a reformist reform that enables ICE to argue that they are better able to care for trans migrants, even as their abuse and neglect of detained trans migrants continues. This final section of the chapter extends my analysis of the role of LGBT NGOs in responding to harms perpetuated by the criminal and immigrant punishment systems, and develops my argument about how these standards can help us think about abolition as a political project.

ICE's recognition of trans migrants as vulnerable populations in immigration detention facilities developed from advocacy work by the National Immigrant Justice Center, the National Center for Transgender Equality, and Immigration Equality, who pushed for the inclusion of standards specific to LGBT migrants in detention. This collaboration with ICE exemplifies the types of relationships that certain national LGBT nonprofits are forming with government agencies around trans and gender nonconforming issues. Aren Z. Aizura notes that these collaborations have contributed to the increasing administrative visibility of trans subjects as vulnerable subjects within governmental and bureaucratic contexts.[107] But as recommendations with no enforcement mechanisms, the PBNDS are likely to have few material effects on the treatment of trans migrants in detention facilities. Their nonenforceability give the standards a mutable character as they circulate and are invoked by immigration agencies and actors, which echo the suspended temporality of detained and immobilized migrants.

The PBNDS are optional to avoid the possibility of creating rights for immigrants; framing the standards as guidelines means that detained migrants cannot sue.[108] At best, it seems as though immigration attorneys might be able to mobilize the standards to help their clients get access to a bond hearing and allow them to be released from detention while their case proceeds.[109] Since the publication of the PBNDS in 2012, human rights and immigrant rights organizations have continued to document the abuses and violations that immigrants experience in detention facilities.[110] The federal government itself has found that ICE is not adhering to the PBNDS in a consistent manner.[111] Thus, the administrative visibility and vulnerability of trans migrants within the PBNDS amounts to a strategy deployed by ICE to avoid accountability for transphobic violence and trans death.[112] As I discussed in my analysis of the PBNDS sections on classification and housing placement for detained trans migrants, administrative visibility does not translate to safety or protection, and more often produces the opposite as it may create more intense conditions of vulnerability.

The nonenforceability of the PBNDS conditions the seductiveness of the standards. Their circulation as nonbinding detention standards can prompt efforts to make them enforceable and make immigration detention facilities accountable to federal regulations. This is the danger of carceral logics, and the response should not be to insist on their enforceability. The purpose of the PBNDS is to make state violence look humane and to normalize immigration detention and immigration enforcement. The PBNDS participate in the naturalization of discourses of immigrant criminality and deportability, and circulate in ways that avoid the interrogation of those same discourses.

Precisely because the standards are not binding or enforceable, the inclusion of transgender-specific guidelines gives us insight into how the incorporation of "transgender" serves as a form of state recognition by government agencies like ICE as well as how the involvement of LGBT nonprofits facilitates these forms of recognition. Cindy Patton's analysis of politics and civil society is helpful here. In her discussion of the "modes for staging politics through identity," Patton contends that civil society produces the categories that the state uses to manage and administer populations.[113] She writes, "the terms for asserting identity *are* the categories of political engagement. The discursive practices of identity and the actors who activate them produce the categories of governmentality that engender the administrative state apparatus, not vice versa."[114] In this formulation, the National Immigrant Justice Center, the National Center for Transgender Equality, and Immigration Equality operate in the role of civil society in their work with ICE on transgender-inclusive guidelines in the PBNDS 2011. These nonprofits are playing a key and complicated role in the continued detention of trans migrants. By helping to shape the administrative category of transgender and the production of transgender vulnerability, they are enabling ICE's response to activist critiques (including the critiques that these particular nonprofits have made) about the violence of immigration detention. The recognition of trans migrants in the PBNDS allows ICE to narrate the state violence of detention as nonviolence, illustrating how vulnerability can be mobilized by state institutions to enact harm. ICE takes up transgender as a biopolitical category to better manage trans migrants and to justify the existence of immigration detention. The collaboration of these LGBT nonprofits with ICE reveal the failure of reformist reforms—like the making of immigration detention more "humane" for trans migrants—to end forms of state violence against trans migrants, let alone achieve any larger political goals of trans liberation.[115]

The inclusion of transgender in the PBNDS functions as a tactic of governance that preserves the detention and deportation system and provides a framework for better managing detained trans migrants. Michel Foucault argues that the instruments of government come to include the use of a variety of tactics: "with government it is a question not of imposing law on men, but of disposing things: that is to say, of employing tactics rather than laws, and even of using laws themselves as tactics—to arrange things in such a way that, through a certain number of means, such and such ends may be achieved."[116] In this instance, the provisions related to trans migrants in the PBNDS and the 2015 ICE "Transgender Care" memo constitute the arrangement of policies to fortify the continued detention of trans migrants. Understanding these tactics of governance puts pressure on legal rights-focused analyses of trans migrants that leave the larger systems of migration, displacement, and criminalization intact. Instead, from a queer and trans abolitionist perspective, we need to recognize how these systems actually form the conditions of possibility for detention.

Even though the PBNDS are nonbinding and nonenforceable, their release in 2012 sparked an outcry from anti-immigration congressional Republicans. On March 28, 2012, Lamar Smith, then Chairman of the Committee on the Judiciary, convened the congressional hearing "Holiday on ICE: The U.S. Department of Homeland Security's New Immigration Detention Standards," during which he claimed that "the Administration's new detention manual reads more like hospitality guidelines for illegal immigrants."[117] Despite many objections to the title and intent of his hearing,[118] Smith refused to rename it and explained, "This hearing is entitled, "Holiday on ICE," because ICE has decided to upgrade accommodations for detained illegal and criminal immigrants. While we would all like to be upgraded, we do not have the luxury of billing American taxpayers or making Federal law enforcement agencies our concierge."[119] Smith's exaggerated and inflammatory rhetoric blatantly ignores the extensive documentation of abuses and inhumane conditions within immigration detention facilities over the previous several decades, including the federal government's own reports on detention conditions. However, his comments exemplify the way that contemporary debates around issues of immigration and citizenship are often framed in terms of ethics and morality by positioning the undeserving immigrant against the deserving citizen. Smith's hyperbolic claims about hospitality in immigration detention echo the logics of asylum that I discuss in chapter 2, in which trans migrants' access to asylum is framed by discourses of sin, grace, and what Mimi Thi Nguyen terms "the gift of freedom."[120] Smith's comments also exemplify the way that "the transformation from nonbeing to legal personhood is always and already framed as someone else's "freely given decision" to relinquish power and privilege in exchange for nothing at all."[121] Furthermore, the criminalization of "illegal" immigrants as violent criminals or as people who do not respect U.S. laws by crossing the border unlawfully not only makes them "ineligible for personhood" in terms of rights and recognition, but it also makes them unworthy of sympathy or compassion. Smith's remarks misrepresent the standards as having the weight of enforceability, pointing to the ways that the standards circulate discursively even when they have little to no material consequences.

While numerous immigration and trans advocacy groups have applauded the PBNDS 2011's acknowledgment of the vulnerabilities trans and queer migrants face in detention facilities, these groups have also criticized the standards for being nonbinding internal policies that have no mechanism for any agency outside of ICE to ensure compliance.[122] In fact, many of the nonprofit organizations that worked with ICE on the standards do recognize the limitations of reforming immigration detention and argue for alternatives to detention. For example, Victoria Neilson, Director of Immigration Equality, responded to the release of the PBNDS 2011 by stating, "Immigration Equality has consistently advocated for DHS to utilize alternatives to detention for vulnerable populations, including LGBT people. Despite improvements within the detention system, it is unjust to hold individuals who have violated civil immigration laws in prison-like conditions. More humane conditions are an important step forward, but we must all continue to work towards an end to immigration detention."[123] This statement underscores the dangers of the nonprofitization of queer and trans social movements under neoliberalism and the tenuous position of many LGBT nonprofits. Even as Neilson's response calls for the dismantling of immigration detention, Immigration Equality's collaboration with ICE contributes to the legitimation of that same system of incarceration and highlights the limits of formal legal equality. Reform and inclusion constitute a hallmark of neoliberalism's use of rights discourse to obscure and maintain the unequal distribution of wealth and life chances along racial and gender stratification. Like asylum law and marriage law, immigration detention policies work to define, regulate, and distribute conditional forms of recognition for trans migrants, and illustrate the risks of looking toward the law for social justice and equality when it is the law that is the source of much of the subjugation that trans subjects face.

The PBNDS 2011 are an administrative response that propose reform within normative boundaries of sovereign governance under neoliberalism. Julia Morris notes that "it is largely because of neoliberal shifts that detention reforms fail to diverge from dominant political strategies of governance."[124] The reformist reforms of the PBNDS 2011 do not require DHS or ICE to make any material changes to already existing facilities or to detain fewer immigrants. In fact, these reforms facilitate the proliferation of the new "humane" detention facilities, such as the Karnes County Civil Detention Center and the T. Don Hutto Residential

Center in Texas,[125] as well as the dedicated protective custody unit for gay and trans migrants who are detained at the Santa Ana County Jail in southern California.[126] In May 2016, ICE opened a new detention facility in Alvarado, Texas, that includes a unit specifically created for trans migrants, following ICE's transgender care guidelines.[127] Yet as Human Rights Watch and others have documented, special units do not insulate detained trans migrants from abuse and violence by prison staff, nor negate the realities of being indefinitely incarcerated.

Radical queer and trans immigrant justice groups that are more critical of legal recognition recognize these relationships and the necessity of abolitionist approaches to immigration detention. In response to the 2015 ICE's "Transgender Care Memorandum," members of the #Not1More campaign—Familia: Trans Queer Liberation Movement, Transgender Law Center, GetEQUAL, and Southerners on New Ground—issued a press release denouncing ICE and DHS for failing to provide safety for trans migrants and calling for the release of trans immigrants and other vulnerable populations from immigration detention. Their press release insists that the best response to the harm and abuse experienced by detained trans migrants is the end of the detention and deportation system as a whole.[128] This abolitionist response notes that the ICE memo and other kinds of guidance documents are rarely implemented and are themselves limited responses to the harms experienced by trans migrants in detention. The #Not1More campaign members strategically use the abuse of trans migrants to argue for an end to detention for all migrants and for "long-term solutions regarding their residency, employment, and citizenship status." The press release positions the ending of "all immigration detention as a crucial step to combating the criminalization faced by immigrants, Black people, other people of color, women, and LGBTQ folks." This statement exemplifies the theoretical and political strengths of abolitionist approaches, which recognize the interconnectedness of larger structural oppressions. Connecting immigration detention to the criminalization of Black people and other people of color in the United States and to the criminalization of trans and queer people through the policing of sexual and gender deviance makes clear the need to challenge and dismantle these systems simultaneously.

The incarceration of trans asylum seekers in immigration detention is often held up as an example of the injustice and violence of detention, since trans asylum seekers already fleeing state-sanctioned violence in their countries of origin are then confronted with domestic state-sanctioned violence in the United States. Yet the detention of trans asylum seekers illustrates how trans migrants as a larger population are criminalized inside and outside immigration detention and how their criminalization mediates their access to citizenship and national belonging. This perspective allows us to recognize how the racially and

class-privileged trans subject gains rights and recognitions by virtue of her distinction from the undocumented trans subject, the gender nonconforming subject, the trans subject of color. Understanding how the inclusion of transgender
in the PBNDS exemplifies the U.S. immigration regime's carceral logics is one
step toward imagining a world without a punitive immigration system that
reproduces racial, sexual, and gender violence.

Coda

This book has traced the consolidation and incorporation of transgender into key areas of immigration law and policy in the first decades of the twentieth-first century, to argue that a consideration of trans migrants in the areas of asylum law, marriage and immigration law, and immigration detention policies illustrates the centrality of im/mobility to the construction of the legal category of transgender. These three areas of the law interface with each other to determine the grounds for recognition and differential inclusion for trans migrants in the United States, and reveal how the im/mobility of trans migrants helps us understand how binary sex/gender structure racialized categories of citizenship and national belonging. Asylum offers the promise of recognition and protection to those few trans migrants who can prove and perform the requisite trauma to fit into established categories of gender and sexuality. The exceptional status of asylum legitimates the mass detention and removal of other trans migrants and immigrants caught in the rapidly expanding immigration detention system, and the inclusion of transgender in federal detention standards is deployed as a tactic of governmentality under the rhetoric of protection. Marriage provides access to citizenship for those more privileged trans migrants who are able to meet to normative requirements for inclusion but also illustrates how incorporation into the national body politic subjects trans migrants to forms of state discipline.

Mobility has functioned as an organizing theme across the chapters, which have highlighted the connections between changes in sex/gender embodiment, the movements of trans bodies across borders, shifting legal statuses, and the circulation of the category of transgender in different areas of immigration law and policy. Using mobility as a critical lens enables a multiscalar analysis of the racial, class, and gender dynamics of trans movements and migrations. This book has emphasized the relative mobility of legal documents, court decisions, and the legal category of transgender compared to the immobility of many actual trans migrants. Carceral state logics of immigration circulate to constrain the mobility of trans migrants who encounter militarized borders and are captured by border patrol agents, who are excluded by draconian immigration enforcement policies, whose sex/gender embodiment may be illegible to existing legal paradigms, who do not have the resources required to navigate the asylum system, who are held in cages in detention facilities, who lack economic mobility due to racism and transphobia, or who cannot afford access to gender-affirming health care.

In a relatively short period of time, trans migrants' legibility in immigration law and policy shifted from Geovanni Hernandez-Montiel's classification as a "gay man with a female sexual identity" by the Ninth Circuit Court of Appeals in 2000 to the recognition of vulnerable transgender migrants in national immigration detention standards in 2011. My tracking of transgender inclusion in immigration law has illustrated the importance of a strategic investment in legibility and recognition paired with an understanding of how sex/gender categorizations operate as forms of state power that can be used against marginalized populations like trans migrants. As I have shown in the previous chapters, the classification and categorization of trans migrants in the law, while intended to provide protection and relief from forms of violence, often enacts further harm, even as the law fails to provide protections. I began the research for this book with an awareness of the regulatory function of the law but also with an appreciation of the desire for the law and the ways that legal recognition can have real material effects in trans people's lives. Holding that balance—critiquing the law for the violence it perpetuates and for the ways that legal reform does not address systemic issues while still taking seriously trans migrants' efforts for legal recognition—has meant not dismissing the law as a repressive force. Instead, this project has attempted to point to some of the ways that a trans politics can include strategic uses of the law but not look to legal recognition and rights as the solution to the racism, sexism, and transphobia experienced by trans migrants in their encounters with state institutions and in everyday life.[1]

In this way, I hope this book contributes to the ongoing conversations by queer and trans studies scholars and activists who have theorized the limits of visibility and identity politics, and push instead for the necessity of trans politics to attend to issues of economic and racial justice, not state recognition. Inclusion operates as another form of state violence and regulation. As Eric A. Stanley points out, "[t]he time of LGBT inclusion is also a time of trans/queer death.[2] I started this project under the Obama administration, writing in reaction to the advances in trans rights and recognitions that were occurring alongside Obama's expansion of immigration enforcement and the deportation regime. At the time, many in the mainstream LGBT movement were celebrating the passage of federal hate crime prevention legislation, the repeal of "Don't Ask, Don't

Tell," and the elimination of the Defense of Marriage Act. There was much less mainstream attention to Obama's immigration policies, which had earned him the title of "deporter-in-chief" from immigrant justice activists, or to the effects of these policies on LGBTQ immigrants. This disconnect between LGBT rights and immigrant rights in national politics continued into Obama's second term in office and was brought into stark relief by Jennicet Gutiérrez when she used her invitation to a Pride Month reception at the White House in June 2015 as an opportunity to challenge Obama on his inhumane detention and deportation regime. Gutiérrez, an undocumented Latinx trans activist, interrupted Obama's speech to demand the release of trans women and other LGBT migrants in detention centers and an end to the violence and human rights violations of detention. Gutiérrez was shamed and dismissed by Obama, but more tellingly, she was booed and silenced by the other advocates and activists at the reception, who represented some of the most well-resourced national LGBT advocacy organizations in the United States.[3]

The transitory nature of these gains in legal recognition for LGBT people was made clear when Trump took office in 2017 and began to roll back trans-inclusive policies while also intensifying the criminalization, detention, and deportation of immigrants and further militarizing U.S. borders.[4] Many of these anti-immigrant policies continue to be enforced under the Biden administration, in particular the use of Title 42 to remove migrants without due process and the expansion of immigration detention facilities. This recent history underscores the need for a successful trans politics to move beyond a restricted focus on "trans" in relation to the politics of recognition.[5]

We can look towards the work of several trans immigrant justice organizations in the United States to see productive examples of this approach. Organizations like Familia: Trans Queer Liberation Movement, the Black LGBTQIA+ Migrant Project (BLMP), El/La Para TransLatinas, the Queer Detainee Empowerment Project, and Mariposas Sin Fronteras are doing vital organizing and advocacy work at the intersections of LGBTQ justice and immigrant justice. These organizations center trans migrant issues and politics in radical abolitionist analyses of the detention, deportation, and criminal legal systems in the United States, and they effectively combine advocacy and policy work with community organizing and empowerment.

Familia describes itself as a "national transgender and queer Latinx LGBTQ rights, immigrant rights, and racial justice organization" that is active at local and national levels, dedicated to advocacy and organizing as well as community-building and education. In southern California, Familia successfully organized with other immigrant justice groups to pressure the Santa Ana City Council to end its contract with Immigration and Customs Enforcement (ICE) after it expired in 2020.[6] The Santa Ana City Jail detention center was the first detention facility to create a pod especially for LGBTQ detainees, and in 2011, ICE began to transfer queer and trans immigrants from other detention facilities across the country to the unit in Santa Ana. Familia started a local campaign in 2012 to shut down the special unit, working with other LGBT rights organizations and immigrant rights organizations to draw national attention to the issue. This campaign strategically called for the end of the detention and deportation of trans women in the special pod as a starting point for ending deportation and detention for all migrants at the Santa Ana City Jail.[7]

The Black LGBTQIA+ Migrant Project (BLMP) also engages in national organizing coordinated with building local networks of community activists. Based in Oakland, California, and fiscally sponsored by the Transgender Law Center (TLC), BLMP works at the intersections of criminal justice and immigrant justice movements to raise awareness and action around issues related to Black LGBTQ migrants. Both Familia and BLMP illustrate the importance of a politics of solidarity and the need for trans movements to build broad-based coalitions. In 2015, BLMP and the TLC partnered with Familia and Mijente[8] to launch the #EndTransDetention campaign as part of the larger national movement to end the criminalization and deportation of all migrants and to abolish ICE. The #EndTransDetention campaign coordinated more actions, including a hunger strike, at the Santa Ana City Jail as well as Jennicet Gutiérrez's disruption of President Obama's Pride event at the White House. In addition to direct actions, the strategies of the #EndTransDetention campaign include using social media to focus attention on individual detained trans migrants to push for their release, organizing formerly detained trans migrants to write letters to President Biden and Department of Homeland Security (DHS) officials, and documenting and amplifying the deaths of trans migrants in ICE custody due to medical and other forms of neglect.[9] In 2019, Familia and BLMP also joined with the National Immigrant Justice Center, Arcoiris, Jardin, and others to start the LGBTQ Border Project, which provides LGBTQ asylum seekers on the U.S.–Mexico border with humanitarian, legal, and medical support. In response to the growing crisis at the border caused by the Trump administration's draconian and inhumane "Remain in Mexico" policy, this project aims to build a "long-term advocacy and grassroots organizing infrastructure along the U.S.–Mexico border."[10] The #EndTransDetention campaign and the LGBTQ Border Project exemplify trans and queer migrant politics that engage in the variety of tactics needed to combat the violence of the immigration system.

Community organizations like Mariposas Sin Fronteras and the Queer Detainee Empowerment Project (QDEP) also respond to the immediate needs of detained and incarcerated queer and trans migrants, guided by abolitionist politics focused on ending the immigration detention and prison systems. Based in New York City, QDEP provides detention visitation, post-release support, and direct services to detained LGBTQ migrants and their families.[11] In Tucson, Arizona, Mariposas Sin Fronteras supports LGBTQ people in immigration detention through visits to detention facilities, letter writing, case support, fundraising for bonds, and coordinating post-detention hospitality and housing.[12] Mariposas Sin Fronteras is a member-based organization led by LGBTQ immigrants, many of whom have been detained, and QDEP's member base is represented on the organization's advisory board and is heavily involved in decision-making processes. Mariposas Sin Fronteras and QDEP show how interventions in the immigration and criminal legal systems must extend beyond a narrow engagement with law reform.

Similarly, the work of El/La Para TransLatinas in San Francisco, California, which I discuss in chapter 2, exemplifies how grassroots activism provides alternatives to the liberal rights-seeking strategy of inclusion pushed by many well-resourced national trans legal advocacy organizations. While El/La is primarily a HIV/AIDS prevention organization for translatinas, it integrates that work with its immigrant justice organizing and activism. *Translatina* functions as a collective term to create community amongst Spanish-speaking trans women from different countries in Central and South America. Alexandra Rodriguez de Ruiz, one of the cofounders of El/La, comments that "the term *translatina* became a way of empowerment and a way of including and a way of giving visibility to a community that was always in the background."[13] El/La's programming is directed by the needs of its translatina participants, which allows the organization to address the myriad issues facing Latinx trans migrants, not just those issues immediately related to legal status.

The advocacy and activist work of these grassroots organizations expands our analysis and understanding of trans migrant politics beyond the limited legal archive this book addresses. Although these organizations strategically engage with immigration law and policy, they refuse to legitimate the normative frameworks of the law and the underlying carceral logics of the immigration regime, resisting the criminalizing binary of deserving/undeserving immigrants and discourses of national security. As the previous chapters have shown, focusing on legal and policy reform and high-impact litigation alone cannot address the needs of trans migrants and will not challenge or transform the ways that transphobia, racism, and misogyny structure the U.S. immigration regime. In contrast, these organizations illustrate the robustness required from trans migrant politics in the contemporary moment. They highlight the connections between the criminal legal system and immigration law and policy, and argue for a trans politics that is committed to racial, economic, and immigrant justice. The breadth of strategies deployed by Familia, BLMP, Mariposas Sin Fronteras, QDEP, and El/La develops from the priorities of trans migrants themselves. Furthermore, these organizations center community-building, leadership training, empowerment, and healing for trans migrants, many of whom have survived incarceration and detention. This work becomes as important as concurrent legal advocacy work, because it acknowledges the fullness of trans migrants' lives and creates the foundation for large-scale transformative change that does not end with legal recognition and formal inclusion. As such, this organizing work embodies Alisa Bierria's description of abolitionist politics as "the practice of presence" based on feminist relations of care.[14] These grassroots activist organizations attend to the immediate needs of trans migrants while simultaneously working toward abolitionist futures in which the ending of immigration detention and the creation of a more just immigration system will make possible collective justice and liberation not just for trans migrants but for all trans people.

ACKNOWLEDGMENTS

The writing of this book has taken many years and was only made possible through the support of advisors, colleagues, friends, and loved ones. This project started as a doctoral dissertation, and I am thankful for the support and guidance I received from my dissertation committee during that early stage of my thinking and writing. I appreciated Caren Kaplan's critical questions and her ability to mentor me through a strategic balance of kind encouragement with pressure and accountability. Marcia Ochoa pushed my theoretical analysis and helped me think through complicated political questions. Mark Jerng continually offered enthusiastic and generative feedback as well as a willingness to read the roughest of drafts. And Jennifer M. Chacón helped me understand the intricacies of asylum and immigration law, while consistently providing detailed feedback on my writing and legal arguments.

I would also like to thank other faculty at UC Davis who supported me during my time as a graduate student, including Omnia El Shakry, Cathy Kudlick, Beth Freeman, Eric Smoodin, and Juana María Rodríguez, who continued to be a generous mentor after she left Davis. I am thankful for the institutional support I received as a graduate student through a Dissertation Year Fellowship from the UC Office of the President, as well as research funding from the Office of Graduate Studies and from the American Studies Department at UC Davis.

My dissertation process was enhanced and supported by a collaborative writing group that included Toby Beauchamp, Ben D'Harlingue, Liz Montegary, Abbie Boggs, Christina Owens, Tallie Ben Daniel, David Michalski, and Hilary Berwick. While at UC Davis, I also appreciated the friendship and conversation I shared with fellow Cultural Studies graduate students Cathy Hannabach, Sarah McCullough, Sandy Gomez, Magalí Rabasa, Ingrid Lagos, and Andrew Ventimiglia about the pain and pleasure of graduate school. Over fifteen years later, I continue to value the queer family I found in Davis, in the form of Liz, Abbie, Ben, Tallie, Toby, and Cynthia Degnan.

I am grateful to the attorneys and legal advocates who were willing to correspond and talk with me about the legalities and politics of trans asylum, including Margarita Manduley, Noemi Calonje, Robert Gerber, Joseph Landau, Cara Jobson, Meredith Wallis, Allegra McLeod, Angela Lam, Dusty Araujo, and

Chelsea Haley Nelson. Special thanks to those who shared the case files that formed the basis of my analysis of trans asylum: Noemi Calonje, Robert Gerber, Angela Lam, Margarita Manduley, Allegra McCloud, and Meredith Wallis.

I completed the final stages of writing this book while teaching and working at Sacramento State University. I have benefited from the feedback of colleagues in two faculty scholarship communities who read and commented on sections of early chapter drafts, in particular Paula C. Austin, Mark Ocegueda, Mark Brown, Hellen Lee, Rosa Martinez, Christine Lupo, Mercedes Valadez, and Kathy Jamieson. I am thankful for the institutional support I received from the Sacramento State Research and Creative Activity Faculty Awards Program, which provided me with valuable summer salaries for the completion of this manuscript. I would also like to thank my colleagues in the Department of Women's and Gender Studies, especially Sujatha Moni, Cara Jones, and Rita Cameron Wedding, for our collective discussions about feminist pedagogy and politics.

Thanks to Craig Willse for his insightful and generative feedback on an unwieldy draft of chapter 4. Craig's critical questions helped me identify more precisely the central threads of my analysis and radically restructure the chapter. I would also like to thank the two anonymous readers for Rutgers University Press who provided very detailed constructive criticism during the revision process, which has strengthened the book immeasurably. I have appreciated Kimberly Guinta's enthusiasm for the project and her understanding and flexibility around deadlines. Thanks to Sherry Gerstein for production editorial support, to Maxine Idakus for copyediting, and to Jac Nelson for indexing the book.

Friends and colleagues have provided much needed encouragement over the years. Christina Owens and Cindy Bello, my intermittent writing partners in Oakland, have been willing to listen to rants and complaints about trying to write while teaching too many classes. I am thankful for the friendship and support of Paula C. Austin, who has pushed me to finish while sharing helpful advice about the writing and revision process. I continue to value our conversations over cocktails and our shared cat admiration. Some of my biggest thanks go to Abbie Boggs and Liz Montegary, two of the best friends I could have ever hoped to meet in graduate school. I am especially grateful for Liz's generosity in sharing her writing and teaching expertise with me, as well as her willingness to field frantic last-minute questions, and for Abbie's emotional and intellectual support and solidarity.

I have relied on the love and care of my mom, Sally-Anne Jackson, and my sister, Carla Josephson. In the early years of the project, my mom shared advice and expertise from her own dissertation writing experience and has exercised restraint over these last few years in not asking too often whether I was done yet. Carla has offered long-distance support from London and a sympathetic ear as well as her own editorial expertise about the writing process.

mónica enríquez-enríquez has been there from the beginning and with me every step of the way, providing inspiration through their art and activism. They have been one of my closest political interlocutors over the past twenty years. I value their faith in my process and loving support. And finally, my love and thanks to Kryst Muroya, who did not quite realize what he was getting into when we first met, but who has done a tremendous job educating himself about the strange and stressful world of academia in order to perfect his writing cheerleading and stress management support skills. Kryst has taught me much about the pleasures of being in the world, and I thank him for sharing his life with me.

An earlier, partial version of chapter 3 was previously published as "Trans Citizenship: Marriage, Immigration, and Neoliberal Recognition in the United States," *Law, Culture and the Humanities* 12, no. 3 (2014): 647–668.

A section of chapter 2 was previously published as "Desiring the Nation: Transgender Trauma in Asylum Declarations," in *Mobile Desires: The Politics and Erotics of Mobility Justice*, edited by Liz Montegary and Melissa Autumn White, 67–79, Basingstoke, UK: Palgrave Macmillan, 2015.

NOTES

INTRODUCTION

1. *Geovanni Hernandez-Montiel v. INS*, 225 F.3d 1084 (9th Cir. 2000).
2. Steinmetz, "The Transgender Tipping Point."
3. Immigration and Nationality Act of 1965, Pub. L. No. 89-236, 79 Stat. 911 (1965).
4. Cott, *Public Vows;* Stevens, *Reproducing the State;* Franke, *Wedlocked.*
5. Anna M. Agathangelou, M. Daniel Bassichis, and Tamara L. Spira make a similar argument in their analysis of the "promises" and "nonpromises" presented in the service of empire: "Offering certain classes of subjects a tenuous invitation into the folds of empire, there are always the bodies of (non)subjects that serve as the raw material for this process, those whose quotidian deaths become the grounding on which spectacularized murder becomes possible" ("Intimate Investments," 123).
6. Susan Stryker and Aren Z. Aizura note that transgender critique challenges the presumed naturalness of normative categories of female, male, woman, and man to make clear "their historicity and cultural contingency" ("Introduction," 9). Similarly, Toby Beauchamp argues for using trans as a mode of analysis that "can also successfully intervene into the naturalization of race, disability, and citizenship" (*Going Stealth*, 13).
7. In her reflections on the early articulation of the field of transgender studies in the 1990s and 2000s, Susan Stryker identifies this as central to the project of trans studies. She notes that trans studies should "articulate and disseminate new epistemological frameworks, and new representational practices, within which variations in the sex/gender relationship can be understood as morally neutral and representationally true, and through which anti-transgender violence can be linked to other systemic forms of violence such as poverty and racism" (Stryker, "(De)Subjugated Knowledges," 10).
8. For critiques of trans travel narratives, see Prosser, "Exceptional Locations: Transsexual Travelogues;" Halberstam, *Female Masculinity;* and Aizura, *Mobile Subjects*, 29–92.
9. Aizura, *Mobile Subjects*, 3.
10. Aizura, *Mobile Subjects*, 19.
11. Within the robust body of research on queer and trans migrations, work that focuses on immigration law and policies includes edited collections like *Queer Diasporas,* ed. Patton and Sánchez-Eppler; *Queer Globalization,* ed. Cruz-Malavé; *Queer Migrations,* ed. Luibhéid and Cantú Jr.; *Passing Lines,* ed. Epps, Valens, and Johnson; *Transgender Migrations,* ed. Cotten; and *Queer and Trans Migrations,* ed. Luibhéid and Chávez. See also single-author monographs like Luibhéid, *Entry Denied;* Cantú Jr., *The Sexuality of Migration;* Shah, *Stranger Intimacy;* Chávez, *Queer Migration Politics;* Murray, *Real*

Queer?; Giametta, *The Sexual Politics of Asylum*; Beauchamp, *Going Stealth*; Camminga, *Transgender Refugees and the Imagined South Africa*.

12. See particularly Luibhéid's *Entry Denied* and "Sexuality, Migration, and the Shifting Line."

13. Cotten, "Introduction: Migration and Morphing," 2.

14. Kaplan, "Transporting the Subject." See also Kaplan's *Questions of Travel*.

15. Sheller, *Mobility Justice*, 11.

16. See for example Sheller and Urry, "The New Mobilities Paradigm;" Urry, *Mobilities*; and Cresswell, *On the Move*.

17. Latour, "Visualisation and Cognition," 7.

18. U.S. Immigration and Customs Enforcement, *Performance-Based National Detention Standards 2011*.

19. Dudziak and Volpp, "Introduction."

20. Rodríguez, *Queer* Latinidad.

21. Valentine, *Imagining Transgender*, 60–62.

22. Valentine, *Imagining Transgender*, 178.

23. Foucault notes that disciplinary power and biopower are "not mutually exclusive and can be articulated with each other" (*"Society Must Be Defended,"* 250).

24. Mbembe, "Necropolitics."

25. Haritaworn, Kuntsman, and Posocco, "Introduction." See also Shakhsari, "The Queer Time of Death."

26. Snorton and Haritaworn, "Trans Necropolitics," 68.

27. Snorton and Haritaworn, "Trans Necropolitics," 74.

28. Butler, *Excitable Speech*; Brown, "Wounded Attachments."

29. Povinelli, *The Empire of Love*, 13.

30. Reddy, *Freedom with Violence*.

31. Spade, *Normal Life*. See especially chapter 2, "What's Wrong with Rights?," 38–49.

32. See Mosse, *Nationalism and Sexuality;* Anderson, *Imagined Communities*; Alexander, *Pedagogies of Crossing*; Kaplan, Alarcón, and Moallem, *Between Woman and Nation*. I have also found useful Marcia Ochoa's analysis of how transformistas in Venezuela negotiate the relationships between marginalization, political participation, affect, and citizenship. See Ochoa, *Queen for a Day*.

33. Berlant, *The Queen of America Goes to Washington City*.

34. For example, see Alexander, "Not Just (Any) Body Can Be a Citizen," and Canaday, *The Straight State*.

35. Carbado, "Racial Naturalization."

36. Luibhéid, "Sexuality, Migration, and the Shifting Line;" De Genova, "The Deportation Regime." See also Andrijasevic, "Sex on the Move," and De Genova, Mezzadra, and Pickles, "New Keywords: Migration and Borders."

37. Luibhéid, *Pregnant on Arrival*.

38. Chavez, *The Latino Threat*, 3.

39. See, for example, Ngai, *Impossible Subjects*; Gómez, *Manifest Destinies*; Molina, *How Race Is Made in America;* Hernandez, *Migra!*; and Garcia, *Seeking Refuge.*

40. In addition to *Hernandez-Montiel v. INS*, a large proportion of later precedential trans asylum cases center on trans migrants from Central and South America. These

include Reyes-Reyes v. Ashcroft, 384 F.3d 782 (9th Cir. 2004); Ornelas Chavez v. Gonzalez, 458 F.3d 1052 (9th Cir. 2006); Morales v. Gonzalez, 472 F.3d 689 (9th Cir. 2007); N-A-M v. Holder, 587 F.3d 1052 (10th Cir. 2009); Gutierrez v. Holder, 730 F.3d 900 (9th Cir. 2013); and Avendano-Hernandez v. Lynch, 800 F.3d 1072 (9th Cir 2015).

41. In the last few months of the Trump administration in late 2020, ICE targeted Haitians and other Black migrants for deportation; this continued throughout 2021 and into 2022 under the Biden administration. While there was some media attention to this, it was mostly immigrant justice activists and Black activists who made the connections between the policing of immigrants and the criminalization of Black people in the United States.

42. Jordan, "Un/Convention(al) Refugees," 171–172.

43. Declaration of Alejandro, dated 2007, paragraphs 28–29 and 47. Most of the declarations I received were redacted, although a few included the initials or first names of the applicants. When referencing unpublished asylum declarations, I use pseudonyms for the asylum applicants to protect their privacy.

44. Berg and Millbank, "Developing a Jurisprudence of Transgender Particular Social Group," 125–127.

45. See the most recent Department of Homeland Security factsheet on refugees and asylees at https://www.dhs.gov/sites/default/files/publications/immigration-statistics/yearbook/2018/refugees_asylees_2018.pdf.

46. Hartman, "Venus in Two Acts," 4.

47. Hartman, "Venus in Two Acts," 10–11.

48. Hartman, "Venus in Two Acts," 6.

49. This approach is also inspired by Hartman's methodology in *Scenes of Subjection*, 10–11.

50. Crenshaw, "Mapping the Margins."

51. Cover, "Violence and the Word," 293. Cover focuses on the specific material effects of legal interpretation by judges in criminal cases, but his argument can be extended to the interpretative work of a scholar outside of a juridical context: "it is precisely this embedding of an understanding of political text in institutional modes of action and distinguishes *legal* interpretation from the interpretation of literature, from political philosophy, and from constitutional criticism" (296).

52. Brown, "Suffering the Paradoxes of Rights," 428.

53. Grossberg, *Cultural Studies in the Future Tense*.

54. Hartman, "Venus in Two Acts," 11.

55. Knox and Davies describe the cultural studies of law as "moving beyond textual analysis by attending to the networks of social practices through which law is constitutive of cultures just as culture and cultural analyses shape, resist and interrogate legal regulation, exception and norms" ("Introduction," 1).

CHAPTER 1   VISIBILITY AND IMMUTABILITY IN ASYLUM LAW AND PROCEDURE

1. *Geovanni Hernandez-Montiel v. INS*, 225 F.3d 1084 (9th Cir. 2000).

2. There have only been a small number of published Circuit Court of Appeals decisions involving trans asylum seekers. This include *Luis Reyes-Reyes v. John Ashcroft*, 384 F.3d 782 (9th Cir. 2004); *Francisco Ornelas-Chavez v. Alberto Gonzales*, 458 F.3d 1052 (9th Cir. 2006); *Nancy Arabillas Morales v. Alberto Gonzales*, 472 F.3d 689 (9th Cir. 2007); *Edgar*

Lacsina Pangilinan v. Eric H. Holder, 568 F.3d 708 (9th Cir. 2009); *N-A-M v. Eric H. Holder*, 587 F.3d 1052 (10th Cir. 2009); *Armando Gutierrez v. Eric H. Holder*, 730 F.3d 900 (9th Cir. 2013); *Edin Carey Avendano-Hernandez v. Loretta E. Lynch*, 800 F.3d 1072 (9th Cir. 2015); and *Yasmick Jeune v. U.S. Attorney General*, 810 F.3d 792 (11th Cir. 2016). The fact that most of these cases were decided by the Ninth Circuit is probably not coincidental, since the Ninth Circuit is one of the most liberal circuit courts. The Ninth Circuit covers Alaska, Washington, Idaho, Montana, Oregon, Nevada, California, Arizona, Hawaii, Guam, and the Northern Mariana Islands, and hearings are held in Pasadena (southern California), San Francisco (northern California), Portland (Oregon), and Seattle (Washington). It is not unusual for queer and trans people to migrate within the United States to be able to file their claims within the geographical jurisdiction of the Ninth Circuit.

3. Latour, "Visualisation and Cognition."

4. Refugee Act of 1980, Pub. L. 96-212, 94 Stat. 102 (1980).

5. Before the Refugee Act was passed, refugees were admitted through the discretionary parole power of the Attorney General. When the Attorney General had sole power of parole, Congress was excluded and had no say in the admittance of tens of thousands of refugees each year. Much conversation in the congressional hearings in the late 1970s was dedicated to discussing how to institutionalize a consultation process between the Attorney General, the President, and Congress in refugee matters.

6. A very explicit instance of this discourse occurred in a May 3, 1979, hearing in which Attorney General Griffin B. Bell renarrates U.S. history through human rights discourse. Bell argues that the United States is "the only country in history that's ever been founded for the purpose, not to seek wealth and comfort, but to seek human rights. That's why people came here. They didn't have as much freedom as they wanted. In the beginning that's why they came. Later they came to avail themselves of life's comforts. But they came here in the beginning seeking rights. And that's why we all believe so strongly in rights—human rights, the Bill of Rights, all rights." *Refugee Act of 1979: Hearings on H.R. 2816, Day 1, Before the Subcommittee on Immigration, Refugees, and International Law of the Committee on the Judiciary*, 96th Cong. 26 (1979) (statement of Griffin B. Bell, Attorney General of the United States).

7. *Hearing on H.R. 3056, Day 2, Before the Subcommittee on Immigration, Citizenship, and International Law of the Committee on the Judiciary*, 95th Cong. 91 (1977) (statement of Hon. Leonard F. Chapman, Jr, Commissioner of the INS).

8. See *Refugee Act of 1979: Hearing on H.R. 2816, Before the Subcommittee on Immigration, Refugees, and International Law of the Committee on the Judiciary*, 96th Cong. (1979) and *Hearing on H.R. 2816, Before the Subcommittee on International Operations of the Committee on Foreign Affairs*, 96th Cong. (1979).

9. These priorities also guide the initial implementation of refugee policy in the Reagan era. Carl Bon Tempo argues that under the Reagan administration in the 1980s, the admission of refugees shrunk significantly since Reagan's anticommunist, anti-Soviet foreign policy played a central role in admissions, rather than the human rights principles that had contributed to the writing of the Refugee Act (*Americans at the Gate*, 167). See also Legomsky, *Immigration and Refugee Law and Policy*, and Legomsky, "The Making of United States Refugee Policy," as well as Mertus, "The State and the Post-Cold War Refugee Regime."

10. The specific procedures for asylum law were only established in June 1980, three months after the Refugee Act passed. In the congressional hearings leading up to the

Refugee Act, the focus was on the figure of the refugee, and asylum was almost like an afterthought. In fact, witnesses from outside agencies, namely, the U.N. High Commissioner for Refugees, Amnesty International, and the American Civil Liberties Union (ACLU), had to remind the committees in the Senate and the House of Representatives that the proposed legislation should include the right to apply for asylum as well as establish uniform procedures for the treatment of asylum seekers, who should all have access to a hearing before an administrative judicial officer. *Refugee Act of 1979: Hearing on H.R. 2816, Before the Subcommittee on Immigration, Refugees, and International Law of the Committee on the Judiciary*, 96th Cong. 188–189 (1979) (statement of David Carliner, ACLU).

11. All asylees have to fit this definition of refugee, but then they are subject to different bureaucratic mechanisms for processing asylum. Asylum is available to persons who enter the United States and then apply, unlike refugee applications, which are processed abroad. As I discuss later, asylum applications are filed in one of two ways. Persons who are in the United States through a student visa or a tourist visa, and who then decide to apply for asylum, file an affirmative application while they are still in status. Defensive applications are those filed by persons who have been deemed deportable or excludable, and who then argue an asylum claim as a defense.

12. Legomsky, *Immigration and Refugee Law and Policy*, 928–929.

13. For an extensive analysis of the articulation of gender- and sexuality-based asylum claims using "membership in a particular social group," see McKinnon, *Gendered Asylum*.

14. Reddy, "Asian Diasporas, Neoliberalism, and Family," 112.

15. Reddy, "Asian Diasporas, Neoliberalism, and Family," 112.

16. See Ngai, *Impossible Subjects*, and Luibhéid, *Entry Denied*.

17. *Nancy Arabillas Morales v. Alberto Gonzales*, 472 F.3d 689 (9th Cir. 2007). The Ninth Circuit's implicit acceptance of that category as constituting a particular social group, as well as the fact that the claim was based directly on transsexual identity and not sexual orientation or sexual identity, are especially significant. Although the court did not specifically address whether "male-to-female transsexual" constitutes a particular social group, it did not challenge this formulation either, so this case could be used as a precedent for other asylum cases to argue for recognition of "transsexual" as a particular social group.

18. *Edin Carey Avendano-Hernandez v. Loretta E. Lynch*, 800 F.3d 1072 (9th Cir. 2015). This Ninth Circuit Court of Appeals decision established the legal precedent that gender identity is a separate category from sexual identity, and that the country conditions in Mexico constitute a basis for asylum claims for trans people.

19. Many attorneys and legal practitioners with whom I corresponded had successfully represented trans asylum seekers as "transgender" in the early 2000s. For a discussion of the myriad ways that "particular social group" has been constructed for trans asylum seekers in multiple asylum-granting countries, see Berg and Millbank, "Developing a Jurisprudence of Transgender Particular Social Group."

20. See, for example, Report of the Office of the United Nations High Commissioner for Human Rights, "Discrimination and violence against individuals based on their sexual orientation and gender identity," May 4, 2015, http://www.un.org/en/ga/search/view_doc.asp?symbol=A/HRC/29/23&referer=/english/&Lang=E. For examples of this discourse from the U.S. government, see U.S. Secretary of State Hillary Clinton's

famous "gay rights are human rights" speech on International Human Rights Day speech in Geneva on December 6, 2011, https://2009-2017.state.gov/secretary/20092013clinton /rm/2011/12/178368.htm. See also President Barack Obama's Presidential Memorandum— International Initiatives to Advance the Human Rights of Lesbian, Gay, Bisexual, and Transgender Persons, December 6, 2011, https://obamawhitehouse.archives.gov/the -press-office/2011/12/06/presidential-memorandum-international-initiatives-advance -human-rights-l, and National Security Advisor Susan E. Rice's remarks at American University on Global LGBTQ Rights, "Promoting and Protecting LGBT Rights," October 26, 2016, https://obamawhitehouse.archives.gov/the-press-office/2016/10/26/remarks -national-security-advisor-susan-e-riceamerican-university.

21.   Gruberg and West, *Humanitarian Diplomacy*, 9.

22.   USCIS, "Guidance for Adjudicating Lesbian, Gay, Bisexual, Transgender, and Intersex (LGBTI) Refugee and Asylum Claims," 2011.

23.   Data from Immigration Equality and Human Rights First show that affirmative asylum applicants are more successful, mainly because immigration detention has a negative impact on asylum grant rates (Gruberg and West, *Humanitarian Diplomacy*, 24).

24.   To apply for asylum affirmatively, a person completes Form I-589, Application for Asylum, Withholding of Removal, and for relief under the UN Convention Against Torture (CAT), and submits it to the U.S. Citizenship and Immigration Services (USCIS). The application includes a declaration by the applicant, which tells the applicant's story in her own words and is probably the most important piece of evidence in an asylum case. After the application is received, the applicant is scheduled for an interview with an asylum officer. This interview is intended to be nonadversarial and takes place in the office of the asylum officer, who asks the applicant to talk about many of the questions on the application form, such as why the applicant is applying for asylum, what kinds of harm the applicant experienced in the country, what the applicant thinks will happen if she is forced to return to her country of origin, as well as how the applicant came to realize and express her gender and sexual identity. This interview usually lasts between one and two hours. If the applicant has an attorney, the attorney is present in the interview, but does not play a major role. The attorney will usually only ask questions about important incidents that the officer neglected to discuss and then make a closing statement.

25.   Detention has become an integral part of the U.S. asylum process as a result of the immigration reforms of 1996, namely, the Anti-Terrorism and Effective Death Penalty Act (AEDPA), Pub. L. 104–132, 110 Stat. 1214, and the Illegal Immigration Reform and Immigrant Responsibility Act (IIRIRA), INA §§ 303(b), 306(c), 309, 505, 553, 642, 644.

26.   There are three possible outcomes for an immigration court hearing: (1) the immigration judge can grant asylum to the applicant; (2) the immigration judge can grant withholding of removal or protection under CAT, if the immigration judge considers the case to be strong but there are problems such as the applicant exceeded the one-year filing deadline or has certain criminal convictions; (3) the immigration judge can deny the claim and issue an order of removal. In the third situation, the applicant has thirty days to file an appeal with the BIA.

27.   Foucault argues that confession has become one of the West's most highly valued methods for producing truth and that it functions as a ritual of discourse that takes place within a power relationship. Confession—in the case of asylum, testimony— occurs in the presence of another person who is the authority and who requires the confession/testimony in order to judge and intervene in it. The agency of domination

does not reside in the person who speak, because she or he is constrained, but rather in the person who questions (Foucault, *The History of Sexuality*, 59–62).

28. Spade, "Mutilating Gender." More recently, see shuster, *Trans Medicine*.

29. Immigration and Nationality Act, INA § 208(b)(1)(B)(ii).

30. Immigration and Nationality Act, INA § 208(b)(1)(B)(iii).

31. *In re* Geovanni Hernandez-Montiel (A 72 994 275), Hearing before Kenneth Bagley, Immigration Judge (January 2, 1996), San Diego, California, 69.

32. *In re* Geovanni Hernandez-Montiel (A 72 994 275), Hearing before Kenneth Bagley, Immigration Judge (January 2, 1996), San Diego, California, 10; and *In re* Geovanni Hernandez-Montiel, Decision of the Board of Immigration Appeals, April 27, 1998, 5.

33. The BIA is part of the Executive Office for Immigration Review (EOIR), which is run by the Department of Justice. The Homeland Security Act of 2002 gave the Attorney General the power to review individual decisions of the BIA, which are binding on immigration judges as well as all DHS officers and employees (Legomsky, *Immigration and Refugee Law and Policy*, 4–5).

34. The names and biographies of the BIA members are available at https://www.justice .gov/eoir/board-of-immigration-appeals-bios.

35. On the rare occasions in which the BIA will hear oral arguments for an appeal, those proceedings usually take place at the EOIR headquarters in Falls Church, Virginia. However, these rare courtroom proceedings do not feature the asylum applicant, only the attorneys arguing the case. Since 2002, the majority of appeals to the BIA have been decided through the process of single-member adjudication, which means that each case is read and considered by only one member of the BIA, who will review questions of law de novo (that is, consider questions of the law afresh) but does not review questions of fact. 8 C.F.R. § 1003.1(d)(3)(ii) and (iii).

36. Due to an immense backlog of cases—about 56,000 in the beginning of 2002—resulting from what the Department of Justice termed "an inefficient adjudication process," in 2002 Attorney General John Ashcroft codified a "streamlining" process. Among other rules about timely adjudication, this "Final Rule" reaffirms the single member adjudication process in which most appeals are read and decided by only one Board member. See the Department of Justice's press releases at https://www.justice.gov/sites /default/files/eoir/legacy/2002/08/29/BIARulefactsheet.pdf and https://www.justice .gov/sites/default/files/eoir/legacy/2002/08/26/BIARestruct.pdf.

The process of single member adjudication, in combination with the enormous backlog of appeals, means that the BIA routinely affirms immigration judge decisions either without a written opinion or with a summary opinion. In order to minimize the chances of the BIA rubber-stamping the immigration judge's opinion, attorneys should argue for a three-member panel to consider the appeal, which will make it more likely that the decision will be overturned. There are six categories of issues for which the BIA will use a three-member panel such as if there are inconsistencies among the rulings of different immigration judges, if the case has precedential value, or if the immigration judge made a clearly erroneous factual determination. For more information on these categories, see the *BIA Practice Manual* at http://www.justice.gov /eoir/vll/qapracmanual/apptmtn4.htm.

37. The potential for winning an asylum case decreases as the litigation process develops, so immigration and asylum legal manuals emphasize the importance of presenting the strongest possible application from the beginning. In part, this is due to the

increasing abstraction of the asylum applicant as the process continues, since the BIA and circuit courts proceedings occur in the physical absence of the applicant. The overburdened court system and increasingly stringent immigration and asylum laws also contribute to the increasing abstraction/distance, since judges have less time and limited ability to overturn earlier findings.

38. INA § 242(b)(4)(B); 8 U.S.C. § 1252(b)(4)(B).

39. The court may allow the attorneys for each side to make oral arguments, but they are only given a limited amount of time (about fifteen minutes) in which to do so. There are no witnesses and the parties are not usually not present either.

40. The sources of asylum law in the United States are statute, regulations, BIA decisions, and federal court decisions. Most asylum applications are decided by asylum officers and immigration judges, but their decisions are not precedential and are not easily accessible. Interviews with asylum officers are not recorded or transcribed; if the asylum officers grants asylum, there is no substantive written decision. Asylum hearings in immigration court are usually closed proceedings that are recorded but only transcribed if there is an appeal. The BIA only selects a handful of decisions to publish each year, so the vast majority of them are unpublished and therefore not precedential. This exemplifies the contradictory politics of generosity and scarcity that undergird the institution of asylum in the United States. Similarly, not all circuit court decisions are published; however, recent changes to federal court rules allow some citation of unpublished circuit court decisions (Neilson and Wertz, *Immigration Law and the Transgender Client*, 66).

41. Latour, "Visualisation and Cognition."

42. Latour, "Visualisation and Cognition," 15.

43. Latour, "Visualisation and Cognition," 19, emphasis in the original.

44. Latour, "Visualisation and Cognition," 16.

45. 19 I. & N. Dec. 211 (BIA 1985).

46. Quoted in Musalo, Moore, and Boswell, *Refugee Law and Policy*, 630.

47. A year after *Acosta*, in *Sanchez-Trujillo v. INS*, 801 F.2d 1571 (9th Cir. 1986), the Ninth Circuit Court defined "particular social group" as a collection of people closely affiliated with each other through a common impulse or interest; that is, it contended that "a voluntary associational relationship" was a component of a particular social group. The court argued that this relationship must impart "some common characteristic that is fundamental to their identity as a member of that discrete social group" and that a particular social group is a "cohesive, homogenous group" (Legomsky, *Immigration and Refugee Law and Policy*, 979–980). Before 2000, *Sanchez-Trujillo v. INS* was cited as creating an additional requirement for the definition of particular social group, but in *Hernandez-Montiel v. INS*, the Ninth Circuit modified and clarified this aspect of *Sanchez-Trujillo v. INS*. In this later decision, the court argued that *Sanchez-Trujillo v. INS* provides an additional way to establish social group (rather than rejecting the Acosta test); significantly, the Ninth Circuit does not mention the requirement of homogeneity at all in *Hernandez-Montiel v. INS*.

Hernandez-Montiel v. INS combines the definitions of social group in *Acosta* and *Sanchez-Trujillo V. INS* to define a particular social group that is united by voluntary association, including former association, *or* as a group that is distinguished by any innate characteristic that is so fundamental to the identities and consciences of its members that the members either cannot or should not be required to change it.

This is the broadest definition of social group that has been articulated by any circuit court.

48. Robert Gerber (attorney), in discussion with author, October 6, 2010.

49. In *In re Toboso-Alfonso*, the BIA affirmed an immigration judge's decision to grant withholding of deportation to a gay Cuban man who argued that he was subject to persecution by the Cuban government because of his status as a homosexual, and upheld the immigration judge's determination that homosexuality was an immutable characteristic (20 I. & N. Dec 819 (BIA 1990)). Four years later Attorney General Janet Reno designated *In re Toboso-Alfonso* as precedent, establishing, for the first time, lesbians and gay men as a particular social group for the purposes of asylum. In addition to its precedential value, *In re Toboso-Alfonso* is also significant for how the decision marks sexual identity as distinct from political activity. The BIA claimed that this case was not about gay rights: "This is not simply a case involving the enforcement of laws against particular homosexual acts, nor is this simply a case of assertion of 'gay rights'." The implication here is that if it were a case of gay rights, Toboso-Alfonso's claim for protection would be less compelling, given the criminalization of homosexuality in the United States at that time; the U.S. Supreme Court struck down all remaining state sodomy laws in 2003 (*Lawrence v. Texas*, 539 U.S. 558). This statement by the BIA condenses a lot of the anxieties that circulate around the category of particular social group and highlights the depoliticizing that occurs in relation to this category, which can be seen as an attempt to make these particular asylum seekers less threatening and deviant. This statement also insists on the distinction between "particular social group" and "political opinion" as grounds for asylum.

50. This formulation of "gay man with a female sexual identity" is deployed in two subsequent published Ninth Circuit Court decisions—*Reyes-Reyes v. Ashcroft*, 384 F.3d 782 (9th Cir. 2004), and *Ornelas-Chavez v. Gonzales*, 458 F.3d 1052 (9th Cir. 2006)—and it is only in *Morales v. Gonzales*, 472 F.3d 689 (9th Cir. 2007), that the Ninth Circuit Court uses the language of "male-to-female transsexual" and "transgender," and refers to Morales using female pronouns.

51. *Hernandez-Montiel v. INS*, 225 F.3d 1084, 1095 n.7 (9th Cir. 2000). This footnote goes on to cite Deborah Tussey's definition of "transsexual" as "a person who is genetically and physically a member of one sex but has a deep-seated psychological conviction that he or she belongs, or ought to belong, to the opposite sex, a conviction that may in some cases result in the individual's decision to undergo surgery in order to physically modify his or her sex organs to resemble those of the opposite sex" (Quoting Deborah Tussey, Annotation, *Transvestism or Transsexualism of Spouse as Justifying Divorce*, 82 A.L.R. 3d n2 (1978)).

52. The U.S. Supreme Court has told the Ninth Circuit Court, one of the more liberal circuit courts, to not determine in the first instance certain substantive immigration law questions, including whether certain groups satisfy the particular social group test. For example, see *INS v. Ventura*, 537 U.S. 12 (2002), and *Gonzales v. Thomas*, 126 S. Ct. 1613 (2006).

53. *Edin Carey Avendano-Hernandez v. Loretta E. Lynch*, 800 F.3d 1072 (9th Cir. 2015). Several of the attorneys and legal practitioners with whom I corresponded in 2010–2011 had successfully represented trans asylum seekers as "transgender."

54. Circuit Rule 36-2. Criteria for Publication, *Federal Rules of Appellate Procedure, Ninth Circuit Rules, Circuit Advisory Committee Notes*, June 1, 2019, 152–153, http://cdn.ca9 .uscourts.gov/datastore/uploads/rules/frap.pdf.

55. See Rempell's "Unpublished Decisions and Precedent Shaping" for a discussion of the impact of the low publication rate of asylum cases by the Ninth Circuit Court of Appeals on the consistency of the development of case law.

56. McKinnon, *Gendered Asylum*, 99.

57. McKinnon, *Gendered Asylum*, 101.

58. McKinnon, *Gendered Asylum*, 98–99.

59. For example, in a U.S. context, David Valentine documents how individuals would simultaneously identify as "gay" and as a "woman" and not see those categories as being mutually exclusive (*Imagining Transgender*). See also Martin Manalansan's discussion in *Global Divas* about the complicated relationships between gender and sexuality among diasporic Filipino gay men in New York City, in terms of language and identity categories. More recently, Martha Balaguera uses the term *chicas trans* to capture how her Central American interviewees "often referred to themselves as gay and trans, thus underscoring the importance of sexuality, ambiguity, and the irreducibility of the term *chicas trans* to gender" ("Trans-migrations," 641n1).

60. In *Avendano-Hernandez v. Lynch* (2015), which also involved a transgender woman fleeing persecution and torture in Mexico, the Ninth Circuit Court of Appeals noted the problems with the legal conflation of gender identity and sexual orientation.

61. *Reyes-Reyes v. Ashcroft*, 384 F.3d 782 (9th Cir. 2004).

62. Landau, "'Soft Immutability' and 'Imputed Gay Identity,'" 247.

63. Stefan Vogler makes a similar argument about transgender asylum cases after *Avendano-Hernandez v. Lynch* (2015), which he contends depend on a cis-trans binary in which applicants need to prove that they are "trans enough" ("Determining Transgender").

64. For example, during the Trump administration, Attorney General Jeff Sessions argued that domestic violence and gang violence are not valid grounds for asylum claims. (Benner and Dickerson, "Sessions Says Domestic and Gang Violence Are Not Grounds for Asylum").

65. This concern has been present within debates about asylum from the very beginning, in the congressional hearings leading up to the passage of the Refugee Act. Much attention in these hearings was given to the economics of the proposed refugee legislation, in relation to concerns about illegal immigration, the economic recession, and reduced government spending. Conservative senators like Strom Thurmond and Walter D. Huddleston argued for considering the number of refugees admitted each year alongside the number of "illegal immigrants" who enter the country each year, in terms of the costs to states, resources, and assimilation rates. Given that most of this discussion referred to "Indochinese refugees" from Vietnam, Cambodia, and Laos, these were arguments about the need to protect U.S. citizens and about the maintenance of the class and racial stratification of labor in the United States. Not surprisingly, these discussions about Indochinese refugees focused on the need for the United States to take the lead and set a good example for helping the world's homeless, and there was very little acknowledgment of the ways that the United States contributed to the creation of this refugee situation. *The Refugee Act of 1979: S. 643, Before the Committee on the Judiciary*, 96th Cong. (1979).

The threat of the United States being overwhelmed by an influx of refugees is of course completely unwarranted, since, as historians Bill Hing in *Deporting Our Souls* and Carl Bon Tempo in *Americans at the Gate* note, the codification of refugee and asylum law actually resulted in fewer refugees being admitted than under the previous parole authority of the Attorney General. Furthermore, as Bon Tempo argues in his analysis of the Reagan era, the implementation of a comprehensive legislative refugee policy places more, not fewer, limits on the admission of refugees (*Americans at the Gate*, 167). This has continued to be the case in more recent decades, especially after 2001, in which administrations have consistently accepted far fewer refugees than the annual congressional cap.

66. Cantú Jr. notes that the narratives of asylum seekers often end up reinscribing essentialist notions of lesbian and gay identity ("Well-Founded Fear," 61).

67. *Hernandez-Montiel v. INS*, 225 F.3d 1084, 1087 (9th Cir. 2000).

68. *Hernandez-Montiel* at 1088.

69. *Hernandez-Montiel* at 1088.

70. McKinley, "Cultural Culprits," 105.

71. McKinley, "Cultural Culprits," 105.

72. In fact, several attorneys with whom I spoke contended that expert witness testimony can be the most important component of an asylum case and often holds more weight and authority than the testimony of the applicant. Neilson and Wertz note that expert witness testimony "will often make the difference in a case, especially if the judge has a particular concern, such as whether some regions in the country are safer than others or whether conditions overall are improving" (*Immigration Law and the Transgender Client*, 82). For discussion of the contradictions that structure representations of violence and culture in expert witness declarations, see Portillo Villeda, "Central American Migrants."

73. *In re* Geovanni Hernandez-Montiel (A 72 994 275), Hearing before Kenneth Bagley, Immigration Judge (January 2, 1996), San Diego, California.

74. Davies's personal experiences and knowledge also contribute to his status as an expert witness, even though his personal experience is secondary to his academic research and university affiliation. In the immigration court hearing, when pressed by the INS attorney during cross-examination about his familiarity with the gay community in Mexico, Davies cites two gay friends in Mexico City and his lesbian stepdaughter who is active in the lesbian and gay community. He goes on to name gay bars he's been to in Mexico as well as all the Mexican states in which he has been in contact with gay men. Davies's testimony about his relationship to the gay community in Mexico also works to erase class differences within queer communities. Thanks to Juana María Rodríguez for this last point.

75. Mohanty, "Under Western Eyes."

76. Cantú Jr., "Well-Founded Fear," 64–68; Luibhéid, *Entry Denied*, 113–114.

77. Cantú Jr., *The Sexuality of Migration*, 63.

78. Carrillo, "Leaving Loved Ones Behind," 25–26. Carrillo compares these shifts in attitudes toward gender and sexuality in Mexico to social changes that are occurring in other countries, including the United States. He notes that both the United States and Mexico have segments of their population that oppose LGBT rights and visibility and segments of each population that support greater sexual equality. Moreover, he argues that the gains being made in LGBT rights is comparable in these two countries. In particular, Carrillo cites the approval of civil unions in Mexico City and the development of an antihomophobia campaign by the Mexican federal government as evidence that recent gains in Mexico have exceeded those in the United States, thus complicating the dominant representation of Mexico as culturally and politically

static compared to the United States. In another essay, Carrillo notes that these rights and policy gains may perversely complicate asylum for queer and trans subjects in the United States, since it may be more difficult to argue for persecution in countries like Mexico where the state has granted some legal protection to LGBT populations ("Immigration and LGBT Rights in the USA").

79. *In re* Geovanni Hernandez-Montiel (A 72 994 275), Hearing before Kenneth Bagley, Immigration Judge (January 2, 1996), San Diego, California, 18.

80. *In re* Geovanni Hernandez-Montiel (A 72 994 275), at 26.

81. *Hernandez-Montiel v. INS*, 225 F.3d 1084, 1096 (9th Cir. 2000).

82. *Jorge Soto Vega v. Alberto Gonzales*, 183 F. App'x 627 (9th Cir. 2006), is an oft-cited example of this situation; more recently, the *New York Times* also discussed the issue of asylum seekers not appearing "gay enough" (Bilefsky, "Gays Seeking Asylum"). See also Miller, "Gay Enough," and Murray, *Real Queer?*. This screening of gay and trans asylum applicants based on gender and sexual stereotypes is also related to longer histories of the medical assessment of trans people by therapists and medical doctors.

   The conflation of sex acts, sexuality, and gender presentation that produces Hernandez-Montiel as a "gay" asylum seeker also demonstrates what Andrew Sharpe names the homophobic grounding of transgender bodies of law (*Transgender Jurisprudence*).

83. Robert Irwin notes that contemporary discussions of Mexican male homosexuality frequently cite this construction of Mexican masculinity, which can be traced back to Octavio Paz's 1950s notion that Mexican men must show their masculinity and power by penetrating others, symbolically and literally, in contrast to women who are weak and penetratable (*Mexican Masculinities*, xxxiii). Irwin critiques academics who have given Paz's account undue authority, even though there is other historical evidence that complicates Paz's construction and makes it clear that his is only one (flawed) version of homosexuality and masculinity in Mexico.

   Social scientists have also argued against the reduction of *activo/passivo* as *the* Latino model of homosexuality. See, for example, Vidal-Ortiz, Decena, Carrillo, and Almaguer, "Revisiting *Activos* and *Passivos*," in which Carrillo argues that *activo* and *passivo* have been seen as identity categories and as the only identity categories available to homosexual men in Latin America. His research in Mexico, however, suggests that *activo* and *passivo* are used locally in ways that are similar to top and bottom in the United States, that is, that these terms signify acts and desires, not identities as gay and nongay (258).

84. *In re* Geovanni Hernandez-Montiel (A 72 994 275), at 22.

85. Cacho, *Social Death*, 123. See also Inda and Dowling, "Introduction," 6n9.

86. Rodríguez, *Queer Latinidad*, 88.

87. Cantú Jr., "Well-Founded Fear," 63.

88. For example, whether the applicant should receive a grant of asylum, withholding of removal, or protection under the CAT.

89. Martinez provides the following working definitions of these categories: Substance refers to "rules that control the primary conduct of human beings outside the litigation or lawmaking process" ("Process and Substance," 1020–1021) whereas process/procedure refers to "not only questions of procedure within courts and courtlike tribunals, but also broader questions about how to allocate the authority to make and

apply law among different government actors, including judges, legislators, and executive officials" ("Process and Substance," 1021).

90. Motomura, "The Curious Evolution of Immigration Law," 1630.

91. Motomura's larger critique in this analysis is the plenary power doctrine, which dictates different—and often exclusionary—authority for Congress and the executive branch in immigration matters. As a result, courts have avoided applying constitutional norms and principles to subconstitutional immigration law, and developed exceptions to the plenary power doctrine by framing constitutional claims as "procedural due process."

92. Martinez, "Process and Substance," 1027.

93. Martinez, "Process and Substance," 1017.

94. Martinez, "Process and Substance," 1031.

95. I engage with this question in my introduction, through the rubric of the relationship between law and justice.

96. Gerber, in discussion with author, October 6, 2010.

97. Gerber, in discussion with author, October 6, 2010. Gerber told me that he was surprised by these questions about criminal activity during the trial, since they were unexpected. Gerber had not found any criminal convictions on record for Hernandez-Montiel, even though Hernandez-Montiel had told Gerber about being apprehended by police officers in the United States and being taken to a police station.

98. The immigration judge found that Hernandez-Montiel's use of the Fifth Amendment contributed to a failure to "sustain the burden of establishing that he is entitled to relief in the form of asylum" and, furthermore, that Hernandez-Montiel's undocumented entries into the United States "evidence a strong disrespect for the immigration laws of this country while militates against a favorable exercise of discretion" (11). In his conclusion, the immigration judge reiterated that even if Hernandez-Montiel had established eligibility for asylum, he would have still denied Hernandez-Montiel asylum as a matter of discretion for these reasons. *In re* Geovanni Hernandez-Montiel (A 72 994 275), Hearing before Kenneth Bagley, Immigration Judge (January 2, 1996), San Diego, California.

99. *In re* Geovanni Hernandez-Montiel, Decision and Order of the Immigration Judge, April 3, 1996, 6–7.

100. Gerber, in discussion with author, October 6, 2010.

101. *In re* Geovanni Hernandez-Montiel, Decision of the Board of Immigration Appeals, April 27, 1998, 5.

102. Fred W. Vacca is also the administrative law judge who issued the minority dissenting opinion in *In re Toboso-Alfonso*, the 1990 BIA decision about a gay Cuban man that helped establish precedent for lesbians and gay men as constituting a particular social group for the purposes of asylum.

103. Latour, "Visualisation and Cognition," 27.

104. To be clear, I am not implying that the BIA's decision would have been different had Hernandez-Montiel been present in the courtroom.

105. *In re* Geovanni Hernandez-Montiel, Decision of the Board of Immigration Appeals, at 6. The Ninth Circuit Court of Appeals decision condemns this homophobic and transphobic statement in the BIA decision about Hernandez-Montiel's "conduct": "Perhaps,

then, by 'conduct,' the BIA was referring to Geovanni's effeminate dress or his sexual orientation as a gay man, as justification for the police officers' raping him. The 'you asked for it' excuse for rape is offensive to this court and has been discounted by courts and commentators alike" (*Hernandez-Montiel v. INS*, 225 F.3d 1084, 1098 (9th Cir. 2000)).

106. It also enabled the case to be more widely cited, such as in female genital surgery cases, for example. *Hernandez-Montiel v. INS* was also cited in the gay marriage case by the California Supreme Court (Gerber, in discussion with author, October 6, 2010).

107. Gerber claimed that the BIA opinion was so extreme that it caught the Ninth Circuit Court's attention. When he saw the court calendar for the Ninth Circuit Court, he saw that he had been given twenty minutes for his oral argument—whereas attorneys are usually given ten minutes—and knew that the case was going to be important. The government had sent out Alice Loughran, an assistant attorney general from Washington, D.C., to argue the prosecution. When the case came up before the judges, all of the Ninth Circuit Court clerks came into the courtroom to hear the argument (Gerber, in discussion with author, October 6, 2010).

108. *Hernandez-Montiel*, at 1099.

109. Final outcome of the case provided by Gerber (in discussion with author, October 6, 2010).

110. Immigration Equality, http://www.immigrationequality.org/; National Center for Lesbian Rights, http://www.nclrights.org/.

111. Gerber was interviewed on *The O'Reilly Factor* ("Mexican National Requests Asylum") and on the BBC's *Outlook* radio program. He received the Tom Homann Law Association's President Award in 2000 for his work on the case (http://www.sheppardmullin.com/press-releases-19.html/). Articles about *Hernandez-Montiel v. INS* also appeared in the *L.A. Times* (Weinstein, "Persecuted Gay Man Wins Asylum Case"), the *New York Times* (Stout, "Court Rules Cross-Dresser Can Stay in the U.S."), and in *Newsweek* (France and Figueroa, "A Gay Refugee Finds Shelter in Court").

112. When I asked Gerber if he knew why Hernandez-Montiel had disappeared, he responded that some people think that they will come to the United States and escape persecution but that it is just as tough here in different ways. Perhaps a person will not experience the same types or intensities of violence and abuse in the United States, but she or he will still experience harassment and discrimination. Gerber told me that he never asked Hernandez-Montiel why she left San Diego after the BIA decision, but in Gerber's opinion, she was not welcomed in conservative San Diego. Gerber mentioned that Los Angeles has a much more active and larger gay and transgender community and implied that might have factored into Hernandez-Montiel's relocation. Gerber, in discussion with author, October 6, 2010.

113. Many of the more recent restrictions around judicial review have been a result of Congress trying to limit the power of the judiciary because it thinks that there are too many rights that noncitizens can access, so this is part of the bigger move to decrease access to process for noncitizens.

114. As Juana María Rodríguez discusses in her analysis of *In re Tenorio* in *Queer* Latinidad, the queer asylum subject also comes to represent various political agendas for different constituents, and then of course disappears again into the everyday realities of queer immigrant life in the United States. The more recent citation of *Hernandez-Montiel v. INS* in the gay marriage case in the California Supreme Court is an example

of the way that queer and trans asylum seekers (and their cases) are taken up by mainstream LGBT organizations for other means.

CHAPTER 2   DESIRING THE NATION

1. All the names associated with the declarations I discuss in this chapter are pseudonyms. Most of the declarations I received were redacted, although a few included the initials or first names of the applicants.

2. Declaration of Claudia, paragraph 59.

3. Declaration of Ana, paragraph 29.

4. *Geovanni Hernandez-Montiel v. INS*, 225 F.3d 1084 (9th Cir. 2000).

5. Povinelli, *The Empire of Love*, 4.

6. Yurchak, *Everything Was Forever, Until It Was No More*, 28.

7. Ramji-Nogales, Schoenholtz, and Schrag found that whether or not an asylum seeker has legal representation is the most important factor that determines the outcome of an asylum case. Asylum seekers who had legal representation were granted asylum at a rate of 45.6 percent, compared to those without legal counsel who had a grant rate of 16.3 percent ("Refugee Roulette," 340). See also Gruberg and West, *Humanitarian Diplomacy*, 22–24.

8. TransLatin@Coalition, *TransVisible*, 10.

9. Balaguera, "Trans-migrations."

10. Cvetkovich, *Archive*, 3.

11. Cvetkovich, *Archive*, 18.

12. Cvetkovich, *Archive*, 47.

13. Miller, "Gay Enough," 165. Emphasis in the original. Miller tends to endorse human rights as a remedy to the violence experienced by asylum seekers and reproduced by asylum advocacy. In doing so, she fails to consider how the human rights regime relies on and requires the presence of an injured body as the basis for claiming rights.

14. Cvetkovich, *Archive*, 17.

15. Cvetkovich, *Archive*, 44.

16. Foucault, *The History of Sexuality*, 58.

17. Foucault, *The History of Sexuality*, 58–59.

18. Brooks writes, "What we are today—the entire conception of the self, its relation to interiority and to others—is largely tributary to the confessional requirement" (*Troubling Confessions*, 101). Furthermore, Brooks's analysis suggests that sexuality is central to confession, as many of his examples focus on sex.

19. Foucault, *The History of Sexuality*, 66.

20. Declaration of Ines, dated August 2006, paragraph 2.

21. Connie Oxford discusses how hegemonic narratives about persecution and violence shape how immigrant service providers, immigration attorneys, and translators work with asylum applicants to produce asylum narratives ("Acts of Resistance").

22. McGuirk, "(In)credible Subjects."

23. Foucault, *The History of Sexuality*, 62.

24. Fassin and d'Halluin, "The Truth from the Body."

25. Bohmer and Shuman, "Producing Epistemologies of Ignorance," 621, 624. David A. B. Murray also discusses the ways that as asylum seekers are seen as less credible, letters from experts, including those from LGBT refugee support groups, become important forms of evidence. In providing letters that support asylum applicants' credibility as sexual and gender minorities, LGBT refugee support groups become complicit with repressive and exclusionary mechanisms of state surveillance and participate in reproducing norms of homonationalism (Murray, "Queer Forms").

26. Psychological Evaluation by Diane D., LCSW, who met with Gloria at the Corrections Corporation of America (CCA) immigration detention facility in Otay Mesa, CA, to conduct a clinical interview and administer two symptoms checklists. Diane D. diagnosed Gloria with symptoms of depression and anxiety but also notes that a diagnosis of PTSD is most appropriate, given that she has "been retraumatized by police and community members during her recent visit to Mexico, and now living with daily reminders in the form of CCA officials as well as fellow detainees who are verbally and emotionally abusive [,] some of whom treat her as less than a human being" (3). Case files from Margarita Manduley.

27. Rodman makes this statement based on photographs provided by Rosa's attorney, Margarita Manduley, and on a telephone interview with Rosa, who was also incarcerated at the CCA detention facility in Otay Mesa, CA (Debra H. Rodman, "Expert Declaration in Support of the Asylum Declaration of R.S," April 7, 2009, paragraph 30).

28. Noll notes that this construction of the asylum seeker works to the benefit of host states, since "it allows them to neutralize the political agency of asylum seekers and to recast them either as mere impostors or as mere 'victims-to-be-saved'" ("Salvation by the Grace of State?," 197).

29. Bettcher, "Evil Deceivers and Make-Believers."

30. Dolnick, "Immigrants May Be Fed False Stories to Bolster Asylum Pleas."

31. Mehta, "The Asylum Seeker," 36.

32. Here I am thinking about Sara Ahmed's analysis in *The Cultural Politics of Emotion* about how affect circulates and sticks to certain racialized bodies to mark them as other and as threats to the nation.

33. Noll, "Salvation by the Grace of State?," 211.

34. Schoenholtz, Schrag, and Ramji-Nogales, *Lives in the Balance*, 143–176.

35. This is similar to Wendy Brown's argument about injury as a basis for claims on the state in "Wounded Attachments."

36. Noll, "Salvation by the Grace of State?," 214.

37. President Biden suspended Trump's Migrant Protection Protocols (MPP) when he entered the White House in 2021, but in December 2021, the Fifth Circuit Court of Appeals ordered the Department of Homeland Security to negotiate with Mexico to reinstate the program (*State of Texas; State of Missouri v. Joseph R. Biden, Jr.*, No. 21-10806 (5th Cir. 2022)). In April 2022, the U.S. Supreme Court is scheduled to review lower court decisions holding that the Biden administration did not have the legal authority to end MPP.

38. The Department of Health and Human Services issued an emergency regulation to implement Section 265 of U.S. Code Title 42 on March 20, 2020, which enabled the Centers for Disease Control to issue an order that effectively closed down the U.S. borders with Canada and Mexico to asylum seekers and other migrants (Centers for Disease Control and Prevention and Department of Health and Human Services, "Control

of Communicable Diseases; Foreign Quarantine: Suspension of Introduction of Persons Into United States From Designated Foreign Countries or Places for Public Health Purposes," 85 Fed. Reg. 16,559 (March 24, 2020), https://www.federalregister.gov/documents/2020/03/24/2020-06238/control-of-communicable-diseases-foreign-quarantine-suspension-of-introduction-of-persons-into). Immigrant legal advocates and immigrant justice groups continue to challenge the Biden administration's use of Title 42. One victory came on March 4, 2022, when the District of Columbia Circuit Court of Appeals decided *Nancy Gimena Huisha-Huisha v. Alejandro Mayorkas*, No. 21-5200 (D.C. Cir. 2022), which prohibits the federal government from using Title 42 to summarily expel families seeking asylum who are fleeing danger in their countries of origin.

39. Declaration of Ines, dated August 2006, paragraph 3.

40. The Transgender Law Center and Cornell University Law School LGBT Clinic note that for some transgender women, the labels of "gay" and "transgender" are not mutually exclusive, and point out that the root cause of violence for both trans women and feminine gay men is "likely the combination of cultural gender norms, misogyny in general and the particular vitriol targeted at people who express femininity despite being assigned a male sex at birth." However, the authors argue that it is important for asylum adjudicators to understand the distinctions between sexual orientation and gender identity (*Report on Human Rights Conditions*, 6).

41. In her analysis of different accounts of political violence and U.S. asylum law, Coutin also notes that "successful asylum narratives do follow a prototypical plot line" as "plot holes" might discredit the applicant ("The Oppressed, the Suspect, and the Citizen," 84).

42. In his ethnographic research with sexual orientation and gender identity (SOGI) refugees in Canada, Murray found that many SOGI refugees engaged in a similar "migration-to-liberation nation" narrative, "which may be due in part to their investment in articulating a narrative that meets the homonormative definitions of SOGI refugee identity demanded by their engagement with the refugee determination system" ("The Challenge of Home," 134).

43. Valentine, *Imagining Transgender*, 226–228. Valentine also points out that this construction of transgender ignores the larger structures of systemic violence that shape the life chances of many trans people.

44. See, for example, Lamble, "Retelling racialized violence," and Stanley, "Near Life, Queer Death."

45. Butler, *The Psychic Life of Power*, 100.

46. Shuman and Bohmer, "Representing Trauma," 403.

47. Butler, *The Psychic Life of Power*, 100.

48. Macpherson argues that the concept of possession shaped seventeenth-century ideas of freedom, rights, obligation, and justice, and that these assumptions have remained in modern liberal theory (*The Political Theory of Possessive Individualism*).

49. Coutin, "The Oppressed, the Suspect, and the Citizen," 87.

50. See Coutin ("The Oppressed, the Suspect, and the Citizen," 87) and Einolf, *The Mercy Factory*. Shuman and Bohmer also found in their ethnographic research with asylum seekers that "the asylum process itself is an emotional struggle comparable to the experiences of persecution" from which applicants have fled ("Representing Trauma," 406).

51. Illegal Immigration Reform and Immigrant Responsibility Act of 1996, Pub. L. 104-206, 110 Stat. 3009-546 (1996). Gruberg and West found that the one-year filing deadline disproportionately affects LGBT asylum seekers (*Humanitarian Diplomacy*, 22). See also

Schoenholtz, Schrag, and Ramji-Nogales's discussion of the one-year filing deadline (*Lives in the Balance,* 41–68).

52. Randazzo, "Social and Legal Barriers," 48.

53. Declaration of Carolina, dated July 2009, paragraph 49.

54. Declaration of Bárbara, dated May 2006, paragraph 19A.

55. Declaration of Verónica, dated 2005, paragraph 56.

56. Declaration of Patricia, dated August 2007, paragraph 22.

57. Declaration of Patricia, dated August 2007, paragraph 29.

58. This performance of good citizenship will never lead to legal U.S. citizenship, however, since this asylum seeker was granted withholding of removal. Withholding of removal has a higher standard of proof than asylum and does not provide applicants with the benefits of asylum: it does not allow successful applicants to apply for legal permanent residence status; it does not allow for travel outside the United States; and it does not grant benefits to spouses or children.

59. The expert witness declarations that I obtained for my archive in this chapter produce similar discourses about asylum applicants' countries of origin. In his testimony in support of Gloria's asylum claim, Stephen O. Murray states that "in the majority Mexican culture there is a category of males who are considered to be failed men," those who are "not conventionally masculine." Murray continues: "there is a cultural mandate to punish both gender and sexual nonconformity, either of which implies the other to most Mexicans" (Declaration of Stephen O. Murray, January 26, 2008, paragraph 6). However, Murray also notes that this is a political issue when he describes widespread police harassment and immunity: there is a "culture of police lawlessness that is more pervasive in Mexico than in any other country in the Americas now" (paragraph 8), in which "persecution, extortion, physical and sexual violence from the police is ubiquitous" (paragraph 9).

   Similarly, Debra Rodman, who provided an expert witness statement for Rosa, writes, "In Latin America, homophobia and transphobia are inextricably intertwined with the cultural phenomenon of machismo," and she argues that "While homosexuality is not illegal in Costa Rica, being a "gender variant"—an effeminate male homosexual, transvestite (cross-dresser), or transsexual or transgender (gender displacement)—is not socially acceptable" ("Expert Declaration in Support of the Asylum Application of R.S.," April 7, 2009, paragraph 15).

60. Nguyen, *The Gift of Freedom,* 20.

61. Nguyen, *The Gift of Freedom,* 5.

62. Nguyen, *The Gift of Freedom,* 181.

63. For an analysis of this tension in relation to asylum claims based on female genital surgery, see Piot, "Representing Africa."

64. Coutin, "The Oppressed, the Suspect, and the Citizen," 82.

65. Here I am referring to my point in chapter 1 about the determination of credibility being a highly subjective process as well as to the requirement of "reasonable fear." As Coutin notes, this requirement ignores the fact that people (i.e., most immigration judges) who have not experienced state repression will have difficulty understanding what that situation would feel like ("The Oppressed, the Suspect, and the Citizen," 83).

66. Grewal, *Transnational America,* 121. The limited objectives of many human rights discourses are susceptible to absorption within a neoliberal frame. As David Harvey

notes in *A Brief History of Neoliberalism*, because human rights regimes individualize rights and freedoms, they privilege the values of neoliberalism that center on the right to private property and profit.

67. Asylum law can also be critiqued at the level of the legality of the law itself, since policy makers and asylum adjudicators in the United States often ignore international human rights law. Key examples include the measures enacted in the Illegal Immigration Reform and Immigrant Responsibility Act of 1996, Pub. L. 104-206, 110 Stat. 3009-546 (1996), which established mandatory detention, expedited removal, and a one-year filing deadline, all of which have been legally challenged for violating international human rights law. According to the Refugee Act of 1980, Pub. L. 96-212, 94 Stat. 102 (1980). U.S. asylum decision-making should adhere to the standards of the *Refugee Handbook* issued by the United Nations High Commissioner for Refugees. Miller argues that asylum adjudicators in the United States "appear to have remained obdurately parochial in their incorporation of, or reference to, the decision-making philosophy of other countries on how to give effect to the common standards of the handbook" ("Gay Enough," 182n29). In contrast to the ways that courts in the United States ignore both the decision-making processes of other countries and international law, the decision-making of the United States is given a lot of attention by the courts of other countries, illustrating the legal imperialism and exceptionalism that structures U.S. legal proceedings.

68. Declaration of Verónica, dated 2005, paragraph 58.

69. Povinelli, *The Empire of Love,* 4.

70. Povinelli, *The Empire of Love,* 4.

71. Declaration of Gloria, dated 2009, paragraph 8. Other scholars' analyses of Mexican trans women's asylum testimonies found similar themes of family rejection and violence in schools, communities, and by the police. See Cheney et al., "Living Outside the Gender Box in Mexico," and Barnes, "Within the Asylum-Advocacy Nexus."

72. For example, the Transgender Law Center and the LGBT Clinic at Cornell University Law School has documented the pervasive violence and discrimination experienced by trans women and analyzes the social and cultural factors that lead to these forms of violence (*Report on Human Rights Conditions*). Similarly, Amnesty International has documented the gender-based violence that gay men and trans women experience in the countries of the Northern Triangle, as well as in Mexico, as asylum applicants ("No Safe Place"). Romero and Huerta found that high levels of gender-based violence in Honduras and El Salvador push many trans women to seek asylum in Mexico, where they also experience sexual and gender violence and discrimination but have more access to support networks and community ("Seeking Protection as a Transgender Refugee Woman").

73. This dynamic is sometimes reflected in academic scholarship. Nielan Barnes notes that much of existing scholarship on trans immigrants and asylum seekers fails to engages in a comparative analysis of the contexts of both the country of origin and the country granting asylum ("Within the Asylum-Advocacy Nexus," 6–7).

74. McKinley, "Cultural Culprits," 110.

75. Aizura, "The Persistence of Transgender Travel Narratives," 152.

76. Jay Prosser argues that the tension between always already being and becoming is the "founding dynamic" of transsexuality, a dynamic that is resolved through (and necessitated) by autobiography (*Second Skins*, 118–119). He writes that autobiography enables

transsexuals to create a coherent subject by joining the split of the past and the present: "over the course of the recounting, the narrative continuity, the trajectory of autobiography (tracing the story of a single self), promises, like the transsexual transition itself, to rejoin this split into a single, connected "life"" (102). Prosser's analysis of transsexual autobiography and his investment in what he calls "the politics of home," tend to universalize the transsexual subject and fail to engage with the ways these narratives are raced and classed.

77. Aizura, "The Persistence of Transgender Travel Narratives," 142.

78. Aizura, "The Persistence of Transgender Travel Narratives," 149.

79. Aizura, "The Persistence of Transgender Travel Narratives," 153.

80. Declaration of Sofía, no date, paragraph 47.

81. Declaration of Martina, no date, paragraph 44.

82. Declaration of Martina, no date, paragraph 60.

83. Declaration of Ines, dated August 2006, paragraph 28.

84. Mexico is a good example of this. The Transgender Law Center and Cornell University Law School's LGBT Clinic's country conditions report on Mexico was published in response to the denial of grants of asylum to Mexican trans women. Immigration judges were denying asylum applications with the assumption that recent legal advances for same-sex couples in Mexico have improved conditions for trans women. In fact, the report argues the opposite. The report's authors argue that these progressive legal changes have increased the visibility of LGBT communities and created a backlash in which instances of homophobic and transphobic violence have become more frequent, with trans women being particularly vulnerable (The Transgender Law Center and Cornell University Law School's LGBT Clinic, *Report on Human Rights Conditions*).

85. Inderpal Grewal emphasizes how the United States has used human rights as a "tool of geopolitics to assert its supremacy and its imperial projects" (*Transnational America*, 149).

86. Because the asylum declaration is a mediated text that develops from a collaborative process between attorney, translator, and applicant, it would be difficult to pinpoint agency with a particular person. In thinking about issues of agentival capacity in the context of asylum declarations, I am not thinking about the intentions of the asylum seeker per se (other than the intention to apply for asylum in the first place), but rather about what the declaration as a performative text itself does.

87. Saleh, "Transgender as a Humanitarian Category," 43.

88. Yurchak, *Everything Was Forever,* 25.

89. Yurchak, *Everything Was Forever,* 28.

90. Yurchak, *Everything Was Forever,* 28.

91. Berlant, *The Queen of America,* 11.

92. Berlant, *The Queen of America,* 1–2.

93. Somerville, "Notes toward a Queer History of Naturalization," 661.

94. Yurchak, *Everything Was Forever,* 23.

95. Yurchak, *Everything Was Forever,* 24–25.

96. As I note in chapter 1, these details are usually included in declarations as evidence of an immutable (trans)gender identity.

97. White, "Archives of Intimacy and Trauma," 87.

98. Declaration of Luisa, dated 2009, paragraph 43.

99. Shuman and Bohmer, "Representing Trauma," 406.

100. Bohmer and Shuman also point to the importance of "relevant" details in asylum testimonies. They argue that the narrative of persecution and torture experienced by an asylum applicant needs to have a specific plot that makes sense to asylum adjudicators: "For the officials this is a level on which things make sense, that is, it is in a narrative that has a beginning, a middle, and an end and contains the appropriate number of personal and political details" (Bohmer and Shuman, "Producing Epistemologies of Ignorance," 616).

101. Declaration of Ines, dated August 2006, paragraph 28.

102. Cvetkovich, *Archive of Feelings*, 16.

103. Declaration of Ines, dated August 2006, paragraph 11.

104. Ethnographic research on what "home" means for LGBT and SOGI migrants has documented how migrants' constructions of home often complicate neocolonialist hierarchies that position countries in the Global South as spaces of violence and oppression and the United States and Canada as spaces of liberation and safety. For example, Sandibel Borges highlights the ways that LGBTQ Latinx migrants in Los Angeles and LGBTQ Mexican migrant returnees in Mexico City engage in homing practices both with immediate family and with chosen families ("Home and Homing as Resistance"). And David A. B. Murray argues that narratives of home for SOGI refugees in Toronto entail "a tense, complex, and fluid arrangement between space, identity, and belonging, rendering possible multiple or simultaneous (albeit not always aligned complementarily) homes that track towards and away from dominant homonationalist discourses (White 2013)" ("The Challenge of Home," 138).

105. Declaration of Ana, no date, paragraph 29.

106. For example, see Miranda Joseph's *Against the Romance of Community,* where she argues that community is supplementary, not oppositional, to neoliberal political and capitalist economy.

107. D'Aoust, "Moving Stories: Love at the Border."

108. Povinelli, *Empire of Love*, 221.

109. Molina, *How Race Is Made in America,* 21–22.

110. Smiley, "Border Crossers."

111. Smiley, "Border Crossers."

112. Southern Poverty Law Center, "Federation for American Immigration Reform," http://www.splcenter.org/get-informed/intelligence-files/groups/federation-for-american-immigration-reform-fair#.UajyUoVSXig.

113. *SF Weekly* Letters: Web Extra, December 10, 2008, http://www.sfweekly.com/2008-12-10/news/sf-weekly-letters/.

114. Smiley, *SF Weekly* Letters: Web Extra, December 10, 2008, http://www.sfweekly.com/2008-12-10/news/sf-weekly-letters/.

115. Smiley, "*SF Weekly* Challenges *Guardian* Op-Ed on "Border Crossers."

116. Victoria Neilson (Immigration Equality), Noemi Calonje and Shannon Minter (National Center for Lesbian Rights), Dusty Araujo and Eric Berndt (National Immigrant Justice Center), *SF Weekly* Letters: Web Extra, December 10, 2008, http://www.sfweekly.com/2008-12-10/news/sf-weekly-letters/full/.

117. Transgender Advisory Group (TAG), *SF Weekly* Letters: Web Extra, December 10, 2008, http://www.sfweekly.com/2008-12-10/news/sf-weekly-letters/full/.

118. *SF Weekly* Letters: Web Extra, December 10, 2008, http://www.sfweekly.com/2008-12 -10/news/sf-weekly-letters/full.

119. El/La Para TransLatinas, https://ellaparatranslatinas.org/.

CHAPTER 3   TRANS CITIZENSHIP

1. *In re* Lovo, 23 I & N Dec. 746 (BIA 2005).

2. *In re Lovo* is cited as precedent in a later BIA decision that confirms immigration benefits for same-sex marriages. *In re Zeleniak*, 26 I & N Dec. 158 (BIA 2013) holds that the U.S. Supreme Court's decision in *United States v. Windsor*, 133 S. Ct. 2673 (2013), now requires the recognition of same-sex marriages for purposes of immigration benefits if those marriages were valid in the jurisdiction in which they were entered into.

3. See Cott, *Public Vows*; Pascoe, *What Comes Naturally*; Stevens, *Reproducing the State*; Schaeffer, *Love and Empire*; Franke, *Wedlocked*.

4. Kerry Abrams uses the term "citizen spouse" to describe the ways that marriage structures citizenship in the United States. She argues that the persistence of the nineteenth century derivative domicile rule means that the status of marriage often has a greater impact on a legal decision than the status of state citizenship (Abrams, "Citizen Spouse").

5. For a discussion of the cultural politics of neoliberalism and citizenship, see Duggan, *The Twilight of Equality?*, and Harvey, *A Brief History of Neoliberalism*. I am also drawing on Dan Irving's work on the role of neoliberalism and capitalist systems of power in the formation of trans subjectivities. He argues the "emphasis on the transsexual as an economically productive body" shapes contemporary theorizations of transsexual subjectivities and transsexuality is embedded within "a discourse of productive citizenship" (Irving, "Normalized Transgressions," 40, 49).

6. Latour, "Visualisation and Cognition."

7. In addition to a few discussions on legal news websites and blogs, the only reference to *In re Lovo* in the gay press I was able to find was an article in New York City's *Gay City News* (Leonard, "Panel Oks Transgendered Marriage").

8. These violations include overstaying an authorized stay or working without legal documents in the country; marriage will not "forgive" entry without inspection (crossing a border without documents).

9. *United States v. Windsor*, 133 S. Ct. 2673 (2013).

10. Defense of Marriage Act, Pub. L. 104–199, 110 Stat. 2419 (1996), § 3 Definition of Marriage.

11. *Obergefell v. Hodges,* 135 S. Ct. 2584 (2015).

12. *In re* Estate of Gardiner, 42 P.3d 120 (Kan 2002); *Littleton v. Prange*, 9 S.W.3d 223 (Tex. Ct. App. 1999), *cert. denied*, 531 U.S. 872 (2000); *Kantaras v. Kantaras*, 884 So. 2d 155 (Fla. Dist. Ct. App. 2004).

13. *M.T. v. J.T.*, 355 A.2d 204 (N.J. Superior Ct. Appellate Division 1976).

14. Tenn. Code Ann. § 68-3-203(d) (2006); *In re* Ladrach, 32 Ohio Misc. 2d 6, 513 N.E.2d 828 (Ohio Prob. Ct. 1987), which interpreted Ohio's birth certificate statute to be only a correction statute that does not encompass correction of sex on birth certificates for

individuals who have changed their sex by surgical procedure; Idaho Admin. Code r. 16.02.08.201 (2006). See Spade, "Documenting Gender," 832n181.

15. Spade, "Documenting Gender," 767–768.

16. For example, in California and Virginia, surgeries other than genital surgeries can be used as proof of sex reclassification for birth certificates (Spade, "Documenting Gender," 768).

17. The U.S. National Transgender Survey presents statistics about the prevalence of types of transition-related surgeries amongst various trans populations, and discusses the correlation between surgeries and the ability to change identity documents (James et al., *The Report of the 2015 U.S. Transgender Survey*, 87–89, 100–103).

18. Currah, "The Transgender Rights Imaginary," 712.

19. Currah, "The Transgender Rights Imaginary," 712.

20. Legal scholarship on trans marriage law tends to focus on the relationship of trans marriage to same-sex marriage, on marriage as part of a larger push for transgender equality, or on analysis of specific cases. Legal scholars who address trans marriage law include Rose, "Sign of a Wave?;" Flynn, "'Transforming' the Debate;" and Robson, "A Mere Switch or a Fundamental Change?" Less has been written about trans subjects at the intersection of immigration and marriage law, although some legal scholars have discussed the implications of *In re* Lovo. These include Martinez, "Open Window;" Haines, "Fear of the Queer Marriage;" Lorenz, "Transgender Immigration;" and Tomchin, "Bodies and Bureaucracy."

21. Neilson and Wertz, *Immigration Law and the Transgender Client.*

22. See Abrams, "Immigration Law and the Regulation of Marriage," for an extensive overview of how immigration law shapes marriage, as well as Pascoe, *What Comes Naturally*; Ngai, *Impossible Subjects*; and Inda, *Targeting Immigrants.*

23. Cott, *Public Vows*, 133.

24. The first federal legislation to restrict immigration was the Page Act, Pub. L. 43-141, 18 Stat. 477, Chap. 141 (1875), which criminalized the entry and importation of all prostitutes but targeted Chinese women immigrants. This was followed by the Chinese Exclusion Act, Pub. L. 47-126, 22 Stat. 58 (1882), which excluded most Chinese immigrants with the exception of a few categories of merchants, diplomats, and students, and prohibited the naturalization of Chinese immigrants. The Immigration Act of 1907, Pub. L. 59-96, 34 Stat. 898 (1907), mandated that any American woman who married a foreigner would lose her U.S. citizenship. The Johnson-Reed Act, Pub. L. 68-139, 43 Stat. 153 (1924), the first comprehensive immigration restriction law that created national origin quotas, established that the terms "husband" and "wife" did not apply to proxy marriages or "picture marriages," which were commonly used by Japanese and Korean male immigrants (Cott, *Public Vows*, 143–144, 151–154).

25. Villazor, "The Other Loving."

26. Personal Responsibility and Work Opportunity Reconciliation Act of 1996, Pub. L. 104-193, 110 Stat. 2105 (1996).

27. Anti-Terrorism and Effective Death Penalty Act (AEDPA), Pub. L. 104–132, 110 Stat. 1214 (1996).

28. Illegal Immigration Reform and Immigrant Responsibility Act of 1996, Division C of Pub. L. 104-208, 110 Stat. 3009-3546 (1996).

29. DOMA was a preemptive move against the possibility of Hawaii legalizing same-sex marriage. A state court decision in Hawaii promised to recognize same-sex marriage under Hawaiian law, but before the Hawaiian Supreme Court could rule on the issue, voters in 1998 amended the state constitution to define marriage as only between a man and a woman.

30. This section is questionable constitutionally, since each state is supposed to give "full faith and credit" to the public acts of other states.

31. The section states "the word 'marriage' means only a legal union between one man and one woman as husband and wife, and the word 'spouse' refers only to a person of the opposite sex who is a husband or a wife." Defense of Marriage Act, Pub. L. 104–199, 110 Stat. 2419 (1996), § 3 Definition of Marriage. This is the section that the U.S. Supreme Court declared unconstitutional in *United States v. Windsor*, 133 S. Ct. 2673 (2013).

32. PRWORA (Pub. L. 104-193, 110 Stat. 2105 (1996)) instigated the most extensive restructuring of the U.S. welfare state since the New Deal. The Act replaced Aid to Families with Dependent Children (AFDC), a federal entitlement program providing assistance to low-income single mothers, with Temporary Assistance to Needy Families (TANF), a federal block grant program that gave states control over welfare eligibility and benefits. PRWORA placed a five-year lifetime limit on benefits and required recipients to begin working after two years of receiving benefits. It instituted stricter eligibility requirements, reductions in immigrant welfare assistance, and promoted marriage through stricter paternity identification practices, enhanced enforcement of child support, and the discouragement of out-of-wedlock births. Gwendolyn Mink understands the PRWORA as the culmination of over thirty years of efforts by both Republicans and Democrats to suppress poor women's welfare rights (*Welfare's End*).

33. In fact, the legislation makes this claim quite explicitly at the end of the first section: "Therefore, in light of this demonstration of the crisis in our Nation, it is the sense of Congress that prevention of out-of-wedlock pregnancy and reduction in out-of-wedlock births are very important Government interests" (PRWORA, Pub. L. 104-193, 110 Stat. 2105, § 101 (1996)).

34. Scholars like Gwendolyn Mink and Dorothy Roberts have shown how historically state institutions have used marriage to structure social welfare programs that reinforce racial and gender stratification in the United States. See Mink, *Welfare's End*, and Roberts, *Killing the Black Body*.

35. Kandaswamy, "State Austerity," 707.

36. Kandaswamy, "State Austerity;" Reddy, *Freedom with Violence*, 182–218.

37. Luibhéid, "Sexuality, Migration, and the Shifting Line between Legal and Illegal Status," 300.

38. Spade, *Normal Life*, 13.

39. Johnson-Reed Act, Pub. L. 68-139, 43 Stat. 153 (1924).

40. AEDPA (Pub. L. 104–132, 110 Stat. 1214 (1996)) was a direct response to the 1995 bombing of a federal office building in Oklahoma City. The Act imposed mandatory detention and deportation—even for long-term U.S. residents—for drug offense convictions (including the possession of small amounts of marijuana) and eliminated the right of those facing deportation under these terms to judicial review. IIRIRA (Division C of Pub. L. 104–208, 110 Stat. 3009–3546) was embedded into a budget bill and signed into law with very little debate. This Act amended some of AEDPA's provisions, but overall

made things worse for noncitizen criminal offenders. IIRIRA made the law retroactive and reiterated the authority of the federal government to deport immigrants for minor crimes; it also restricted humanitarian relief and access to asylum, which I discuss in chapter I. The Act limited the power of federal courts to review deportation decisions and made detention mandatory for everyone in deportation hearings while simultaneously broadening the definition of "aggravated felony" (the level of crime that leads to deportation) to include many nonviolent offenses. AEDPA and IIRIRA worked as precursors to the USA PATRIOT Act of 2001 (Pub. L. 107-56, 115 Stat. 272), which was passed quickly after the terrorist attacks on September II and which restricts judicial review even further to encompass executive action.

41. Cacho, *Social Death*, 95.

42. Coutin, *Nations of Emigrants*, 8.

43. *American Baptist Churches v. Thornburgh*, 760 F. Supp. 796 (N.D. Cal. 1991).

44. Immigration Act of 1990, Pub. L. 101-649, 104 Stat. 4978 (1990).

45. Nicaraguan Adjustment and Central American Relief Act in 1997, Pub. L. 105-100, title II, III Stat. 2193 (1997).

46. Coutin, *Nations of Emigrants*, 61–72.

47. Coutin, *Nations of Emigrants*, 8–9.

48. Pierce and Bolter, *Dismantling and Reconstructing the U.S. Immigration System*, 82–83.

49. Lahoud, "Ninth Circuit Allows for the End of Temporary Protected Status."

50. Pierce and Bolter, *Dismantling and Reconstructing the U.S. Immigration System*, 68–77.

51. *In re Lovo*, 23 I & N Dec. 746, 747 (BIA 2005). Many of the laws regulating changing sex designation on identification documents depend on the medical model of transsexuality and require evidence of surgery. These surgery requirements reflect sexist and homophobic standards. Many trans people do not want or cannot afford surgery. Trans scholars and advocates point out that genital status, in particular, is not relevant in day-to-day gendered activities for both trans and non-trans people. For a critique of surgery standards, see Spade, "Resisting Medicine," 16–26.

52. Neilson and Wertz, *Immigration Law*, 37.

53. See Jasbir Puar's *Terrorist Assemblages* for analysis of the configurations of sexuality, race, gender, and nation that animate contemporary discourses of national security and terrorism.

54. Beauchamp, *Going Stealth*, 7.

55. William R. Yates, "Adjudication of Petitions and Applications Filed by or on Behalf of, or Document Requests by, Transsexual Individuals," Interoffice Memorandum, U.S. Citizenship and Immigration Services, April 16, 2004.

56. Yates, "Adjudication of Petitions," 1.

57. Yates, "Adjudication of Petitions," 2.

58. Yates, "Adjudication of Petitions," 2.

59. This policy only applies to marriages. The Yates memo clearly states that in the adjudication of other immigration petitions or applications for which the gender of the individual is not relevant, USCIS personnel will not take into account an applicant's trans status. For example, the applications of trans immigrants with work visas for a permanent resident card will be considered, as long as the individual can provide the required medical and legal documentation for a change of name and gender.

60. The memo instructs USCIS officers to look for "a name that would normally be used by the opposite sex" (Yates, "Adjudication of Petitions," 3). This "objective indicator" of course rests on the assumption that the gender associated with a name is self-evident, an assumption that becomes even more complicated in an immigration context in which names may reflect specific linguistic and cultural norms with which the USCIS officer may not be familiar.

61. In her supplemental brief in support of Lovo-Ciccone's appeal, ACLU attorney Sharon M. McGowan remarks on the fact that the director did not cite the Yates memo in his initial denial, and notes that in response to Lovo-Ciccone's appeal, the federal government does cite the memo in support of the director's decision. McGowan argues that the Yates memo and other USCIS memoranda on marriages involving trans people are unconstitutional because they violate the due process and equal protection clauses. *Supplemental Brief in Support of Petitioner's Appeal, In re Gia Teresa Ciccone-Lovo and Jose Mauricio Lovo-Lara*, A95-076-067 (Nebraska Service Center).

62. *In re* Lovo, 747.

63. *In re* Lovo, 748.

64. *In re* Lovo, 753.

65. The BIA found that the marriage can be the basis for benefits under section 201(b)(2)(A)(i) of the Immigration and Nationality Act, 8 U.S.C. § 1151(b)(2)(A)(i) (2000).

66. *In re* Lovo, 753.

67. *In re* Lovo, 753n5.

68. Neilson and Wertz, *Immigration Law and the Transgender Client*, 39.

69. Chávez, "Homonormativity and Violence against Immigrants," 132.

70. My citations in this chapter come from the published book version of *Immigration Law and the Transgender Client*, but the complete text was also available on Immigration Equality's website. After the Supreme Court decisions in *Windsor v. United States*, 133 S. Ct. 2673 (2013), and *Obergefell v. Hodges*, 135 S. Ct. 2584 (2015), the content of the handbook on the website was updated and reorganized.

71. Neilson and Wertz, *Immigration Law and the Transgender Client*, 39.

72. *In re* Widener, A95-347-685, 2004 WL 2375065 (BIA Sept. 21, 2004), 10.

73. *In re* Widener, A95-347-685, 2004 WL 2375065 (BIA Sept. 21, 2004), 9.

74. *In re* Widener, A95-347-685, 2004 WL 2375065 (BIA Sept. 21, 2004), 9.

75. Neilson and Wertz, *Immigration Law and the Transgender Client*, 49.

76. This illustrates the narrowness of struggles for legal rights, not only in terms of separating out trans struggles from lesbian and gay struggles but also in terms of separating queer and trans justice from immigration justice. Immigration Equality, one of the authors of *Immigration Law and the Transgender Client*, spearheaded the push for legal recognition of same-sex binational couples in the United States, which was largely disconnected from the larger immigrant justice movement. Karma R. Chávez points out that after the 2013 *Windsor v. United States* U.S. Supreme Court decision, which allowed U.S. citizens and legal permanent residents who lived in states with legal marriage to sponsor their same-sex partners for immigration, the leadership team of Immigration Equality left the organization. Chávez argues that this "reflects the way the gay and lesbian movement relied on the immigration movement to achieve its ends, but then abandoned immigrants not connected to U.S. citizens as

the broader struggle for immigration overhaul continues" ("Homonormativity and Violence against Immigrants," 133).

77. See for example, Saleh, "Transgender as a Humanitarian Category" and Camminga, *Transgender Refugees and the Imagined South Africa.*

78. Aizura, "Transnational Transgender Rights and Immigration Law," 141.

79. Aizura, "Transnational Transgender Rights and Immigration Law," 145.

80. Aizura, "Transnational Transgender Rights and Immigration Law," 140.

81. Luibhéid, "Sexuality, Migration, and the Shifting Line Between Legal and Illegal Status," 304.

82. IIRIRA requires the U.S. citizen to prove an annual income of at least 125 percent of the U.S. poverty line income in order to sponsor the migrant spouse, while PRWORA restricts welfare and public benefits for immigrants (IIRIRA, Division C of Pub. L. 104–208, 110 Stat. 3009–3546, Sec. 551. Requirements for Sponsor's Affidavit of Support).

83. Tomchin, "Bodies and Bureaucracy," 818.

84. *Kantaras v. Kantaras*, 884 So. 2d 155 (Fla. Dist. Ct. App. 2004).

85. Neilson and Wertz, *Immigration Law*, 46.

86. Neilson and Wertz, *Immigration Law*, 47.

87. In 2013, the USCIS began to develop the *USCIS Policy Manual*, a centralized online repository for its immigration policies. In May 2020, the USCIS retired its *Adjudicator's Field Manual* (AFM), and incorporated its content into the USCIS Policy Manual: https://www.uscis.gov/policy-manual.

88. U.S. Citizenship and Immigration Services, "PM-602-0061: Adjudication of Immigration Benefits for Transgender Individuals; Addition of *Adjudicator's Field Manual* (AFM) Subchapter 10.22 and Revisions to AFM Subchapter 21.3 (AFM Updated AD12-02)," Policy Memorandum, April 10, 2012. https://www.uscis.gov/sites/default/files/document/memos/Transgender_FINAL.pdf.

89. Sharpe, *Transgender Jurisprudence.*

90. USCIS, Policy Memorandum, April 10, 2012, 2.

91. USCIS, Policy Memorandum, April 10, 2012, 4.

92. USCIS, Policy Memorandum, April 10, 2012, 5.

93. USCIS, Policy Memorandum, April 10, 2012, 5.

94. Immigration Equality and National Center for Transgender Equality, "Victory for Trans Immigration Documents and Marriage Benefits: NCTE and Immigration Equality Applaud President Obama for Taking Important Action," Press release, April 13, 2012, https://web.archive.org/web/20120419191217/https://www.immigrationequality.org/2012/04/victory-for-trans-immigration-documents-marriage-benefits/.

CHAPTER 4   TRANSFER POINTS

1. Arellano was arrested by police for driving under the influence on April 9, 2007, and placed in deportation proceedings because she was undocumented (Ehrenreich, "Death on Terminal Island").

2. See, for example, Hernandez, "A Lethal Limbo"; Hernandez, "Denied Medication, AIDS Patient Dies in ICE Custody"; Feinberg, "Death of Trans Immigrant in Detention Forges United Protests"; Fears, "3 Jailed Immigrants Die in a Month."

3. Unfortunately it has not been the last. Since Arellano's death in 2007, there have been more reported deaths of trans women in ICE custody. In 2017, Roxsana Hernandez, a trans asylum seeker from Honduras, died under similar circumstances in the Cibola County Correctional Center, run by CoreCivic.

4. Human Rights Watch recounts Arellano's story in detail in its report *Chronic Indifference: HIV/AIDS Services for Immigrants Detained by the United States.*

5. Bernstein, "New Scrutiny as Immigrants Die in Custody"; Fears, "Illegal Immigrants Received Poor Care in Jail."

6. *Detention and Removal: Immigration Detainee Medical Care, Before the Immigration, Citizenship, Refugees, Border Security, and International Law Subcommittee of the Committee on the Judiciary,* 110th Cong. (2007).

7. I found Saidiya Hartman's discussion of the ethics of representing the violence of slavery in *Scenes of Subjection* helpful for my thinking here. Hartman grapples with the ways that these representations often uncritically present the spectacle of "the slave's ravaged body" (3). She asks, "In light of this, how does one give expression to these outrages without exacerbating the indifference to suffering that is the consequence of the benumbing spectacle or contend with the narcissistic identification that obliterates the other or the prurience that too often is the response to such display?" (Hartman, *Scenes of Subjection,* 4).

8. Snorton and Haritaworn, "Trans Necropolitics," 6.

9. Ehrenreich highlights this when he notes that the advocacy organizations that "championed" Arellano after she died were the same organizations who told Olga Arellano, Arellano's mother, that they could not help her when Olga called them for assistance in the last few weeks of her daughter's life ("Death on Terminal Island," 10).

10. Sarah Lamble discusses this universal trans subject in relation to the Transgender Day of Remembrance. She argues that the focus on transphobia as the "definitive cause of violence" obscures how race and class increase the vulnerability of particular gender variant populations to violence and that as a result, "transgender bodies are universalized along a singular identity plane of victimhood and rendered visible primarily through the violence that is acted upon them" (Lamble, "Retelling Racialized Violence," 24).

11. Arellano's death continues to circulate in the second decade of the twenty-first century. For example, her experience in detention is described at length in the U.S. Commission on Civil Rights' September 2015 Statutory Enforcement Report, *With Liberty and Justice for All.* The news coverage of trans migrants in ICE custody has increased since 2007. Many media sources, from Fusion and Buzzfeed to the *Advocate* and the *New York Times* now regularly report on trans migrants in detention. This increased coverage results from the continued activism and advocacy from grassroots organizations and trans legal organizations.

12. The complete PBNDS 2011 are available at https://www.ice.gov/detain/detention-management/2011. In 2016, ICE revised the some of these detention standards to be compliant with federal regulations, and the standards available on their website reflect these updates.

13. I am indebted to the political and theoretical work of abolitionist grassroots organizations like Critical Resistance in my analysis of reformist reforms.

14. Sheller and Urry, "The New Mobilities Paradigm," 210.

15. As I discuss in the Introduction and in chapter 1, the Illegal Immigration Reform and Immigrant Responsibility Act of 1996 requires the routine detention of asylum

seekers while their cases proceed, which means that trans migrants who are seeking asylum or other forms of relief, such as withholding from removal, will be detained with "criminal aliens" and other undocumented immigrants who are facing deportation proceedings as well as with nonimmigrants who are incarcerated on criminal charges.

16. Cresswell, *On the Move,* 151.

17. Cresswell argues that U.S. Supreme Court justices have constructed corporeal mobility as a right of citizenship, despite the absence of formal constitutional protections (*On the Move,* 151–159). For example, *Crandell v. Nevada,* 73 U.S. 35 (1865), centered on the question of whether a tax on passengers leaving the state of Nevada on public transport was constitutional. Cresswell argues that this case articulated a particular relationship between the federal government and its citizens, such that "citizens needed to be able to travel throughout the country in order to be citizens" (*On the Move,* 152). Another case, *United States v. Guest,* 383 U.S. 745 (1966), addressed the issue of whether the extended harassment of Black citizens in Athens, Georgia, by a group of white men denied the Black citizens their constitutional and legal rights and privileges. The opinion of the Court by Justice Stewart argued that the group of white men had conspired to deny Black citizens their right to travel freely to and from the state of Georgia on interstate highways. Cresswell notes that Justice Stewart affirms the freedom to travel as a basic right under the Constitution even as he admits that the source of such a right is not clear (*On the Move,* 155).

18. Engin Isin makes this argument about the logic of exclusion in relation to citizenship in *Being Political: Genealogies of Citizenship.*

19. De Genova, "The Deportation Regime," 50.

20. Loyd, Burridge, and Mitchelson, "Thinking (and Moving) Beyond Walls and Cages," 90.

21. Cornelisse, "Immigration Detention and the Territoriality of Universal Rights," 101.

22. Inda and Dowling, "Introduction: Governing Migrant Illegality," 5.

23. Inda and Dowling, "Introduction: Governing Migrant Illegality," 4.

24. Keaney and Friedland, "ICE ACCESS Programs." The Criminal Alien Program (CAP) allows ICE agents to screen inmates in federal, state, and local jails and prisons for immigration status. Secure Communities enables local and state police to run the fingerprints of individuals they arrest through DHS immigration databases. The 287(g) program empowers state and local enforcement agencies to function as immigration agents. For an in-depth analysis of the impact of the CAP on migrants and how mass incarceration has transformed immigration enforcement in the United States, see Macías-Rojas, *From Deportation to Prison.*

25. Transactional Records Access Clearinghouse, *Deportations Under ICE's Secure Communities Program.*

26. U.S. Customs and Border Protection, "DHS Launches 'Operation Streamline II': Enforcement Effort Focusing on Prosecuting and Removing Illegal Aliens in Del Rio, Texas," News release, December 16, 2005, http://www.cpb.gov/xp/cgov/newsroom/news _releases/archives/2005_press_releases/122005/12162005.xml. "Operation Streamline" launched in Texas in 2005 but has spread throughout the Southwest border and allows DHS to criminally prosecute immigrants for illegal entry. This means that migrants who are caught crossing the border for the first time can receive misdemeanor charges resulting in up to six months in jail and those caught (re)entering

after they have been deported can be charged with felonies that can carry up to twenty years in prison.

27. Inda and Dowling, "Governing Migrant Illegality," 18.

28. De Genova, "Migrant 'Illegality' and Deportability in Everyday Life;" Golash-Boza, *Deported*.

29. Gehi, "Struggles From the Margins," 323. Dean Spade also outlines the various means by which trans immigrants are often targeted for crimes that lead to detention ("Compliance Is Gendered," 217, 229, 232). See also Medina, "Immigrating While Trans."

30. The Sylvia Rivera Law Project has produced a helpful flowchart that diagrams how trans immigrants are disproportionately detained and deported. "Disproportionate Deportation," https://srlp.org/resources/flow-chart-disproportionate-deportation/.

31. Spade, *Normal Life*, 146–147.

32. Hickey, "Policing Gender and Sexuality." See also James et al., *U.S. Transgender Survey*.

33. Gehi, "Gendered (In)security," 369–372.

34. Human Rights Watch, *'Do You See How Much I'm Suffering Here?,'* 8–9.

35. Spade, *Normal Life*, 148.

36. Bernstein, "U.S. to Reform Policy on Detention for Immigrants." See César Cuauhtémoc García Hernández's "Immigration Detention as Punishment" for an analysis of the punitive origins of the immigration detention system.

37. Schriro, *Immigration Detention*. The report was based on information gathered from tours of twenty-five facilities; discussion with detained migrants and employees; meetings with NGOs and federal, state, and local officials; reviews of data and reports from government agencies (Government Accountability Office, Department of Homeland Security, the United Nations); the American Bar Association; and human rights organizations.

38. Schriro, *Immigration Detention*, 2.

39. Schriro, *Immigration Detention*, 4.

40. Schriro, *Immigration Detention*, 21.

41. Spade, "Laws as Tactics," 55–56.

42. *Moving Towards More Effective Immigration Detention Management, Before the Subcommittee on Border, Maritime, and Global Counterterrorism of the Committee on Homeland Security*, 111th Cong. 2 (2009) (statement of Mark E. Souder, congressional Republican, Indiana).

43. Schriro, *Immigration Detention*, 2.

44. Schriro, *Immigration Detention*, 4.

45. Schriro, *Immigration Detention*, 5.

46. The PBNDS apply to the network of dedicated immigration facilities in the United States. ICE has a separate set of standards for the state and local facilities (jails, prisons, and United States Marshals Service facilities) with which the agency contracts to house detained immigrants. These *National Detention Standards for Non-Dedicated Facilities* can be found at https://www.ice.gov/detain/detention-management/2019.

47. PBNDS 2011, Preface, i.

48. This is evidenced by the first footnote in each section of the PBNDS, which references the corresponding section of the ACA Standards. The footnotes cite the ACA's *Performance-based Standards for Adult Local Detention Facilities*, 4th ed. (Lanham, MD: American Correctional Association, 2004).

NOTES TO PAGES 98-100

49. PBNDS 2011, Preface, i.

50. Victoria Neilson, "DHS Issues New Detention Standards," March 1, 2012, Press release, http://www.immigrationequality.org/2012/03/dhs-issues-new-detention-standards/ (no longer available).

51. PBNDS 2011, sec. 7.5 Definitions, 394.

52. ICE revised the PBNDS 2011 in 2016 to be compliant with federal regulations, namely, with regard to the Prison Rape Elimination Act of 2003, Pub. L. 108-79, 117 Stat. 972 (2003), and section 504 of the Rehabilitation Act of 1973, Pub. L. 93-112, 87 Stat. 355 (1973), which prohibits discrimination on the basis of a disability and requires accommodations for persons with disabilities. The addition of section 2.11 "Sexual Abuse and Assault Prevention and Intervention" in the 2016 revisions mentions transgender migrants in several places. The revised PBNDS are available at https://www.ice.gov /doclib/detention-standards/2011/pbnds2011r2016.pdf.

53. National Immigrant Justice Center and Physicians for Human Rights, *Invisible in Isolation*.

54. National Immigrant Justice Center and Physicians for Human Rights, *Invisible in Isolation*, 19.

55. For example, McHenry County Jail in Illinois has a policy of segregating HIV-positive migrants when "detainee/inmate behavior may require staff to take actions that may tend to identify them as HIV-positive [. . .] In such cases, the health and safety of staff and other detainees/inmates will take precedence over the detainee/inmate's right to freedom of movement or privacy, and that individual may be confined in Administrative Segregation indefinitely for preventive purposes" (cited in National Immigrant Justice Center and Physicians for Human Rights, *Invisible in Isolation*, 20).

56. National Immigrant Justice Center (NIJC) and Physicians for Human Rights (PHR) found that "solitary confinement in immigration detention facilities is often arbitrarily applied, significantly overused, harmful to detainees' health, and inadequately monitored" (*Invisible in Isolation*, 4). In its 2011 complaint to the DHS's Office for Civil Rights and Civil Liberties on behalf of thirteen gay and trans detained migrants, the National Immigrant Justice Center notes that at least one court, *Medina-Tejada v. Sacramento County* (2006 WL 463158 (E.D. Cal. 2006)), has found that a blanket policy of administrative segregation for trans migrants in detention, without specifying the particular need to do so, violates due process rights ("Submission of Civil Rights Complaints," 5). See also Gruberg, *Dignity Denied*.

57. The NIJC and PHR found that detained migrants in solitary confinement were more vulnerable to excessive force, harassment, and abuse by corrections officers (National Immigrant Justice Center and Physicians for Human Rights, *Invisible in Isolation*, 11). For detained trans migrants, this harassment often takes the form of purposeful misrecognition of gender identity, for example, guards insisting on calling trans women "mister" or "sir."

58. The dangers of solitary confinement have been well documented in prison populations. The effects of what is known as "prison psychosis"—the psychological effects of solitary confinement—may be irreversible after prolonged periods of isolation. The harmful effects of solitary confinement can be more pronounced for individuals who have already suffered trauma such as detained migrants who have survived persecution and torture in their countries of origin or sexual and physical violence in the United States (National Immigrant Justice Center and Physicians for Human Rights, *Invisible in Isolation*, 12–13). See Stop Prisoner Rape's report, *In the Shadows*, for a

discussion of the trauma that trans migrants experience while in detention and their experiences with post-traumatic stress disorder afterward.

59. PBNDS 2011, sec. 2.2 Custody Classification System, 62.

60. PBNDS 2011, sec. 2.2 Custody Classification System, 64.

61. PBNDS 2011, sec. 2.2 Custody Classification System, 64.

62. PBNDS 2011, Appendix 2.2.A: ICE Custody Classification Worksheet, 69.

63. PBNDS 2011, Appendix 2.2.A: ICE Custody Classification Worksheet, 70–71.

64. Detained migrants classified as "medium-low" may be housed with those classified as "low-custody" and detained migrants classified as "medium-high" may be housed with those classified as "high-custody," but the standards note that "Low custody individuals may never be housed with high custody individuals, or medium custody individuals who have any history of assaultive or combative behavior" (PBNDS 2011, Appendix 2.2.A: ICE Custody Classification Worksheet, 710).

65. Arkles, "Safety and Solidarity," 518.

66. Dayan, "Held in the Body of the State," 197. Published under Joan Dayan.

67. Conlon and Hienstra, "Mobility and Materialisation of the Carceral."

68. Dayan, "Held in the Body of the State," 209.

69. Dayan, "Held in the Body of the State," 203.

70. Office of Inspector General, Department of Homeland Security, *U.S. Immigration and Customs Enforcement's Alternatives to Detention (Revised)*, 4–5, 11. For more detailed analysis of the RCA, see Koulish, "Using Risk to Assess the Legal Violence of Mandatory Detention."

71. Gruberg, "No Way Out," and Gruberg, "ICE Officers Overwhelmingly Use Their Discretion to Detain LGBT Immigrants."

72. *Detention and Removal: Immigration Detainee Medical Care, Before the Immigration, Citizenship, Refugees, Border Security, and International Law Subcommittee of the Committee on the Judiciary*, 110th Cong. 54 (2007) (statement of Tom Jawatz, ACLU).

73. Ehrenreich, "Death on Terminal Island."

74. Martin, "Getting Out and Getting In," 155.

75. Human Rights Watch, *Locked Up Far Away*, 21.

76. Attorneys are not usually notified before their clients are transferred. Before ICE launched an online tracking system for migrants in detention in 2010, attorneys would have to spend hours or days tracking down clients who had been suddenly transferred.

77. Human Rights Watch, *A Costly Move*, 2.

78. Human Rights Watch, *Chronic Indifference*, 5.

79. PBNDS 2011, sec. 2.1 Admission and Release, 55. Emphasis in the original.

80. PBNDS 2011, sec. 2.10 Searches of Detainees, 124–125.

81. For one example, see the complaint of Community Initiatives for Visiting Immigrants in Confinement (CIVIC) in January 2015 to the DHS's Office for Civil Rights and Civil Liberties on behalf of thirty-one trans women held in ICE custody in the Santa Ana City Jail (CIVIC, "Complaint").

82. See especially, Human Rights Watch, *'Do You See How Much I'm Suffering Here?,'* 28–31.

83. Thomas Homan, "Further Guidance Regarding the Care of Transgender Detainees," Interoffice Memorandum, U.S. Citizenship and Immigration Services, June 19, 2015,

https://www.ice.gov/sites/default/files/documents/Document/2015/TransgenderCare
Memorandum.pdf.

84. The memo states that it "may not be relied upon to create any right or benefit, substantive or procedural" (Homan, "Further Guidance Regarding the Care of Transgender Detainees," 6).

85. Homan, "Further Guidance Regarding the Care of Transgender Detainees," 2.

86. Homan, "Further Guidance Regarding the Care of Transgender Detainees," 3.

87. Homan, "Further Guidance Regarding the Care of Transgender Detainees," 4.

88. *Detention and Removal: Immigration Detainee Medical Care, Before the Immigration, Citizenship, Refugees, Border Security, and International Law Subcommittee of the Committee
on the Judiciary*, 110th Cong. 1–2 (2007) (statement of Zoe Lofgren, Chairwoman of the
Subcommittee, congressional Democrat, California).

89. Johnson-Reed Act, Pub. L. 68-139, 43 Stat. 153 (1924).

90. Ngai, *Impossible Subjects*, 3.

91. Ngai, *Impossible Subjects*, 4. Emphasis in the original.

92. Detention and Removal Operations (DRO) was renamed Enforcement and Removal
Operations (ERO) in 2010.

93. *Detention and Removal: Immigration Detainee Medical Care, Before the Immigration, Citizenship, Refugees, Border Security, and International Law Subcommittee of the Committee
on the Judiciary*, 110th Cong. 6 (2007) (statement of Gary Mead, Assistant Director for
Detention and Removal Operations (DRO) for U.S. Immigration and Customs Enforcement, and Timothy Shack, M.D., Medical Director of Immigrant Health Services).

94. *Detention and Removal: Immigration Detainee Medical Care, Before the Immigration, Citizenship, Refugees, Border Security, and International Law Subcommittee of the Committee
on the Judiciary*, 110th Cong. 3 (2007) (statement of Steve King, congressional Republican, Iowa).

95. *Problems with Immigration Detainee Medical Care, Before the Subcommittee on Immigra-
tion, Citizenship, Refugees, Border Security, and International Law of the Committee on the
Judiciary*, 110th Cong. 5 (2008) (statement of Steve King, congressional Republican,
Iowa).

96. Cacho, *Social Death*, 6.

97. PBNDS 2011, sec. 4.3 Medical Care, 239.

98. PBNDS 2011, sec. 4.3 Medical Care, 243.

99. PBNDS 2011, sec. 4.3 Medical Care, 249.

100. The U.S. Transgender Survey, conducted by the National Transgender Center for
Equality, documents disparities in health and health care among trans people in the
United States. The survey's key findings about trans people's access to routine and
transition-related health care included the following: 25 percent of respondents had
problems with insurance coverage, such as being denied coverage for a transition-
related care; 33 percent of respondents had had a negative encounter with a health
care provider in the previous year; and although 78 percent of respondents wanted
hormone therapy, only 49 percent had received access to hormone therapy (James
et al., *U.S. Transgender Survey*, 93).

101. Roxsana Hernandez's case was widely reported and taken up by trans immigrant
activist organizations. In November 2018, the Transgender Law Center and the Law
Office of Andrew R. Free filed a Notice of Wrongful Death Tort Claim in New Mexico

to hold all parties accountable for her death. See https://transgenderlawcenter.org /legal/immigration/roxsana.

102. Human Rights Watch, *Chronic Indifference*, 5. See also Human Rights Watch, *"Do You See How Much I'm Suffering Here?"*, 42–44.

103. Human Rights Watch, *Chronic Indifference*, 5. See also Human Rights Watch, *"Do You See How Much I'm Suffering Here?"*, 42–44.

104. Human Rights Watch, *"Do You See How Much I'm Suffering Here?"*, 45–47.

105. The Trump administration began separating children from families crossing the U.S.–Mexico border without legal documentation in October 2017. See Human Rights Watch, "Q&A: Trump Administration's 'Zero Tolerance' Immigration Policy, August 16, 2018, https://www.hrw.org/news/2018/08/16/qa-trump-administrations-zero-tolerance -immigration-policy.

106. See generally, Angela Davis's work on prisons and the work of Critical Resistance. Also see Stanley and Smith, eds., *Captive Genders*.

107. Aizura, "Affective Vulnerability and Transgender Exceptionalism," 123.

108. The legal question of whether detained migrants can claim constitutional protections is unclear. Detained migrants are not explicitly covered by the Eighth Amendment's protections against cruel and unusual punishment, since they are in civil detention rather than criminal detention. The Due Process Clause of the Fifth Amendment may apply to detained migrants, according to the U.S. Commission on Civil Rights. The Commission notes that under the Fifth Amendment, (1) immigrants should not be detained in a manner that violates the Due Process clause; (2) immigrants should not be detained in a manner comparable to punitive incarceration; (3) immigrants should be afforded the ability to obtain legal counsel; and (4) immigrants should have the opportunity to meet with that legal counsel. Based on the Commission's own research and its survey of documented human rights reports and news articles, it found that the federal government's policies, practices, and treatment of detained migrants may be violating Due Process protections; that is, it is possible that a court would find the federal government to be in violation of detained migrants' due process rights (U.S. Commission on Civil Rights, *With Liberty and Justice for All*, 94–123).

109. Dean Spade argues for the importance of using law reform tactically and notes that "legal help can be an excellent point of politicization for trans people, turning individual experiences of harm into a shared understanding of collective struggle" (*Normal Life*, 39). This might be another way to think about the potential value of immigration detention standards, even though they are not binding and serve to justify the continued existence of immigration detention facilities. Arkles, Gehi, and Redfield also discuss this potential in terms of what they call "lawyering for empowerment" ("The Role of Lawyers in Trans Liberation," 579, 601).

110. See, for example, the National Immigrant Justice Center and Detention Watch Network, *Lives in Peril*.

111. U.S. Commission on Civil Rights, *With Liberty and Justice for All*.

112. For example, CoreCivic reference their adherence to the PBNDS in their response to the death of Roxsana Hernandez, a trans asylum seeker from Honduras who died in ICE custody in the Cibola County Correctional Center in May 2018. See "CoreCivic Statement Regarding Roxsana Hernandez," https://www.corecivic.com/-temporary -slug-f146d3c6-81e0-4834-92f6-65aae75958aa.

113. Patton, "Tremble, Hetero Swine!," 145.

114. Patton, "Tremble, Hetero Swine!," 173.

115. See Myrl Beam's *Gay, Inc.: The Nonprofitization of Queer Politics* for analysis of how the LGBT nonprofit system participates in the continuation of inequalities that activists are trying to challenge.

116. Foucault, "Governmentality," 95.

117. *Holiday on ICE: The U.S. Department of Homeland Security's New Immigration Detention Standards, Before the Subcommittee on Immigration Policy and Enforcement of the Committee on the Judiciary*, 112th Cong. 11 (2012) (statement of Lamar Smith, Chairman of the Committee on the Judiciary, congressional Republican, Texas).

118. Those objecting included congressional Democrat Zoe Lofgren (California), who had chaired several hearings in 2007 and 2008 on the lack of medical care in detention facilities; congressional Democrat John Conyers (Michigan); and writer Edwidge Danticat, whose uncle sought asylum in the United States but died in ICE custody after being denied his prescription medication. Danticat published an op-ed in the *New York Times* the day of the hearing, "Detention Is No Holiday."

119. *Holiday on ICE: The U.S. Department of Homeland Security's New Immigration Detention Standards, Before the Subcommittee on Immigration Policy and Enforcement of the Committee on the Judiciary*, 112th Cong. 12 (2012) (statement of Lamar Smith, Chairman of the Committee on the Judiciary, congressional Republican, Texas).

120. Nguyen, *The Gift of Freedom*, 20.

121. Cacho, *Social Death*, 8.

122. For example, Stannow, "When Good Isn't Enough." See also Hoffman, "Transgender Immigrants Still Face Rampant Physical and Sexual Abuse in US Detention Centers."

123. Victoria Neilson, "DHS Issues New Detention Standards," March 1, 2012, Press release, accessed March 13, 2013, http://immigrationequality.org/2012/03/dhs-issues-new-detention-standards. No longer available.

124. Morris, "Power, Capital, and Immigration Detention Rights," 417.

125. The opening of the Karnes County Civil Detention Center received a lot of sensationalist, anti-immigrant coverage from mainstream media sources, which represented it as a "hotel" for detained migrants. See del Bosque, "The Trouble with Karnes County's ICE 'Hotel.'"

   The T. Don Hutto Residential Center, a former state prison near Austin, Texas that is run for profit by the Corrections Corporation of America, was used as a family detention facility from 2006 to 2009 and received critical news coverage and an ACLU lawsuit for its treatment of young children. See Bernstein, "U.S. to Reform Policy on Detention for Immigrants." Since 2009, it has been used as an immigration detention center for women. See "Fact Sheet: T. Don Hutto Residential Center," http://www.ice.gov/news/library/factsheets/facilities-hutto.htm.

126. The creation of a special protective custody unit at the Santa Ana County Jail was a response to a mass civil complaint filed by the National Immigrant Justice Center in April 2011. This unit can house sixty-four gay and trans detained migrants, segregated from the rest of the jail population, and has two-person cells, an indoor day room with natural lighting, and a small outdoor recreational space (Fiahlo, "A Model Immigration Detention Facility for LGBTI?"). Trans immigrant activism led to the ending of this contract with ICE.

127. Rivas, "Immigration Officials to Start Sending Transgender Women to the Middle of Texas."

128. #Not1More Campaign, "ICE Issues New Guidance on Transgender Detainees," Press release, June 29, 2015, https://transgenderlawcenter.org/archives/11723.

CODA

1. In their discussion of the targeting of trans migrants as "criminal aliens," Pooja Gehi and Gabriel Arkles argue for a trans immigration politics that engages with multiple resistance strategies simultaneously—high-impact litigation, bystander intervention, civil disobedience, education, and mutual aid—while being attentive to their effects on those (trans) migrants who are most vulnerable ("The Tacit Targeting," 68).

2. *Atmospheres of Violence*, 6.

3. DeFilippis, "'Building the World That We Want to Live in';" Zecena, "Shameless Interruptions;" DasGupta, "Rescripting Trauma."

4. For a report on the changes made to the immigration system during the Trump administration, see Sarah Pierce and Jessica Bolter, *Dismantling and Reconstructing the U.S. Immigration System.*

5. Aizura also discusses how the problems of relying on a politics of recognition became especially obvious with the establishment of the Trump administration ("Introduction").

6. Kwong, "Immigrant Rights Activists Celebrate ICE Notice to Terminate Santa Ana Jail Contract."

7. DeFilippis, "'Building the world that we want to live in,'" 109.

8. Mijente is a national organization and social movement hub that describes itself as "a political home for Latinx and Chicanx people who seek racial, economic, gender and climate justice" (https://mijente.net/our-dna).

9. Examples include the #FreeValeria, #FreeCristina, and #FreeTiaEva campaigns, which helped push for the release of three trans women from immigration detention; the #JusticeforRoxsana and #JusticeforJohana campaigns, which drew attention to the preventable deaths of Roxsana Hernandez and Johana Medina in ICE and Border Patrol custody; and an open letter to President Biden and DHS Secretary Alejandro Mayorkas demanding the end of detention for trans migrants and HIV+ migrants (https://familiatqlm.medium.com/36-formerly-detained-trans-people-call-on-president-biden-and-dhs-secretary-mayorkas-to-58d9e073d55e).

10. Familia: Trans Queer Liberation Movement, https://familiatqlm.org/programs.

11. See Hammami, "Bridging Immigration Justice and Prison Abolition," as well as Hammani's discussion of QDEP in McGuirk et al., "Centering Intersectional Politics."

12. Mariposas Sin Fronteras, https://mariposassinfronteras.org.

13. Rodríguez de Ruíz and Ochoa, "Translatina Is about the Journey," 162.

14. Alisa Bierria, "Community Accountability as Resistance to Racial Capitalism," talk given at the National Women's Studies Association conference, November 16, 2019, on a panel entitled "Radical Horizons of Care in the Shadows of Carceral Cultures."

BIBLIOGRAPHY

Abrams, Kerry. "Immigration Law and the Regulation of Marriage." *Minnesota Law Review* 91 (2006–2007): 1625–1709.

———. "Citizen Spouse." *California Law Review* 101 (2013): 407–444.

Agathangelou, Anna M., M. Daniel Bassichis, and Tamara L. Spira. "Intimate Investments: Homonormativity, Global Lockdown, and the Seductions of Empire." *Radical History Review* 100 (Winter 2008): 120–143.

Ahmed, Sara. *The Cultural Politics of Emotion.* London: Routledge, 2004.

Aizura, Aren Z. "The Persistence of Transgender Travel Narratives." In *Transgender Migrations: The Bodies, Borders, and Politics of Transition*, edited by Trystan T. Cotten, 139–156. New York: Routledge Press, 2012.

———. "Transnational Transgender Rights and Immigration Law." In *Transfeminist Perspectives in and beyond Transgender and Gender Studies,* edited by A. Finn Enke, 133–151. Philadelphia: Temple University Press, 2012.

———. "Affective Vulnerability and Transgender Exceptionalism: Norma Ureiro in *Transgression.*" In *Trans Studies: The Challenge to Hetero/Homo Normativities*, edited by Yolanda Martínez-San Miguel and Sarah Tobias, 122–139. New Brunswick, NJ: Rutgers University Press, 2016.

———. Introduction to "Unrecognizable: On Trans Recognition in 2017." *South Atlantic Quarterly* 116, no. 3 (2017): 606–611.

———. *Mobile Subjects: Transnational Imaginaries of Gender Reassignment.* Durham, NC: Duke University Press, 2018.

Alexander, M. Jacqui. "Not Just (Any) Body Can Be a Citizen: The Politics of Law, Sexuality and Postcoloniality in Trinidad and Tobago and the Bahamas." *Feminist Review* 48, no. 1 (1994): 5–23.

———. *Pedagogies of Crossing: Meditations on Feminism, Sexual Politics, Memory, and the Sacred.* Durham: Duke University Press, 2006.

Amnesty International. "No Safe Place: Salvadorans, Guatemalans, and Hondurans Seeking Asylum in Mexico Based on Their Sexual Orientation and/or Gender Identity." November 2017. https://www.amnestyusa.org/wp-content/uploads/2017/11/No-Safe-Place-Briefing-ENG-1.pdf.

Anderson, Benedict. *Imagined Communities: Reflections on the Origin and Spread of Nationalism.* New York: Verso, 1991 (1983).

Andrijasevic, Rutvica. "Sex on the Move: Gender, Subjectivity and Differential Inclusion." *Subjectivity* 29 (2009): 389–406.

Arkles, Gabriel. "Safety and Solidarity across Gender Lines: Rethinking Segregation of Transgender People in Detention." *Temple Political & Civil Rights Law Review* 18, no. 2 (2009): 515–560.

Arkles, Gabriel, Pooja Gehi, and Elana Redfield. "The Role of Lawyers in Trans Liberation: Building a Transformative Movement for Social Change." *Seattle Journal for Social Justice* 8, no. 2 (2010): 579–641.

Balaguera, Martha. "Trans-migrations: Agency and Confinement at the Limits of Sovereignty." *Signs: Journal of Women in Culture and Society* 43, no. 3 (2018): 641–664.

Barnes, Nielan. "Within the Asylum-Advocacy Nexus: An Analysis of Mexican Transgender Asylum Seekers in the United States." *Sexuality, Gender & Policy* 2 (2019): 5–25.

Beam, Myrl. *Gay, Inc.: The Nonprofitization of Queer Politics.* Minneapolis: University of Minnesota Press, 2018.

Beauchamp, Toby. *Going Stealth: Transgender Politics and US Surveillance Practices.* Durham, NC: Duke University Press, 2019.

Benner, Katie, and Caitlin Dickerson. "Sessions Says Domestic and Gang Violence Are Not Grounds for Asylum." *New York Times*, June 11, 2018. https://www.nytimes.com/2018/06 /11/us/politics/sessions-domestic-violence-asylum.html.

Berg, Laurie, and Jenni Millbank. "Developing a Jurisprudence of Transgender Particular Social Group." In *Fleeing Homophobia: Sexual Orientation, Gender Identity and Asylum*, edited by Thomas Spijkerboer, 121–153. New York: Routledge, 2013.

Berlant, Lauren. *The Queen of America Goes to Washington City: Essays on Sex and Citizenship.* Durham, NC: Duke University Press, 1997.

Bernstein, Nina. "New Scrutiny as Immigrants Die in Custody." *New York Times*, June 26, 2007. https://www.nytimes.com/2007/06/26/us/26detain.html.

———. "U.S. to Reform Policy on Detention for Immigrants." *New York Times*, August 5, 2009. https://www.nytimes.com/2009/08/06/us/politics/06detain.html.

Bettcher, Talia Mae. "Evil Deceivers and Make-Believers: On Transphobic Violence and the Politics of Illusion." In *The Transgender Studies Reader 2*, edited by Susan Stryker and Aren Z. Aizura, 278–290. New York: Routledge, 2013.

Bilefsky, Dan."Gays Seeking Asylum in U.S. Encounter a New Hurdle." *New York Times*, January 28, 2011. https://www.nytimes.com/2011/01/29/nyregion/29asylum.html.

Bohmer, Carol, and Amy Shuman. "Producing Epistemologies of Ignorance in the Political Asylum Application Process." *Identities: Global Studies in Culture and Power* 14 (2007): 603–629.

Bon Tempo, Carl. *Americans at the Gate: The United States and Refugees during the Cold War.* Princeton, NJ: Princeton University Press, 2008.

Borges, Sandibel. "Home and Homing as Resistance: Survival of LGBTQ Latinx Migrants." *WSQ: Women's Studies Quarterly* 46, nos. 3 & 4 (2018): 69–84.

Brooks, Peter. *Troubling Confessions: Speaking Guilt in Law and Literature.* Chicago: University of Chicago Press, 2000.

Brown, Wendy. "Suffering the Paradoxes of Rights." In *Left Legalism / Left Critique*, edited by Wendy Brown and Janet Halley, 420–434. Durham, NC: Duke University Press, 2002.

———. "Wounded Attachments." In *States of Injury: Power and Freedom in Late Modernity*, 52–76. Princeton, NJ: Princeton University Press, 1995.

Butler, Judith. *Excitable Speech: A Politics of the Performative.* New York: Routledge, 1997.

———. *The Psychic Life of Power: Theories in Subjection.* Stanford, CA: Stanford University Press, 1997.

Cacho, Lisa Marie. *Social Death: Racialized Rightlessness and the Criminalization of the Unprotected.* New York: New York University Press, 2012.

Camminga, B. *Transgender Refugees and the Imagined South Africa: Bodies over Borders and Borders over Bodies.* Cham, Switzerland: Palgrave Macmillan, 2019.

Canaday, Margot. *The Straight State: Sexuality and Citizenship in Twentieth-Century America.* Princeton, NJ: Princeton University Press, 2009.

Cantú Jr., Lionel. *The Sexuality of Migration: Border Crossings and Mexican Immigrant Men.* Edited by Nancy A. Naples and Salvador Vidal-Ortiz. New York: New York University Press, 2009.

Cantú Jr., Lionel, with Eithne Luibhéid and Alexandra Minna Stern. "Well-Founded Fear: Political Asylum and the Boundaries of Sexual Identity in the U.S.-Mexico Borderlands." In *Queer Migrations: Sexuality, U.S. Citizenship, and Border Crossings*, edited by Eithne Luibhéid and Lionel Cantú Jr., 61–74. Minneapolis: University of Minnesota Press, 2005.

Carbado, Devon W. "Racial Naturalization." In "Legal Borderlands: Law and the Construction of American Borders," edited by Mary L. Dudziak and Leti Volpp. Special issue, *American Quarterly* 57, no. 3 (2005): 633–658.

Carrillo, Héctor. "Immigration and LGBT Rights in the USA: Ironies and Constraints in U.S. Asylum Cases." In *Routledge Handbook of Sexuality, Health and Rights*, edited by Peter Aggleton and Richard Parker, 444–452. New York: Routledge, 2010.

———. "Leaving loved ones behind: Mexican gay men's migration to the USA." In *Mobility, Sexuality, and AIDS*, edited by Felicity Thomas, Mary Haour-Knipe, and Peter Aggleton, 24–38. New York: Routledge, 2010.

Chávez, Karma R. *Queer Migration Politics: Activist Rhetoric and Coalitional Possibilities.* Chicago: University of Illinois Press, 2013.

———. "Homonormativity and Violence against Immigrants." *QED: A Journal in GLBTQ Worldmaking* 4, no. 2 (2017): 131–136.

Chavez, Leo R. *The Latino Threat: Constructing Immigrants, Citizens, and the Nation.* 2nd ed. Palo Alto, CA: Stanford University Press, 2013.

Cheney, Marshall K., Mary J. Gowin, E. Laurette Taylor, Melissa Frey, Jamie Dunnington, Ghadah Alshuwaiyer, J. Kathleen Huber, Mary Camero Garcia, and Grady C. Wray. "Living Outside the Gender Box in Mexico: Testimony of Transgender Mexican Asylum Seekers." *American Journal of Public Health*, 107, no. 10 (October 2017): 1646–1652.

Community Initiatives for Visiting Immigrants in Confinement. "Complaint on Behalf of Thirty-one Women in ICE Custody in the Santa Ana City Jail," January 25, 2015. https:// www.prisonlegalnews.org/media/publications/CIVIC%20Complaint%20against%20 ICE%2C%20SACJ%2C%202015.pdf.

Conlon, Dierdre, and Nancy Hienstra. "Mobility and Materialisation of the Carceral: Examining Immigration and Immigration Detention." In *Carceral Mobilities: Interrogating Movement in Incarceration,* edited by Jennifer Turner and Kimberley Peters, 100–114. New York: Routledge, 2017.

Cornelisse, Galina. "Immigration Detention and the Territoriality of Universal Rights." In *The Deportation Regime: Sovereignty, Space, and the Freedom of Movement,* edited by Nathalie Peutz and Nicholas De Genova, 101–122. Durham, NC: Duke University Press, 2010.

Cott, Nancy. *Public Vows: A History of Marriage and the Nation.* Cambridge, MA: Harvard University Press, 2000.

Cotten, Trystan T. "Introduction: Migration and Morphing." In *Transgender Migrations: The Bodies, Borders, and Politics of Transition,* edited by Trystan T. Cotten. New York: Routledge, 2012.

———, ed. *Transgender Migrations: The Bodies, Borders, and Politics of Transition.* New York: Routledge, 2012.

Coutin, Susan Bibler. "The Oppressed, the Suspect, and the Citizen: Subjectivity in Competing Accounts of Political Violence." *Law and Social Inquiry* 26 no. 1 (2001): 63–94.

——. *Nations of Emigrants: Shifting Boundaries of Citizenship in El Salvador and the United States.* Ithaca, NY: Cornell University Press, 2007.

Cover, Robert M. "Violence and the Word." In *On Violence: A Reader*, edited by Bruce B. Lawrence and Aisha Karim, 292–313. Durham, NC: Duke University Press, 2007.

Crenshaw, Kimberlé. "Mapping the Margins: Intersectionality, Identity Politics, and Violence against Women of Color." *Stanford Law Review* 43, no. 6 (1991): 1241–1299.

Cresswell, Tim. *On the Move: Mobility in the Modern Western World.* New York: Routledge, 2006.

Cruz-Malavé, Arnaldo, ed. *Queer Globalization: Citizenship and the Afterlife of Colonization.* New York: New York University Press, 2002.

Currah, Paisley. "The Transgender Rights Imaginary." *Georgetown Journal of Gender and the Law* 4 (Spring 2003): 705–720.

Cvetkovich, Ann. *An Archive of Feelings: Trauma, Sexuality, and Lesbian Public Cultures.* Durham, NC: Duke University Press, 2003.

D'Aoust, Anne-Marie. "Moving Stories: Love at the Border." In *Mobile Desires: The Politics and Erotics of Mobility Justice*, edited by Liz Montegary and Melissa Autumn White, 94–107. New York: Palgrave Macmillan, 2015.

Danticat, Edwidge. "Detention Is No Holiday." *New York Times*, March 27, 2012. https://www.nytimes.com/2012/03/28/opinion/detention-is-no-holiday.html.

DasGupta, Debanuj. "Rescripting Trauma: Trans/Gender Detention Politics and Desire in the United States." *Women's Studies in Communication* 41, no. 4 (2018): 324–328.

Dayan, Joan. "Held in the Body of the State: Prisons and the Law." In *History, Memory, and the Law*, edited by Austin Sarat and Thomas R. Kearns, 183–247. Ann Arbor: University of Michigan Press, 2002.

DeFilippis, Joseph Nicholas. "'Building the World That We Want to Live in': An interview with Jennicet Gutiérrez and Jorge Gutierrez from Familia: TQLM." In *Queer Activism after Marriage Equality*, edited by Joseph Nicholas DeFilippis, Michael W. Yarbrough, and Angela Jones, 105–112. New York: Routledge, 2016.

De Genova, Nicholas. "Migrant 'Illegality' and Deportability in Everyday Life." *Annual Review of Anthropology*, 31 (2005): 419–447.

——. "The Deportation Regime: Sovereignty, Space, and the Freedom of Movement: Theoretical Overview." In *The Deportation Regime: Sovereignty, Space, and the Freedom of Movement*, edited by Nicholas De Genova and Natalie Peutz, 33–65. Durham: Duke University Press, 2010.

De Genova, Nicholas, Sandra Mezzadra, and John Pickles, eds. "New Keywords: Migration and Borders." *Cultural Studies* 29, no. 1 (2015): 55–87.

del Bosque, Melissa. "The Trouble with Karnes County's ICE 'Hotel.'" *Texas Observer*, March 16, 2012. http://www.texasobserver.org/the-trouble-with-karnes-countys-ice-hotel/.

Dolnick, Sam. "Immigrants May Be Fed False Stories to Bolster Asylum Pleas." *New York Times*, July 11, 2011. https://www.nytimes.com/2011/07/12/nyregion/immigrants-may-be-fed-false-stories-to-bolster-asylum-pleas.html.

Dudziak, Mary L., and Leti Volpp. "Introduction." In "Legal Borderlands: Law and the Construction of American Borders," edited by Mary L. Dudziak and Leti Volpp. Special issue, *American Quarterly* 57, no. 3 (2005): 593–610.

Duggan, Lisa. *The Twilight of Equality? Neoliberalism, Cultural Politics, and the Attack on Democracy.* Boston: Beacon Press, 2003.

Ehrenreich, Ben. "Death on Terminal Island." *Los Angeles Magazine*, September 1, 2009. https://www.lamag.com/longform/death-on-terminal-island/.

Einolf, Christopher. *The Mercy Factory*. Chicago: Ivan R. Dee Publishing, 2001.

Epps, Brad, Keja Valens, and Bill Johnson Gonzalez, eds. *Passing Lines: Sexuality and Immigration*. Cambridge, MA: Harvard University Press, 2005.

Fassin, Didier, and Estelle d'Halluin. "The Truth from the Body: Medical Certificates as Ultimate Evidence for Asylum Seekers." *American Anthropologist* 107, no. 4 (2005): 597–608.

Fears, Darryl. "Illegal Immigrants Received Poor Care in Jail, Lawyers Say." *Washington Post*, June 12, 2007.

———. "3 Jailed Immigrants Die in a Month; Medical Mistreatment Alleged; Federal Agency Denies Claims." *Washington Post*, August 15, 2007.

Feinberg, Leslie. "Death of Trans Immigrant in Detention Forges United Protests." *Workers World*, September 8, 2007.

Fiahlo, Christina. "A Model Immigration Detention Facility for LGBTI?" *Forced Migration Review* 42 (April 2013).

Flynn, Taylor. "'Transforming' the Debate: Why We Need to Include Transgender Rights in the Struggle for Sex and Sexual Orientation Equality." *Columbia Law Review* (2001): 392–420.

Foucault, Michel. *The History of Sexuality. Vol. I An Introduction*. Translated by Robert Hurley. New York: Vintage Books, 1990.

———. "Governmentality." In *The Foucault Effect: Studies in Governmentality*, edited by Graham Burchell, Colin Gordon, and Peter Miller, 87–104. Chicago: University of Chicago Press, 1991.

———. *"Society Must Be Defended": Lectures at the College de France, 1975–1976*. Edited by Mauro Bertani and Alessandro Fontana. Translated by David Macey. New York: Picador, 2003.

France, David and Ana Figueroa. "A Gay Refugee Finds Shelter in Court." *Newsweek*, September 11, 2000. https://www.newsweek.com/gay-refugee-finds-shelter-court-159575.

Franke, Katherine. *Wedlocked: The Perils of Marriage Equality*. New York: New York University Press, 2015.

Garcia, Maria Cristina. *Seeking Refuge: Central American Migration to Mexico, the United States, and Canada*. Berkeley: University of California Press, 2006.

Gehi, Pooja. "Struggles from the Margins: Anti-Immigrant Legislation and the Impact on Low-Income Transgender People of Color." *Women's Rights Law Reporter* 30 (2009): 315–329.

———. "Gendered (In)Security: Migration and Criminalization in the Security State." *Harvard Journal of Law & Gender* 35 (2012): 357–398.

Gehi, Pooja, and Gabriel Arkles. "The Tacit Targeting of Trans Immigrants as "Criminal Aliens": Old Tactics and New." In *The Unfinished Queer Agenda after Marriage Equality*, edited by Angela Jones, Joseph Nicholas DeFilippis, and Michael W. Yarbrough, 53–73. New York: Routledge, 2018.

Gerber, Robert. "Mexican National Requests Asylum on the Basis of Homosexuality." Interview by Bill O'Reilly. *The O'Reilly Factor*, Fox News Network, September 25, 2000.

Giametta, Calogero. *The Sexual Politics of Asylum: Sexual Orientation and Gender Identity in the UK Asylum System*. London: Routledge, 2017.

Golash-Boza, Tanya Maria. *Deported: Immigrant Policing, Disposable Labor, and Global Capitalism*. New York: New York University Press, 2015.

Gómez, Laura E. *Manifest Destinies: The Making of the Mexican American Race*. New York: New York University Press, 2018.

Grewal, Inderpal. *Transnational America: Feminisms, Diasporas, Neoliberalisms.* Durham, NC: Duke University Press, 2005.

Grossberg, Lawrence. *Cultural Studies in the Future Tense.* Durham, NC: Duke University Press, 2010.

Gruberg, Sharita. *Dignity Denied: LGBT Immigrants in U.S. Immigration Detention.* Center for American Progress. November 2013. https://www.americanprogress.org/issues /immigration/reports/2013/11/25/79987/dignity-denied-lgbt-immigrants-in-u-s -immigration-detention/.

_____. "No Way Out: Congress' Bed Quota Traps LGBT Immigrants in Detention." *Center for American Progress,* May 14, 2015. https://www.americanprogress.org/issues/lgbt /news/2015/05/14/111832/no-way-out-congress-bed-quota-traps-lgbt-immigrants-in -detention/.

_____. "ICE Officers Overwhelmingly Use Their Discretion to Detain LGBT Immigrants." *Center for American Progress,* October 26, 2016. https://www.americanprogress.org /issues/lgbt/reports/2016/10/26/291115/ice-officers-overwhelmingly-use-their -discretion-to-detain-lgbt-immigrants/.

Gruberg, Sharita and Rachel West. *Humanitarian Diplomacy: The U.S. Asylum System's Role in Protecting Global LGBT Rights.* June 2015. https://americanprogress.org/wp-content /uploads/2015/06/LGBTAsylum-final.pdf?_ga=2.50013989.22619424.1646842101 -1253077272.1646842100.

Haines, Justin L. "Fear of the Queer Marriage: The Nexus of Transsexual Marriages and U.S. Immigration Law." *New York City Law Review* 9 (2005–2006): 209–247.

Halberstam, Jack. *Female Masculinity.* Durham, NC: Duke University Press, 1998.

Hammami, Jamila. "Bridging Immigration Justice and Prison Abolition." In *Queer and Trans Migrations: Dynamics of Illegalization, Detention, and Deportation,* edited by Eithne Luibhéid and Karma R. Chávez, 133–136. Chicago: University of Illinois Press, 2020.

Haritaworn, Jin, Adi Kuntsman, and Silvia Posocco. "Introduction." In *Queer Necropolitics,* edited by Jin Haritaworn, Adi Kuntsman, and Silvia Posocco. New York: Routledge, 2014.

Hartman, Saidiya. *Scenes of Subjection: Terror, Slavery, and Self-Making in Nineteenth-Century America.* Oxford: Oxford University Press, 1997.

_____. "Venus in Two Acts." *Small Axe* 12, no. 2 (2008): 1–14.

Harvey, David. *A Brief History of Neoliberalism.* Oxford: Oxford University Press, 2005.

Hernández, César Cuauhtémoc García. "Immigration Detention as Punishment." *UCLA Law Review* 61 (2014): 1346–1414.

Hernandez, Kelly Lytle. *Migra! A History of the U.S. Border Patrol.* Berkeley: University of California Press, 2010.

Hernandez, Sandra. "Denied Medication, AIDS Patient Dies in ICE Custody." *Los Angeles Daily Journal,* August 9, 2007.

_____. "A Lethal Limbo: Lack of Healthcare Turns Federal Detention into a Death Sentence for Some Immigrants." *Los Angeles Times,* June 1, 2008. https://www.latimes.com /archives/la-xpm-2008-jun-01-op-hernandez1-story.html.

Hickey, Darby. "Policing Gender and Sexuality: Transgender Sex Workers, HIV, and Justice." *Positively Aware,* July/August 2008. http://www.positivelyaware.com/2008/08_04 /policing_gender_sexuality.html.

Hing, Bill. *Deporting Our Souls: Values, Morality, and Immigration Policy.* Cambridge: Cambridge University Press, 2006.

Hoffman, Meredith. "Transgender Immigrants Still Face Rampant Physical and Sexual Abuse in US Detention Centers." *Vice,* July 8, 2015. https://www.vice.com/en/article

/bnpmm3/transgender-immigrants-still-face-rampant-abuse-in-us-detention
-centers-708.

Human Rights Watch. *Chronic Indifference: HIV/AIDS Services for Immigrants Detained by the United States*. December 6, 2007. https://www.hrw.org/report/2007/12/05/chronic -indifference/hiv/aids-services-immigrants-detained-united-states.

_____. *Locked Up Far Away: The Transfer of Immigrants to Remote Detention Centers in the United States*. December 2, 2009. https://www.hrw.org/report/2009/12/02/locked-far -away/transfer-immigrants-remote-detention-centers-united-states.

_____. *A Costly Move: Far and Frequent Transfers Impede Hearings for Immigrant Detainees in the United States*. June 12, 2011. https://www.hrw.org/report/2011/06/14/costly-move/far -and-frequent-transfers-impede-hearings-immigrant-detainees-united.

_____. *"Do You See How Much I'm Suffering Here?": Abuse against Transgender Women in US Immigration Detention*. March 2016. https://www.hrw.org/sites/default/files/report_pdf /us0316_web.pdf.

Inda, Jonathan Xavier. *Targeting Immigrants: Government, Technology, and Ethics*. Oxford: Blackwell Publishing, 2006.

Inda, Jonathan Xavier and Julie A. Dowling. "Introduction: Governing Migrant Illegality." In *Governing Immigration Through Crime*, edited by Julie A. Dowling and Jonathan Xavier Inda, 1–36. Palo Alto, CA: Stanford University Press, 2013.

Irving, Dan. "Normalized Transgressions: Legitimatizing the Transsexual Body as Productive." *Radical History Review* 100 (Winter 2008): 38–59.

Irwin, Robert. *Mexican Masculinities*. Minneapolis: University of Minnesota Press, 2003.

Isin, Engin. *Being Political: Genealogies of Citizenship*. Minneapolis: University of Minnesota Press, 2002.

James, Sandy E., Jody L. Herman, Susan Rankin, Mara Keisling, Lisa Mottet, and Ma'ayan Anafi. *The Report of the 2015 U.S. Transgender Survey*. National Center for Transgender Equality, 2016. https://transequality.org/sites/default/files/docs/usts/USTS-Full-Report -Dec17.pdf.

Jordan, Sharalyn R. "Un/Convention(al) Refugees: Contextualizing the Accounts of Refugees Facing Homophobic or Transphobic Persecution." *Refuge* 26, no. 2 (2009): 165–182.

Joseph, Miranda. *Against the Romance of Community*. Minneapolis: University of Minnesota Press, 2002.

Kandaswamy, Priya. "State Austerity and the Racial Politics of Same-Sex Marriage in the U.S." *Sexualities* 11, no. 6 (2008): 706–725.

Kaplan, Caren. *Questions of Travel: Postmodern Discourses of Displacement*. Durham, NC: Duke University Press, 1996.

_____. "Transporting the Subject: Technologies of Mobility and Location in an Era of Globalization." In *Uprootings / Regroundings: Questions of Home and Migration*, edited by Sara Ahmed, Claudia Casteñeda, Anne-Marie Fortier, and Mimi Sheller, 207–224. Oxford: Berg Publishers, 2003.

Kaplan, Caren, Norma Alarcón, and Minoo Moallem, eds. *Between Woman and Nation: Nationalisms, Transnational Feminisms, and the State*. Durham, NC: Duke University Press, 1999.

Keaney, Melissa and Joan Friedland. "ICE ACCESS Programs: 287(g), the Criminal Alien Program, and Secure Communities." November 2009. https://www.nilc.org/issues /immigration-enforcement/ice-access-2009-11-05/.

Knox, Sara L., and Cristyn Davies. "Introduction." In "The Force of Meaning: Cultural Studies of Law," edited by Sara L. Knox and Cristyn Davies. Special issue, *Cultural Studies* 27, no. 1 (2013): 1–10.

Koulish, Robert. "Using Risk to Assess the Legal Violence of Mandatory Detention." *Laws* 5, no. 3 (2016): 30. https://doi.org/10.3390/laws5030030.

Kwong, Jessica. "Immigrant Rights Activists Celebrate ICE Notice to Terminate Santa Ana Jail Contract." *Orange County Registrar*, February 25, 2017. https://www.ocregister.com /2017/02/25/immigrants-rights-activists-celebrate-ice-notice-to-terminate-santa-ana -jail-contract/

Lahoud, Raymond G. "Ninth Circuit Allows for the End of Temporary Protected Status." *National Law Review,* October 9, 2020. https://www.natlawreview.com/article/ninth -circuit-allows-end-temporary-protected-status.

Lamble, Sarah. "Retelling Racialized Violence, Remaking White Innocence: The Politics of Interlocking Oppressions in Transgender Day of Remembrance." *Sexuality Research and Social Policy* 5, no. 1 (2008): 24–42.

Landau, Joseph. "'Soft Immutability' and 'Imputed Gay Identity': Recent Developments in Transgender and Sexual-Orientation-Based Asylum Law." *Fordham Urban Law Journal* 32, no. 2 (2005): 237–263.

Latour, Bruno. "Visualisation and Cognition: Drawing Things Together." http://www.bruno -latour.fr/sites/default/files/21-DRAWING-THINGS-TOGETHER-GB.pdf.

Legomsky, Stephen H. "The Making of United States Refugee Policy: Separation of Powers in the Post-Cold War Era." *Washington Law Review* 70 (1995): 675–714.

———. *Immigration and Refugee Law and Policy.* 4th ed. New York: Foundation Press, 2005.

Leonard, Arthur S. "Panel Oks Transgendered Marriage." *Gay City News*, May 26–June 1, 2005.

Lorenz, Rachel Duffy. "Transgender Immigration: Legal Same-Sex Marriages and Their Implications for the Defense of Marriage Act." *UCLA Law Review* 53 (2005–2006): 423–559.

Loyd, Jenna, Andrew Burridge, and Matthew Mitchelson. "Thinking (and Moving) beyond Walls and Cages: Bridging Immigrant Justice and Anti-Prison Organizing in the United States." *Social Justice* 36, no. 2 (2009): 85–103.

Luibhéid, Eithne. *Entry Denied: Controlling Sexuality at the Border.* Minneapolis: University of Minnesota Press, 2002.

———. "Sexuality, Migration, and the Shifting Line between Legal and Illegal Status." *GLQ: A Journal of Gay and Lesbian Studies* 14, nos. 2–3 (2008): 289–315.

———. *Pregnant on Arrival: Making the Illegal Immigrant.* Minneapolis: University of Minnesota Press, 2013.

Luibhéid, Eithne, and Lionel Cantú Jr., eds. *Queer Migrations: Sexuality, U.S. Citizenship, and Border Crossings.* Minneapolis: University of Minnesota Press, 2005.

Luibhéid, Eithne, and Karma R. Chávez, eds. *Queer and Trans Migrations: Dynamics of Illegalization, Detention, and Deportation.* Chicago: University of Illinois Press, 2020.

Macías-Rojas, Patrisia. *From Deportation to Prison: The Politics of Immigration Enforcement in Post-Civil Rights America.* New York: New York University Press, 2016.

Macpherson, C. B. *The Political Theory of Possessive Individualism: Hobbes to Locke.* New York: Oxford University Press, 1962.

Manalansan, Martin F. *Global Divas: Filipino Gay Men in the Diaspora.* Durham, NC: Duke University Press, 2003.

Martin, Lauren L. "Getting Out and Getting In: Legal Geographies of US Immigration Detention." In *Carceral Spaces: Mobility and Agency in Imprisonment and Migrant Detention*, edited by Dominique Moran, Nick Gill, and Dierdre Conlon, 149–166. Farmharm, UK: Ashgate, 2013.

Martinez, Grisella. "Open Window: *Matter of Lovo*'s Implications for Transsexual and Immigrant Communities." *Modern American* 2, no. 1 (2006): 28–31.

Martinez, Jenny S. "Process and Substance in the 'War on Terror'." *Columbia Law Review* 108 (June 2008): 1013–1091.

Mbembe, Achille. "Necropolitics." Translated by Libby Meintjes. *Public Culture* 15, no 1 (2003): 11–40.

McGuirk, Siobhán. "(In)credible Subjects: NGOs, Attorneys, and Permissible LGBT Asylum Seeker Identities." *PoLAR: Political and Legal Anthropology Review* 41, no. S1 (2018): 4–18.

McGuirk, Siobhán, Jara M. Carrington, Claudia Cojocaru, Jamila Hammami, and Marzena Zukowska. "Centering Intersectional Politics: Queer Migration Activisms 'after Marriage.'" In *Queer Activism after Marriage Equality,* edited by Joseph Nicholas DeFilippis, Michael W. Yarbrough, and Angela Jones, 130–150. New York: Routledge, 2018.

McKinley, Michelle A. "Cultural Culprits." *Berkeley Journal of Gender, Law & Justice* 24 (2009): 91–165.

McKinnon, Sara L. *Gendered Asylum: Race and Violence in U.S. Law and Politics.* Chicago: University of Illinois Press, 2016.

Medina, Luis. "Immigrating While Trans: The Disproportionate Impact of the Prostitution Ground of Inadmissibility and Other Provisions of the Immigration and Nationality Act on Transgender Women." *Scholar: St. Mary's Law Review on Race and Social Justice* 19 (2017): 253–295.

Mehta, Suketu. "The Asylum Seeker." *New Yorker,* August 1, 2011. https://www.newyorker.com /magazine/2011/08/01/the-asylum-seeker.

Mertus, Julie. "The State and the Post-Cold War Refugee Regime: New Models, New Questions." *Michigan Journal of International Law* 20 (1998): 59–90.

Miller, Alice M. "Gay Enough: Some Tensions in Seeking the Grant of Asylum and Protecting Global Sexual Diversity." In *Passing Lines: Sexuality and Immigration,* edited by Brad Epps, Keja Valens, and Bill Johnson González, 137–187. Cambridge, MA: Harvard University Press, 2005.

Mink, Gwendolyn. *Welfare's End.* Ithaca, NY: Cornell University Press, 1998.

Mohanty, Chandra Talpade. "Under Western Eyes: Feminist Scholarship and Colonial Discourses." In *Dangerous Liaisons: Gender, Nation, and Postcolonial Perspectives,* edited by Anne McClintock, Aamir Mufti, and Ella Shohat, 255–277. Minneapolis: University of Minnesota Press, 1997.

Molina, Natalia. *How Race Is Made in America: Immigration, Citizenship, and the Power of Racial Scripts.* Berkeley: University of California Press, 2014.

Morris, Julia. "Power, Capital, and Immigration Detention Rights: Making Networked Markets in Global Detention Governance at UNHCR." *Global Networks* 17, no. 3 (2017): 400–422.

Mosse, George. *Nationalism and Sexuality: Middle-Class Morality and Sexual Norms in Modern Europe.* Madison: University of Wisconsin Press, 1985.

Motomura, Hiroshi. "The Curious Evolution of Immigration Law: Procedural Surrogates for Substantive Constitutional Rights." *Columbia Law Review* 92, no. 7 (1992): 1625–1704.

Murray, David A. B. "The Challenge of Home for Sexual Orientation and Gendered Identity Refugees in Toronto." *Journal of Canadian Studies / Revue de'études Canadiennes* 48, no. 1 (2014): 132–152.

———. "Queer Forms: Producing Documentation in Sexual Orientation Refugee Cases." *Anthropological Quarterly* 89, no. 2 (2016): 465–484.

———. *Real Queer? Sexual Orientation and Gender Identity Refugees in the Canadian Refugee Apparatus.* London: Rowman and Littlefield, 2016.

Musalo, Karen, Jennifer Moore, and Richard A. Boswell. *Refugee Law and Policy: A Comparative and International Approach.* 3rd ed. Durham, NC: Carolina Academic Press, 2007.

National Immigrant Justice Center. "Submission of Civil Rights Complaints regarding Mistreatment and Abuse of Sexual Minorities in DHS Custody," April 13, 2011. https://immigrantjustice.org/sites/default/files/OCRCL%20Global%20Complaint%20Letter%20April%202011%20FINAL%20REDACTED_0.pdf.

National Immigrant Justice Center and Detention Watch Network. *Lives in Peril: How Ineffective Inspections Make ICE Complicit in Immigration Detention Abuse.* October 2015. http://immigrantjustice.org/sites/default/files/content-type/research-item/documents/2017-03/THR-Inspections-FOIA-Report-October-2015-FINAL.pdf.

National Immigrant Justice Center and Physicians for Human Rights. *Invisible in Isolation: The Use of Segregation and Solitary Confinement in Immigration Detention.* September 2012. https://immigrantjustice.org/sites/immigrantjustice.org/files/Invisible%20in%20Isolation-The%20Use%20of%20Segregation%20and%20Solitary%20Confinement%20in%20Immigration%20Detention.September%202012_7.pdf.

Neilson, Victoria and Kristina Wertz. *Immigration Law and the Transgender Client.* Washington, D.C.: American Immigration Lawyers Association, 2008.

Ngai, Mae M. *Impossible Subjects: Illegal Aliens and the Making of Modern America.* Princeton, NJ: Princeton University Press, 2004.

Nguyen, Mimi Thi. *The Gift of Freedom: War, Debt, and Other Refugee Passages.* Durham, NC: Duke University Press, 2012.

Noll, Gregor. "Salvation by the Grace of State? Explaining Credibility Assessment in the Asylum Procedure." In *Proof, Evidentiary Assessment and Credibility in Asylum Procedures,* edited by Gregor Noll, 197–214. Boston: Martinus Nijhoff Publishers, 2005.

Ochoa, Marcia. *Queen for a Day: Transformistas, Beauty Queens, and the Performance of Femininity in Venezuela.* Durham, NC: Duke University Press, 2014.

Office of Inspector General, Department of Homeland Security. *U.S. Immigration and Customs Enforcement's Alternatives to Detention (Revised),* OIG-15-22. February 4, 2015. https://www.oig.dhs.gov/assets/Mgmt/2015/OIG_15-22_Feb15.pdf.

Oxford, Connie. "Acts of Resistance in Asylum Seekers' Persecution Narratives." In *Immigrant Rights in the Shadows of Citizenship,* edited by Rachel Ida Buff, 40–65. New York: New York University Press, 2008.

Pascoe, Peggy. *What Comes Naturally: Miscegenation Law and the Making of Race in America.* Oxford: Oxford University Press, 2009.

Patton, Cindy. "Tremble, Hetero Swine!" In *Fear of a Queer Planet: Queer Politics and Social Theory,* edited by Michael Warner, 143–177. Minneapolis: University of Minnesota Press, 1993.

Patton, Cindy, and Benigno Sánchez-Eppler, eds. *Queer Diasporas.* Durham, NC: Duke University Press, 2000.

Pierce, Sarah, and Jessica Bolter. *Dismantling and Reconstructing the U.S. Immigration System: A Catalog of Changes under the Trump Presidency.* Migration Policy Institute. July 2020. https://www.migrationpolicy.org/research/us-immigration-system-changes-trump-presidency.

Piot, Charles. "Representing Africa in the Kasinga Asylum Case." In *Transcultural Bodies: Female Genital Cutting in Global Context,* edited by Ylva Hernlund and Bettina Shell-Duncan, 157–166. New Brunswick, NJ: Rutgers University Press, 2007.

Portillo Villeda, Suyapa G. "Central American Migrants: LGBTI Asylum Cases Seeking Justice and Making History." In *Queer and Trans Migrations: Dynamics of Illegalization, Detention, and Deportation,* edited by Eithne Luibhéid and Karma R. Chávez, 67–73. Chicago: University of Illinois Press, 2020.

Povinelli, Elizabeth A. *The Empire of Love: Toward a Theory of Intimacy, Genealogy, and Carnality*. Durham, NC: Duke University Press, 2006.

Prosser, Jay. *Second Skins: The Body Narratives of Transsexuality*. New York: Columbia University Press, 1998.

————. "Exceptional Locations: Transsexual Travelogues." In *Reclaiming Genders: Transsexual Grammars at the Fin de Siécle*, edited by Kate More and Stephen Whittle, 83–114. New York: Continuum, 1999.

Puar, Jasbir K. *Terrorist Assemblages: Homonationalism in Queer Times*. Durham, NC: Duke University Press, 2007.

Ramji-Nogales, Jaya, Andrew I. Schoenholtz, and Phillip G. Schrag. "Refugee Roulette: Disparities in Asylum Adjudication." *Stanford Law Review* 60, no. 2 (2007): 295–412.

Randazzo, Timothy J. "Social and Legal Barriers: Sexual Orientation and Asylum in the United States." In *Queer Migrations: Sexuality, U.S. Citizenship, and Border Crossings*, edited by Eithne Luibhéid and Lionel Cantú Jr., 30–60. Minneapolis: University of Minnesota Press, 2005.

Reddy, Chandan. "Asian Diasporas, Neoliberalism, and Family: Reviewing the Case for Homosexual Asylum in the Context of Family Rights." In "What's Queer About Queer Studies Now?," edited by David L. Eng, Judith Halberstam, and José Muñoz. Special issue, *Social Text* 23, nos. 3–4 (Fall/Winter 2005): 101–119.

————. *Freedom with Violence: Race, Sexuality, and the US State*. Durham, NC: Duke University Press, 2011.

Rempell, Scott. "Unpublished Decisions and Precedent Shaping: A Case Study of Asylum Claims." *Georgetown Immigration Law Journal* 31 (2016): 1–43.

Rivas, Jorge. "Immigration Officials to Start Sending Transgender Women to the Middle of Texas." *Fusion*, May 23, 2016. http://fusion.net/story/305117/transgender-ice-detainees -moving-texas/.

Roberts, Dorothy. *Killing the Black Body: Race, Reproduction, and the Meaning of Liberty*. New York: Vintage Press, 1997.

Robson, Ruthann. "A Mere Switch or a Fundamental Change?: Theorizing Transgender Marriage." *Hypatia* 22, no. 1 (2007): 58–70.

Rodríguez, Juana María. *Queer Latinidad: Identity Practices, Discursive Spaces*. New York: New York University Press, 2003.

Rodríguez de Ruíz, Alexandra, and Marcia Ochoa. "Translatina Is about the Journey: A Dialogue on Social Justice for Transgender Latinas in San Francisco." In *Trans Studies: The Challenge to Hetero/Homo Normativities*, edited by Yolanda Martínez-San Miguel and Sarah Tobias, 154–171. New Brunswick, NJ: Rutgers University Press, 2016.

Romero, María Paula Castañeda, and Sofia Cardona Huerta. "Seeking Protection as a Transgender Refugee Woman: From Honduras and El Salvador to Mexico." In *LGBTI Asylum Seekers and Refugees from a Legal and Political Perspective: Persecution, Asylum and Integration*, edited by Arzu Güler, Maryna Shevtsova, and Denise Venturi, 251–272. Springer, 2019.

Rose, Katrina C. "Sign of a Wave? The Kansas Court of Appeals Rejects Texas Simplicity in Favor of Transsexual Reality." *UMKC Law Review* 70 (2001–2002): 257–301.

Saleh, Fadi. "Transgender as a Humanitarian Category: The Case of Syrian Queer and Gender-Variant Refugees in Turkey." *TSQ: Transgender Studies Quarterly* 7, no. 1 (February 2020): 37–55.

Schaeffer, Felicity Amaya. *Love and Empire: Cybermarriage and Citizenship across the Americas*. New York: New York University Press, 2013.

Schoenholtz, Andrew I., Philip G. Schrag, and Jaya Ramji-Nogales. *Lives in the Balance: Asylum Adjudication by the Department of Homeland Security.* New York: New York University Press, 2014.

Schriro, Dora. *Immigration Detention Overview and Recommendations.* October 6, 2009. https://www.ice.gov/doclib/about/offices/odpp/pdf/ice-detention-rpt.pdf.

Shah, Nayan. *Stranger Intimacy: Contesting Race, Sexuality and the Law in the North American West.* Berkeley: University of California Press, 2013.

Shakhsari, Sima. "The Queer Time of Death: Temporality, Geopolitics, and Refugee Rights." *Sexualities* 17, no. 8 (2014): 998–1015.

Sharpe, Andrew. *Transgender Jurisprudence: Dysphoric Bodies of Law.* New York: Cavendish Publishing, 2002.

Sheller, Mimi. *Mobility Justice: The Politics of Movement in an Age of Extremes.* London: Verso, 2018.

Sheller, Mimi, and John Urry. "The New Mobilities Paradigm." *Environment and Planning A* 38, no. 2 (2006): 207–226.

Shuman, Amy, and Carol Bohmer. "Representing Trauma: Political Asylum Narrative." *Journal of American Folklore* 117, no. 466 (2004): 394–414.

shuster, stef m. *Trans Medicine: The Emergence and Practice of Treating Gender.* New York: New York University Press, 2021.

Smiley, Lauren. "Border Crossers." *SF Weekly*, November 26, 2008, https://www.sfweekly.com/news/border-crossers/.

⸺. "*SF Weekly* Challenges *Guardian* Op-Ed on "Border Crossers." *SF Weekly*, December 4, 2008. http://blogs.sfweekly.com/thesnitch/2008/12/sf_weekly_challenges_guardian.php.

Snorton, C. Riley, and Jin Haritaworn. "Trans Necropolitics: A Transnational Reflection on Violence, Death, and the Trans of Color Afterlife." In *The Transgender Studies Reader 2*, edited by Susan Stryker and Aren Z. Aizura, 66–75. New York: Routledge, 2013.

Somerville, Siobhan. "Notes toward a Queer History of Naturalization." In "Legal Borderlands: Law and the Construction of American Borders," edited by Mary L. Dudziak and Leti Volpp. Special issue, *American Quarterly* 57, no. 3 (2005): 659–675.

Spade, Dean. "Resisting Medicine, Re/modeling Gender." *Berkeley Women's Journal* 18 (2003): 15–37.

⸺. "Compliance Is Gendered: Struggling for Gender Self-Determination in a Hostile Economy." In *Transgender Rights,* edited by Paisley Currah, Richard M. Juang, Shannon Price Minter, 217–241. Minneapolis: University of Minnesota Press, 2006.

⸺. "Mutilating Gender." In *The Transgender Studies Reader*, edited by Susan Stryker and Stephen Whittle, 315–332. New York: Routledge, 2006.

⸺. "Documenting Gender." *Hastings Law Journal* 59 (March 2008): 731–832.

⸺. "Laws as Tactics." *Columbia Journal of Gender and Law* 21 (2011–2012): 40–71.

⸺. *Normal Life: Administrative Violence, Critical Trans Politics, and the Limits of Law.* Durham: Duke University Press, 2015.

Stanley, Eric A. "Near Life, Queer Death": Overkill and Ontological Capture." *Social Text* 29, no. 2 (2011): 1–19.

⸺. *Atmospheres of Violence: Structuring Antagonism and the Trans/Queer Ungovernable.* Durham, NC: Duke University Press, 2021.

Stanley, Eric A., and Nat Smith, eds. *Captive Genders: Trans Embodiment and the Prison Industrial Complex.* 2nd ed. Chico, CA: AK Press, 2015.

Stannow, Lovisa. "When Good Isn't Enough." *HuffPost*, March 6, 2012. https://www.huffpost.com/entry/when-good-isnt-enough_b_1317745.

Steinmetz, Katy. "The Transgender Tipping Point: America's Next Civil Rights Frontier." *Time*, May 29, 2014. https://time.com/magazine/us/135460/june-9th-2014-vol-183-no-22-u-s/.

Stevens, Jacqueline. *Reproducing the State*. Princeton, NJ: Princeton University Press, 1999.

Stop Prisoner Rape. *In the Shadows: Sexual Violence in U.S. Detention Facilities*. 2006. https://justdetention.org/wp-content/uploads/2015/10/In-The-Shadows-Sexual-Violence-in-U.S.-Detention-Facilities.pdf.

Stout, David. "Court Rules Cross-Dresser Can Stay in the U.S. on Asylum Claim." *New York Times*, August 26, 2000. https://www.nytimes.com/2000/08/26/us/court-rules-cross-dresser-can-stay-in-the-us-on-asylum-claim.html.

Stryker, Susan. "(De)Subjugated Knowledges: An Introduction to Transgender Studies." In *The Transgender Studies Reader*, edited by Susan Stryker and Stephen Whittle, 1–17. New York: Routledge, 2006.

Stryker, Susan, and Aren Z. Aizura. "Introduction: Transgender Studies 2.0." In *The Transgender Studies Reader 2*, edited by Susan Stryker and Aren Z. Aizura, 1–12. New York: Routledge, 2013.

Tomchin, Olga. "Bodies and Bureaucracy: Legal Sex Classification and Marriage-Based Immigration for Trans* People." *California Law Review* 101, no. 3 (2015): 813–862.

Transactional Records Access Clearinghouse, Syracuse University. TRAC Report. *Deportations Under ICE's Secure Communities Program*, April 25, 2018. http://trac.syr.edu/immigration/reports/509/#f5.

The Transgender Law Center and Cornell University Law School LGBT Clinic. *Report on Human Rights Conditions of Transgender Women in Mexico*, May 2016. https://transgenderlawcenter.org/wp-content/uploads/2016/05/CountryConditionsReport-FINAL.pdf.

The TransLatin@ Coalition. *TransVisible: Transgender Latina Immigrants in U.S. Society*, 2013. https://static1.squarespace.com/static/55b6e526e4b02f9283ae1969/t/56feaa3eb6aa60ebb6037d03/1459530307297/transvisible_en.pdf.

Urry, John. *Mobilities*. Polity Press, 2007.

U.S. Citizenship and Immigration Services (USCIS). "Guidance for Adjudicating Lesbian, Gay, Bisexual, Transgender, and Intersex (LGBTI) Refugee and Asylum Claims." Refugee, Asylum, and International Operations Directorate (RAIO)—Officer Training. December 28, 2011. https://www.uscis.gov/sites/default/files/document/guides/RAIO-Training-March-2012.pdf.

U.S. Commission on Civil Rights. *With Liberty and Justice for All: The State of Civil Rights at Immigration Detention Facilities*. Statutory Enforcement Report. September 2015. https://www.usccr.gov/files/pubs/docs/Statutory_Enforcement_Report2015.pdf.

U.S. Immigration and Customs Enforcement. *Performance-Based National Detention Standards 2011* (PBNDS 2011). https://www.ice.gov/doclib/detention-standards/2011/pbnds2011r2016.pdf.

Valentine, David. *Imagining Transgender: An Ethnography of a Category*. Durham, NC: Duke University Press, 2007.

Vidal-Ortiz, Salvador, Carlos Decena, Héctor Carrillo, and Tomás Almaguer. "Revisiting *Activos* and *Passivos*: Towards New Cartographies of Latino/Latin American Male Same-Sex Desire." In *Latina/o Sexualities: Probing Powers, Passions, Practices, and Policies*, edited by Marysol Asencio, 253–273. New Brunswick, NJ: Rutgers University Press, 2010.

Villazor, Rose Cuison. "The Other Loving: Uncovering the Federal Government's Racial Regulation of Marriage." *New York University Law Review* 86 (November 2011): 1361–1443.

Vogler, Stefan. "Determining Transgender: Adjudicating Gender Identity in U.S. Asylum Law." *Gender & Society* 33, no. 3 (2019): 439–462.

Weinstein, Henry. "Persecuted Gay Man Wins Asylum Case." *Los Angeles Times*, August 25, 2000. https://www.latimes.com/archives/la-xpm-2000-aug-25-mn-10319-story.html.

White, Melissa Autumn. "Archives of Intimacy and Trauma: Queer Migration Documents as Technologies of Affect." *Radical History Review* 120 (Fall 2014): 75–93.

Yurchak, Alexei. *Everything Was Forever, Until It Was No More: The Last Soviet Generation.* Princeton, NJ: Princeton University Press, 2005.

Zecena, Ruben. "Shameless Interruptions: Finding Survival at the Edges of Trans and Queer Migrations." In *Queer and Trans Migrations: Dynamics of Illegalization, Detention, and Deportation*, edited by Eithne Luibhéid and Karma R. Chávez, 175–191. Chicago: University of Illinois Press, 2020.

INDEX

ABOUT THE AUTHOR

TRISTAN JOSEPHSON is associate professor of women's and gender studies at California State University, Sacramento.